NOTES
FROM THE
COSMOS

NOTES
FROM THE
COSMOS

*A Futurist's Insights Into the
World of Dream Prophecy and Intuition*

By Gordon-Michael Scallion

With Foreword by
Cynthia Keyes

Published by Matrix Institute Inc., W. Chesterfield, NH 03466

Cover Design by Gordon-Michael Scallion
Cover Illustration by Ken Southwick

Published by Matrix Institute, Inc.

For information contact:
Matrix Institute, Inc., P.O. Box 367
West Chesterfield, NH 03466-0367
FAX: (603) 256-6614
Voice: (603) 256-6520
World Wide Web address: http://www.matrixinstitute.com
E-mail address: admin@matrixinstitute.com

If you are unable to order this book from your local bookseller, you may order directly from the publisher. Quantity discounts are available for organizations.

Library of Congress Catalog Card Number: 97-73762

ISBN: 0-9619709-0-1
1. Metaphysics.   2. Autobiography.
3. Occultism.   4. Cosmology.

First printing/ June 1997
Second printing/ September 1997
Third printing/ March 1998

First Edition
Printed in the United States of America

Table of Contents

Acknowledgements

I remember how impressed I was when I saw the first pop-top can. Its simplicity of design made me wonder why someone had not come forward with this idea earlier. My guess then was that everything has its time. When something is ready, it somehow miraculously moves out into the world. Later I read that it had taken years to perfect the design of the can, and it was only through the dedication of a few key people that it succeeded.

Notes from the Cosmos is no different. It took me over six years to produce the first rough draft. And, as in the case of the pop-top can, you would not be reading this book if not for a few insightful, talented, and dedicated people who worked many long hours to help me finish the project. To them, I am forever grateful, and blessed for knowing and working with them:

Cynthia Keyes, who since 1982 has witnessed my journey into the mystical world of consciousness firsthand, and has maintained her sanity throughout, while helping me to maintain my own. Her insights along the way added much to this book, as did her editing and writing skills. I am fortunate to know her as a friend, a wife, a business partner, and as a truly gifted writer.

Krista Haimovitch, who joined our book production team at the beginning of the editing phase and was able to dive right in and add her own unique, logical, and insightful editing talents to the project. The greatest compliment I can give Krista is that I am hopeful we will be able to work together again on new projects in the future.

Foreword

Gordon-Michael Scallion has become known as an intuitive, a futurist, and a modern-day prophet. He is probably most famous for his "future maps" of North America and of the world, as well as his predictions of Earth changes around the globe. When I first met Gordon in 1982, however, he was just getting accustomed to his newfound abilities. Prior to 1979, he had been an ordinary person with ordinary abilities. It was only after experiencing the strange sequence of events, described later in this book, that he suddenly began to develop extraordinary perceptions.

Before we actually met, I knew about him from a mutual acquaintance. I was aware that he could go into a trance-like state and speak about any number of things. In this state he seemed to be a virtual encyclopedia of information about ancient civilizations, reincarnation, health and healing, as well as having insight into a person's spiritual direction or career path. He would even answer such mundane questions as, "What would be the best job for me to take?" or, "Will I ever meet someone who will become my partner in life?"

So when I first met him, I knew something of his capabilities. Sometime in our early conversations, I asked him where he was from. He responded by saying that he was from the same city and the exact street where I had lived as a child. I was startled. I remember looking at him in complete amazement, and he asked me what was the matter.

"Were you reading my mind?" I asked him.

"No. Why?" he asked, surprised at my reaction to what he

thought was a direct answer to a simple, straightforward question.

"Because that's where I lived," I said, in an almost accusatory tone of voice, sure that somehow he had looked into my past, discovered where I lived, and was now feeding that information back to me for some strange reason that I couldn't understand.

"You were reading my mind, weren't you?"

"No, that's where I lived." This time he was quite emphatic.

When he told me the street number, I realized that his house was diagonally across the street from mine. I reluctantly began to believe him ... reluctantly, because I wasn't sure which was more unnerving, thinking that he was reading my mind or discovering the unlikely coincidence that we had once lived on the same street. As we talked, we also discovered that we had moved away to different towns in the very same year. We still couldn't remember each other, but we soon realized that Gordon and my brother Ted had played together as children. Later, when I introduced Gordon to my parents, my mother remembered him immediately. I was stunned to hear her greet him with, "I remember you. You were the one that put my son in the hospital."

It turned out that one time when they were playing "cowboys and indians," Gordon had thrown a rubber tomahawk, and it caught my brother on the forehead, just below his hairline. My mother had taken Ted to the emergency room for stitches, so she had no trouble remembering the incident.

I've since become more relaxed about the so-called coincidences in our lives, but at the time I was somewhat amazed. Growing up as children, we had lived on the same street, moved away, and now years later, with no conscious effort from either of us, our paths had crossed again. Since then, I've come to believe that there is no such thing as coincidence. Some part of us is aware of our spiritual progress and constantly tries to move us onto the path that holds the most challenge and growth for our development. We don't always follow those urgings, but opportunities continue to repeat themselves until we "get it right," even if it takes many lifetimes to achieve our goal. It is a continual journey, but we often don't know our destination and have to feel our way through the maze.

In *Notes from the Cosmos*, you will read about Gordon's journey into awareness and how he learned to understand and use his gifts of prophecy and insight. You will see how he overcame his fear of his newly discovered abilities, and how he dealt with the fears of others. It wasn't always easy for him to live with the intrusion of unwanted thoughts, images and sometimes voices. It wasn't always easy for me to be with him when one of these "transmissions" was coming through, especially in the beginning when he was still learning how to control it. I remember one time when we were at my cousin's wedding. It was in an old inn and we were standing in front of an open fireplace with a big roaring fire in it. All of a sudden, Gordon said, "Did you feel that?"

"What?" I said, thinking, "Oh no, he's going to get weird on me, and right in front of all my relatives."

"Didn't you feel that cold draft?" I had actually just felt a chill, which was kind of odd, given the warmth of the fire. The next thing I knew he said he was hearing a voice. Attempting to look as normal as possible so as to not attract attention, I said, "What did the voice say?"

He described it as a woman's voice. She'd told him her name and said that he should go into the library and look for a particular book. We had only been in the lobby and in the room with the fireplace, and didn't know if there was a library, but we began to wander around the inn looking for it. We no sooner rounded a corner off the main hall when we found ourselves in a small room filled with floor-to-ceiling bookshelves, crammed with what appeared to be very old books. It was also filled with tables for the reception dinner to follow, but at this time people were milling around elsewhere and the room was empty. We squeezed between the tables to get to the shelves so we could hunt for the book. To our amazement, there it was on one of the first shelves we looked at, a small book with yellowed pages. We gingerly took the book off the shelf; as we did so, a single piece of paper fell out and floated to the floor. I quickly picked it up and saw that it was a letter, written in the tiniest script that I had ever seen. The musty, brittle paper was obviously quite old. Gordon and I were speechless as we read the letter silently to ourselves. It was written by a young girl who had apparently lived in the building when it was a private residence. This had been her family home. In the letter, written in the 1800's, she described a relationship she was having with a young black man, and that it had to remain secret for fear of her family learning about it.

Before we could decide what to do with the letter, if anything, the announcement came that it was time to sit down for dinner, and people suddenly began crowding into the library. We had to move so that people could sit in their assigned seats, so we quickly put the letter back into the book, placed it back in the bookcase, and left the room. We intended to go back to the library after dinner and once again examine the letter, but the opportunity never presented itself. We later found a brochure from the inn which confirmed the name of the family and the daughter's name. We could only surmise that after all this time, the girl at last wanted someone to know her secret. It is said that ghosts inhabit places because their spirits are unable to reconcile their deaths, perhaps because of some unfinished business. The spirit of this young girl must have felt a strong need to share her secret, and with Gordon's ability to receive information, she was able to direct him to the letter in the book. We hoped that sharing her secret with us had been enough to allow her to move forward on her journey.

These kinds of experiences were common for Gordon in the early years, and he had to learn how to tune out much of it for the sake of his own sanity. Gradually, he developed the ability to keep it in the background unless he chose to access it. He also learned how to ask for specific information when he wanted it. But, he was never comfortable with information that had to do with events yet to happen. Living with knowledge of the future and the responsibility of what to do with it was never easy for him. Having personal knowledge of some of these events was hard, but trying to decide whether or not the information should be shared with others was even more difficult. The only thing that got him through this time period was the ever-increasing trust he was developing in his inner guidance. Along with his new abilities, he'd also found that he had spiritual guides who could help him deal with this new body of information that he was receiving. These guides made themselves known to him when he needed them, and he eventually learned how to call on them at will.

One of the most important lessons of that early time period was learning how to deal with fear. Gordon first had to deal with his own fear of what was happening to him, and at the same time he became aware of other people's fear of him. In our culture, there is very little credence given to anything of a metaphysical nature, and as a result such things are often misunderstood, and feared. Actually, most people were not so much afraid of Gordon as they were afraid of what he might know about them. People often thought that he had nothing better to do than probe their minds and reveal their innermost thoughts. As soon as they felt assured that he didn't read minds, nor did he want to know about their personal lives, they would relax. Many then proceeded to turn around and pressure him with questions about themselves. As it turned out, these early lessons were precursors of what was to come, only on a much larger scale. Years later, when Gordon's Earth changes predictions were published, we experienced a whole new dimension of fear. This time it affected large groups of people, and we heard from all of them. Along with that fear came, once again, questions relating to people's personal lives: "Where should I move?" "Where will I be safe?" "Will there be an earthquake here?"

We had hoped that by publishing the information on Earth changes (which we began to do in October of 1991), we could help people increase their own awareness, and they would find out for themselves whether or not Gordon's predictions had any validity for them. Instead, we were amazed to find out how readily people would turn over the responsibility for their own lives to someone else. It was not a responsibility that we sought, nor one that we wanted.

Time and time again we addressed this issue of personal responsibility in the *Earth Changes Report*. We advised people never to make decisions based on fear, but to use Gordon's predictions as just another piece of information to be included in what we hoped would be a comprehensive approach to decision-making. We felt so strongly about people determining the paths of their own lives, that we began to offer instruction on intuition, so that people could learn how to fine tune their own innate intuitive abilities.

Throughout this time period, we found that dreams were becoming the common denominator — the doorway into the world of intuition that we had been searching for. Everyone dreams. Even people who are completely resistant to using their own intuitive abilities in the conscious state seem open to insights that take place in the dream state. We began to focus on dreams as a way to help people develop their intuition, thereby giving them another tool to assist them in their decision-making process. We felt that this was an important step, because by now the changes that Gordon had seen for years were beginning to happen, and most likely more were on the way. And so our focus has changed from warning people of possible Earth changes, to helping them develop their own inner guidance — to become confident in their intuitive abilities and to learn to rely on it when making decisions for themselves and their families.

I have known Gordon for some fifteen years. He is my husband, my business partner, and my best friend. We've shared much in our years together, and I've probably been privy to much more information about the future than I ever wanted or needed to know. But through it all, there has been a constant love and mutual support of one another. Together we have journeyed through time, to ancient civilizations long since forgotten, and to probable futures yet to come; we have visited realities beyond time and space, and explored concepts difficult to put into words. Our experiences together have run the emotional gamut — fear, sadness, joy, wonder, and an ongoing mind-expanding awareness — in what I can only describe as the ride of a lifetime. *Notes from the Cosmos* is the story of that journey. We hope you enjoy the ride as much as we have.

— *Cynthia Keyes*

Preface

In 1982 I began work on this book, not with any intent of publishing it, but rather, out of necessity. Three years earlier, my life had changed suddenly and irrevocably within a single period of twenty-four hours. Not only did my friends stop knowing who I was, I found I didn't know myself either. Without warning or acceptance on my part, psychic phenomena had begun to occur in my life on a daily basis. Everything you may have read, watched on television, or seen in the movies regarding paranormal experience — E.S.P., seeing auras, communications with poltergeists, spirits, and other higher intelligences, channeling, psychic healing, astral travel and out-of-body experiences — was happening to me.

To maintain my sanity, I began to keep "notes" on the messages I was receiving from what I could only refer to as "an intelligence from the cosmos." By 1985, I had filled volumes of notebooks and audio-cassette tapes with the information I had received, and with descriptions of the phenomena I had witnessed.

A few years passed, and the onslaught of phenomena slowed down enough so that I felt I could catch my breath. By then it was 1988, and I drafted the first rough version of this book, hoping to release it so that others who might be having similar experiences could benefit from my experiences and research. This was not to be the case, however. No sooner had I made the commitment to release my transcript of *Notes from the Cosmos*, when the phenomena began again, stronger and even more frequently than before. I was now receiving new "notes" each day that would need to be added to the manuscript. Clearly the forces at work here felt I had more to learn; it wasn't yet time to release my manuscript.

I continued to experience this deluge of psychic input for several more years, until 1991, when it all stopped one day, abruptly, much as one might turn off a light switch. My health had deteriorated by then, as a result of what I felt was psychic overload, so it was perhaps a blessing to finally lose this input that I had come to see as valuable and rewarding, even at the expense of my own well-being. But while all the previous phenomena ceased, something new and gentle came to replace them. A new group of intelligences presented themselves to me, and they continue to guide me to this day.

These intelligences have become known to me as my dream guides. They aren't spirits or something outside me; rather, they are within. Have you ever wondered just how the incredible dreams we experience are created? Who creates them? I continue to wonder about this, and can only feel that it is the hand of God, although this power is something to look for inside ourselves, rather than up in the clouds. This mild, simple connection with my dream guides allows me to continue seeking answers beyond our current human knowledge, although it does not affect my health adversely, as previous contacts have done. Experiences are no longer happening *to* me, as they did in the beginning. Instead, my dream guides are working *with* me, in what has become a joyful pursuit of understanding and clarity about the world we live in.

With this new contact made, I once again began to record massive amounts of data on what my dream guides referred to as "the most important body of information for mankind to know today." My guides were referring to the sentient Earth, and our present interactions with her. History-as-we-know-it was going to sustain great changes, very shortly. According to my guides, we — all life on Earth — would help to determine just how this change will come about. The insights of my dream guides continue to be received by me on key nights, and occasionally, while fully awake. Since 1991, I have endeavored to share these insights through my newsletter, the *Earth Changes Report.*

The book you are about to read is the story of my journey into the world of spirituality and intuition. My initiation, if you will. Some of my experiences may strike a chord, and you may discover that you too have had similar experiences. Perhaps a dream that you remembered vividly turned out to be prophetic. Or perhaps you've had a déjà vu experience, a near-death experience, a daydream that gave you the answer to an "unsolvable" problem, or simply a "knowing" that comes over you, showing you the solution to a puzzling issue. In the course of training thousands of people how to use their latent intuitive abilities to their fullest potential, I've learned that all of the experiences mentioned above are not only normal and healthy — they occur to each of us daily! It is up to us whether we ignore this vital part of ourselves, or practice its use until we become comfortable trusting what it has to tell us about our lives here on Earth.

Before you begin this journey into the world of intuition with me, I can suggest one tool that will become an invaluable asset to have on your voyage — a journal to keep track of the feelings and experiences you will have as you read this book. If you have never kept a journal before, now is as good a time as any to start. Just get a blank spiral notebook, and try to write in it each day, making special note of any insights or dreams you have. By the time you reach the chapter, "How to Become a DreamVoyager," you will already have made some progress towards unlocking the power of your intuition. Additionally, I maintain a World Wide Web site on the Internet where interested people can share their experiences. For more information on how to access these sites through your local internet server, please see the resources section at the back of this book.

After you read *Notes from the Cosmos,* you may want to practice honing your own intuitive skills, much in the same manner as I have done. I hope this book helps you get started on the right foot. Remember, everything that happens is part of the journey. The outcome is only a memory of the journey.

Good luck, and may the spirit of life fill your heart with joy.

— *Gordon-Michael Scallion*

CHAPTER ONE

The Awakening

As a young boy, chronic asthma forced me to spend much of my time in bed. The disease appeared out of nowhere, I'm told, at around the age of two. It is possible I've suppressed the memories of these early years of my life, since I recollect little of my growing up, save those stories which were later told to me by relatives. Both the asthma and the social difficulties that resulted from it were painful, to be sure. Summers were spent in make-up classes, catching up for all the school time I had lost during the cold, Connecticut winters that aggravated my asthma. Strenuous activities — sports or just rough playing — were simply not a part of my early life. I do have some vague memories from this time, but most seem as dreams that belong to someone else, like a shared memory.

Around the age of seven, I built my first crystal radio and began to experiment with electronics, possibly because it was something I could do alone at home, even in bed. Over the next few years I taught myself Morse code, just for fun, and proceeded to read everything I could get my hands on relating to antennas, transmitters or receivers. By the time I was thirteen, I had earned my ham radio license and was granted permission by the Federal Communications Commission to operate a transmitter. I look back at these choices now and realize this may have been my first "psychic" or intuitive experience, although I certainly didn't see it that way at the time. These interests would dovetail rather neatly with the experiences that were to come, almost as if I had some latent knowledge of the path I would later find myself on. Even as a child, there were unseen forces guiding me toward something ... as they do for all of us. Sometimes it's simply a matter of stopping to look back and see what was there all along.

My interest in electronics continued as I grew to adulthood, first taking correspondence courses and later attending night school for four years majoring in electronics at a local university. With a new family and a full-time job taking up more and more of my time, however, I withdrew from night school and continued my studies on my own, as I had earlier in life.

Until 1979, my life could have been considered self-indulgent and average. I was, however, always amazed at what seemed to be an almost uncanny ability to analyze technical problems intuitively, especially in electronics, where problems might be caused by any one of hundreds of different circuits. If you aren't familiar with electronics, imagine trying to find the single burned out bulb on a string of Christmas tree lights. Now imagine going straight to the bad bulb, replacing it, and having the whole strand light up in your hands. It was like that with me all the time. With a dozen circuit boards to choose from, somehow I always managed to go straight for the culprit within a failing system, not just identifying which board the problem was with, but the exact point of failure. This enabled me to work quickly, to feel satisfied by my work, and as a result, to prosper.

By the mid-1970s, when I was in my thirties, the symptoms

of my asthma had reduced somewhat. I was no longer dependent on medications to control it, but I still had to watch for major outbreaks. Exposure to cold air — something we had plenty of in New England — could easily bring on a respiratory attack that would last for an hour or more.

I began to experience strong urges to travel to foreign countries around this time, not for any particular reason other than as an experience, and by this time I had been divorced for about a year, so I had no reason not to follow these instincts. Partly due to my ongoing struggle with asthma, warm places were at the top of my list, especially during wintertimes in New England, where snowbanks grew to several feet in height and temperatures could drop to sub-zero ranges. Mexico and Canada were the destinations which seemed within reach and budget, and Mexico sounded the warmer and more pleasant of the two, so in 1975 I embarked on a venture to Mexico with friends. We planned no itinerary, only the point at which we would cross the border, my camper crammed full with the three of us, plus our gear and supplies. Off we went, and some days later we found ourselves in Mexico City, attending a bullfight. It was here I encountered my first negative intuitive reaction. I found myself in shock, watching the bloody spectacle. But I wasn't simply judging the culture that could create this thing. At the same time, I felt a new feeling I could not ever remember having had in my lifetime — as if I was watching something I had watched before. I don't mean on television or in books, but somehow I felt I had actually seen such events in the past. I shrugged it off, telling myself I had probably dreamed about it, (even though it was not a dream I could remember). I don't know why I thought it might have been a dream, but this was all my rational mind could come up with as an explanation. Having satisfied my need for logic with this theory, I let it go.

Returning to our camper, I scanned the brochures we had picked up at the border. Two jumped out at me: the pyramids of Teotihuacán, and the Popocatépetl volcano. We talked it over, and the group was open to a journey, though my friends wondered why I had selected these locations so definitively. I couldn't answer for sure, I only knew that somehow I was drawn to them. I would have gone alone if necessary, the feelings were that strong. A few days later we arrived at the pyramids of Teotihuacán. My heart raced as we entered the area. My eyes began blinking rapidly, and I rubbed them, not understanding my reaction. Blue sparks appeared in my peripheral vision. I wrote it off to the pressure I was applying to my eyes. None of this experience agreed easily with my view of the world up to that point, but I made it all conform to concepts I could accept. I had a pretty good idea of how things worked, chemistry, physics and such. How could anything happen that did not fit with the immutable laws of science?

As I walked towards the Temple of the Sun, I felt an electrical sensation run all over my body. The blue flashes which had left now returned, seeming to dance about at the edge of my field of vision. I sat down, believing it was the high altitude, some ten thousand feet above sea level. Once again the same feeling of familiarity I'd experienced while watching the bullfight came over me. My eyes began to blink rapidly again. With a loud pop-like sound, I was suddenly transported back in time. I could see the ancient street as it once looked, with buildings on both sides, and the pyramids at the end of the road. Teotihuacán is reported to be over four thousand years old (though there is now some controversy over its age — some scientists believe it may be more than five thousand years old). Most of it has been unearthed and reconstructed during this century. As I blinked, I could see thatched roofs where none now exist. The walls of buildings which are now just piles of stone were covered with a coating of stucco, reddish-orange in color. Murals detailed some of the larger buildings which stood atop embankments adjacent to the Temple of Sun and Moon. My imagination was playing tricks with me, I thought. But regardless of how I justified what I was experiencing, I simply wrote it off to thin air and the exotic nature of the locale. If I had ever had any interest in pyramids or ancient cultures, I would have had an easier time explaining away my feelings and visions as creative daydreams, but I had never cared about these things at all. I had read very little on the subject, and studied nothing. Still, it was probably just the altitude.

My friends and I completed the tour and left for a nearby campground. The next morning we set off for Popocatépetl, about a half-day's drive away. Once there we, like most everyone else who visits, climbed the volcano. Hiking up to the summit, we walked on pumice and ash left from the last eruption, some thirty years earlier. This was a dormant volcano, but once again the feeling of déjà vu — a term I'd heard before, but something I'd never experienced — came over me. My eyelids fluttered, and I could feel my eyes moving in a rapid, REM-like fashion. I could actually see the volcano erupting! I shut my eyes tightly and slowly opened them, only to find large rocks thrusting up into the air from where the crater was, the top looking like a fountain of fireworks at Fourth of July. I turned to a stranger in our group and uttered something very odd: "This is not going to be dormant for long." Coming from me at that time, I see now that it was truly one of the strangest things I'd ever said to another person. Then, as quickly as the vision had occurred, it vanished. We rested on the mountain for an hour or so, and left for our next campground. I never told my friends about what I had experienced; I could barely accept it myself. Some years later, in 1994, Popocatépetl erupted, after more than five decades of silence, requiring evacuations in excess of seventy-five thousand people. It has remained active since then, and in 1997, (as this book was going to press) the volcano has erupted once again, causing the evacuation of thousands of people.

* * * * *

After a month in Mexico, we returned to New England, to our jobs and our everyday lives, and for the next few years everything in my life seemed to be the same as before. I did think about the trip often, and on occasion even mused about the strange phenomena I'd experienced, but I continued to dismiss them as the effects of high altitude on my brain. Several years later I found myself having an increasingly difficult time breathing in the winter, and finally made the decision to move to a warmer climate. My asthma was significantly reduced whenever I spent time by the warm ocean, so one day I decided to play "pin the tail on the donkey" with a map of Florida. I closed my eyes, and went for the map. The pin landed on Venice, Florida, and a few weeks later I moved there.

By February 1979, I had been happily ensconced in Florida for a couple of years. I was single, living on a thirty-foot sailboat, and had started an electronics consulting business that was doing extremely well. Basking in the warmth of the days, less afflicted by asthmatic problems than I'd ever been, I knew Florida was the right place to be. My life was pleasant, my work was both lucrative and satisfying, and I thought I was about as happy as a person could be.

One day, while in the middle of a conversation with a client, my vocal chords suddenly refused to work. It was as if someone had pulled my voice out of my throat, and though I opened my mouth, moved it, and had every intention of speaking, not a sound came out. My client was alarmed at first, thinking I was having a heart attack, and as I was nearing age forty, that possibility crossed my mind as well. There was no pain, though, no discomfort, just silence. Soon we terminated the meeting and the client left, never to return. And still I had no voice.

By evening, I'd finally made contact with a local doctor, who had then referred me to an intern at the hospital. Not being able to use the telephone, this had taken awhile. The young intern who was attending to me seemed both competent and sympathetic. I attempted to explain what had happened in a sign language of my own devising. He looked at me with a smile on his face, one that I assumed was intended to make me feel at ease. When he examined me, however, he could find nothing wrong, and he suggested that I check into the hospital overnight for some more rigorous tests.

That night I lay in the hospital, immobilized by IV needles in both arms. I felt hungry, and a bit fearful, anticipating what they might find. I turned on the television and watched it idly, meanwhile jotting down a list of things I meant to get done once I was released from the hospital. I kept a notebook handy, by the side of my bed. I noticed the "Tonight Show" would be coming on soon, and thought I might watch it before going to sleep.

Around 11:00 p.m. I observed a strange glow at the end of my room. It appeared to be emanating from outside my door, and beyond the swinging door which opened into the hall. My first thought was that they were using some sort of equipment out in the hallway, taking x-rays or even flash photographs. Unconcerned, I went back to watching TV. A few minutes later, though, I noticed that the glow was now penetrating my room. Soon a circular ball was hovering near the end of my bed. It was a foot in diameter and purple in color, with indigo sparks glowing and flickering about its surface. I thought it was a reflection of some sort, because I was still not willing, at that point in my life, to think it might be anything else.

The glow had hardly been there for more than a few seconds when a clear vision — definitely not a reflection — appeared where the sphere had been and then moved out and floated over my bed, about two feet above my knees. It was the face of an elderly woman, perhaps in her seventies, with silver hair. Beams of light radiated from her, appearing to penetrate the ceiling and floor, although none of the rays were coming towards me. Her lips were moving, but there was no sound.

At this point I really wanted the nurse call button, because I knew something really strange was happening to me, but I just couldn't reach it. The IV was starting to pull my arm, and I was trying to somehow hold onto it with my right hand while I went for the button. It was a real predicament, because I couldn't yell, I couldn't speak, and I couldn't reach the button that would summon help.

By this time, I was terrified. Not knowing what was happening, I pushed myself back in the bed, digging my feet in. But the way my mind worked, even in the middle of that extreme fear, I needed to find some rational reason for why this was happening. I wasn't ready to accept the fact that I had maybe gone off the deep end, suddenly become schizophrenic or that I was hallucinating on my own; I couldn't accept those possibilities as reality. What I could accept was that perhaps what was in the IV was somehow altering my perceptions. I didn't know much about drugs, because I hadn't participated in the sixties' drug scene, so I'd never experienced a lot of the things that I had read about, and I thought maybe this was an answer. I told myself, "Okay, this is what's happening ... the medicine in the IV is distorting my sense of reality." My body relaxed completely, as soon as I felt like I had an answer that made sense to me. I just gave myself over to the situation at that point.

As I stared at the woman, I heard her speak. But I realized that I was hearing her voice inside my head, not through my ears. She said, "Write down what I'm going to show you." Having accepted the experience as drug-induced, I was able to go along with this. She proceeded to show me things to write down — events she said would occur in the future, some within the next lunar cycle and some within my lifetime. I had no idea what a lunar cycle was, but I wrote it down anyway. Some of the things that she said were going to happen sooner rather than later included an airline crash, a small earthquake which would be accompanied by certain weather conditions, and a specific economic situation that would occur. She also showed me pictures of ancient civilizations. It was all so real and three-dimensional that it felt as if I was experiencing some kind of time-travel, as if I were actually there amongst the people and places she was showing me.

She then told me that, beginning in the late 1980s, there would be major Earth changes throughout the world, beginning with an increase in earthquakes, volcanic activity, tsunamis, and other occurrences of this nature. By the early nineties, she stated, these would increase in number and intensity each year, and that people would begin to blame God for these things, and each other, and their governments, and that it was to be a time of great choosing. And she called this period "tribulation."

I watched all of this, and I wrote it all down. You have to remember where I was coming from, too. I didn't know what metaphysics was; I didn't know what psychic phenomena was; I didn't believe in UFOs. I really didn't have a belief system at all. While I had a Catholic upbringing, at age seventeen I had left home and gone out on my own. I had never really formed a belief system of my own, never really explored anything of this nature. I was convinced that what I was experiencing was a drug-induced eruption of suppressed beliefs. I figured maybe I had been having too good a time in life, living on my sailboat, making money, and so on. Remembering the religious teachings of my early childhood that seemed to focus so much on sacrifice and suffering, I thought "If you have too good a time in life, somehow you have to pay a price." So here I was, laying in the hospital, paying the price. Again, I had constructed a rationalization I could handle.

When the woman in my vision had completed her message, she stopped talking, and a new phenomenon began. The light beams that emanated from the sphere became prismatic, and appeared to be moving from within, as if the light was speeding away from the woman, penetrating the floor, walls and ceiling with increasing intensity. Finally, the color bars became a blur, and near the left side of the old woman's face there appeared mathematical formulas and symbols, as if written on an invisible chalkboard. I could see each one of these clearly, but then it too would speed up and eventually disappear in a blur, only to be followed by another and another. Then, when this part of the experience had reached an extreme in intensity, as quickly as it had started, everything ended. Just disappeared!

As I regained focus, I could hear Ed McMahon saying, "Heeeeere's Johnny," and realized the TV was still on, just as it had been. I was now exhausted. I put aside the notes I had taken and watched Carson for a while, and then shut off the lights and television and went to sleep.

The next thing I knew, the windows were being opened by a very cheerful nurse who was saying, "Good morning! How are you today?"

Without thinking, I said, "I'm doing fine, thank you."

Surprised, she scanned my chart, exclaiming, "You can talk!"

I was just as surprised as she was, and gingerly explored my neck and throat area with one hand. "I guess I can." Then, remembering the experience of the night before, I asked, "By the way, can you tell me what's in these IVs?"

She said I would have to talk to my doctor.

When the doctor appeared, he reported that my tests had turned up nothing, but more tests might help. He added, however, that his sense was that my problem was not physical, but what he called "an emotional restriction." I had an inkling of what he was getting at. He gave me the name of another doctor to see — a psychiatrist, as it turned out — and released me from the hospital.

I decided I had had enough new experiences for twenty-four hours, and badly needed to get back to my boat. As I left the hospital, I was amazed by the brightness of the sun. I saw an Irish setter, and around her body were shades of amber and orange, tinged with blue. Still rationalizing, I thought, "I need to get some sunglasses." I also observed a similar brightness around other objects — people, cars, palm trees, dogs. I attributed this phenomenon to the experience I had just gone through. The number of explanations I was being forced to devise for myself to make sense of it all were growing by the hour. But I was pretty desperate to leave my beliefs unexamined, and to pick up my good life in Florida where I'd left it the day before.

I was picked up at the hospital by a friend who was a psychologist. I asked him to find out what kind of drugs I had been given. He assured me they wouldn't have given me any drugs without running more tests, nor without telling me about it. I told him the name I had noticed on the IV bottles, and he explained that this was just a glucose solution to keep me from getting dehydrated. My whole drug-trip theory vanished before my eyes. I realized I had to face the fact that I may indeed have experienced "an emotional restriction," and that maybe I would have to talk to a psychiatrist after all. Instead, I went sailing and tried to put the last twenty-four hours out of my mind. Later that evening, I shared what I had written down at the hospital with my friend, trying to make light of it. I was no longer "going with the experience," but I was willing to laugh about it. Frankly, I was willing to do anything that would help make it go away.

Later that week, my friend called and asked me if I'd seen the newspaper. "No. Why?" I asked. He was excited, and proceeded to tell me that some of the events that I'd written down during my strange vision at the hospital had actually taken place. I was greatly alarmed by this, and refused to discuss it with him. Many years would go by before I was finally able to accept what had been happening to me, at which point I began to keep records of my premonitions. I wish now that I had done so in the beginning, but at the time I just wanted it to stop. Not only did I discard the original notes I'd taken, but I actively avoided any news that might have proved their accuracy. Quite simply, I wanted nothing to do with it.

For days, I withdrew into myself and became very quiet. I had stopped seeing colors around animals and people, at least. And I could still talk! Happily, no more glowing balls visited me at night, although I did find myself checking the sky frequently and thinking that there might be life out there after all. I couldn't forget what had happened to me, but I couldn't accept it either. I decided that the only way to get out of this thing was to leave Florida immediately. In a way, I was hoping Florida would be like a haunted house where I could leave the ghosts behind, if I just got out. So in a matter of months I moved back to my hometown in New England.

But Florida was not a haunted house, and these were not ghosts I was dealing with. The visions followed me home.

CHAPTER TWO

Looking for Answers

ack in Connecticut, the good friends I had known before
leaving seemed distant to me. I no longer felt connected to
many elements of my life, and found myself unable to simply
pick up the pieces and continue on with the lifestyle I had
thought of as comfortable and satisfying. Changes were occurring rapidly, and I noticed new ones almost daily, although I
still didn't understand why this was happening to me. I was
not consciously choosing to change my life; change was
choosing me.

It seemed to start with food. Helplessly, I relinquished one
favorite after another. The first to go was my daily enjoyment
of a burger, large fries, and a vanilla shake for lunch, which
now made me violently ill. (Nowadays, this may seem an
obvious dietary faux pas, but this was early 1980; healthy food
had not become nearly so mainstreamed into the mass-con-

sciousness of our culture at that time, and I was especially uninitiated to the concept of a balanced diet. For many years I had succumbed to noontime "Big Mac attacks" with no ill effects. So I was truly surprised to find my stomach turning on me, literally!) The first time it happened, I wrote it off to a "twenty-four-hour bug" and tried again, with the same results. I found I could now tolerate neither red meat nor fried foods, instead finding myself drawn to vegetable soups and leafy salads. Fortunately, desserts seemed "allowed" to remain on the menu, although lighter portions and lower sugar levels were now more appealing. I was forced to give up milk, but could still drink coffee, now black, instead of the splash of java I used to add to my cream and sugar. I lost all tolerance for alcohol, too, so that even two beers over the course of an evening now made me feel sick and slightly drunk. As my physical body began to make these decisions about what was best for me, my conscious mind played a perpetual game of catch-up, grudgingly going along with the lifestyle changes my body now insisted upon, all the while wishing for my life to just "go back to normal."

At the same time, other phenomena were occurring. I tried to ignore anything that seemed out of the ordinary, afraid that the doctor in Florida had been right in suggesting I was becoming unstable. Actually, he had not said anything of the sort, only that what I had experienced was not physical, and that mental causes would be the next thing to check out. But I was — as most of us are — extremely uncomfortable with the idea that my mind might not be working exactly as I would like it to work, and I preferred to deny the possibility completely. I busied myself with short-term consulting jobs, living mostly from the proceeds I'd earned from selling my company in Florida. Fear was something I began to put more and more energy into denying; it sapped the enthusiasm I'd always applied to my interest in electronics, my work and my leisure activities. It took a great deal of energy to keep myself from looking in a new direction.

Often, I would see movements out of the corner of my eye,

at the outer reaches of my peripheral vision. I would turn, expecting to see whatever it was that had moved, but nothing would be there. These experiences would continue for between ten seconds and two minutes, depending upon how long I was willing to spend before blocking the incident from my mind and going back to the safety of my denial. Afterwards I would usually have a headache.

Of course, whenever I allowed myself to acknowledge the frequency of this particular phenomenon, I saw it as the unfolding of real trouble. But I was convinced I could diagnose what was happening to me in a technical manner. Science would provide me with a rational explanation, an indisputable formula, which I could then use to some personal advantage. I comforted myself with the old adage, "Only truly sane people question their own sanity, whereas insane people are always absolutely positive that they are perfectly sane." I was questioning these weird occurrences, in proper scientific fashion, so I deduced that I must be all right. Still operating from a place of fear, I had begun to admit that these "flashes" in my peripheral vision were bona fide experiences, not figments of my imagination; however, I continued to see this Outer Peripheral Vision (or "OPV," as I had begun to call it) as a physical ailment, a problem to be confronted and stopped. I decided to look for certain details in the experience, the symptoms as it were, and in that way find a cure. Was it something in the eyelids, perhaps? Could it be that the headaches were mild migraines, and the OPV was an early warning sign? I would get to the bottom of this. I vowed that the next time the OPV happened, I would stop everything I was doing and pay attention to every nuance of feeling until the headache came. Then I would be able to go to my doctor with an explicit description of my malady, he would immediately identify it, give me a prescription and send me home. I would be cured, and I could go back to eating my cheeseburgers in peace. This decision made, I was ready.

It was the spring of 1981, three days before Easter, when it happened. I was shopping in the supermarket, rushing around on Thursday at 5:30 p.m., along with everyone else who was trying to get stocked up for the holiday weekend. I was locked into the meat section, where a queue for Easter hams and turkeys was making maneuvering difficult for everyone involved. There was a feeling of mass exasperation in the air, and I was no exception.

The flash came, just outside my field of vision, as usual. This time I wasn't going to run away. I froze in the middle of the aisle, immediately giving myself over to awareness of any feelings or sensations I might be having. Did I have a headache? Were my eyes fluttering? People were undoubtedly backed up in the aisle all around me, but I didn't hear or see anything. I was tuning in only to my problem.

Then a very interesting thing happened. I call it "interesting" because that has become the word I use to describe events that might be considered out of the ordinary, even when they are extremely unusual, even extraordinary. Suddenly, the vision changed from a sense of movement just outside my peripheral vision to something I could actually see out of the corner of my eye. A whole scene began to unfold at the edge of my vision. I saw land and cities, between which various aircraft — not planes — were flying. These craft looked like large balloons with finely woven baskets suspended under them. They were similar to dirigibles, but had no propellers, although they traveled horizontally and with purpose, unlike a hot-air balloon. The cities that I saw glistened. They had rounded, oval, and dome-shaped buildings. Captivated by the image, I started to "pull" the vision into my full field of view, but I became aware of the headache at just that point, and as I tried to move the image, the headache became much more intense. I tried to disregard it, but it was quite painful. I then lost the image anyway, as suddenly as it had come. I snapped back into awareness of my surroundings. I was still there in the supermarket, now with a number of irate people attempting to push around me. Having no idea how much time had elapsed, and feeling somewhat embarrassed for having "spaced out" in a public place, I just shuffled my cart on down the aisle, leaving the crowd and the butcher behind me. Inside, I felt proud that I had prepared for the event and met it, and though the experience had certainly been stranger than expected, I now had some data stored away that would hopefully be useful in identifying my problem.

My experiments would continue in the coming months, each one giving me more information. As I allowed the visions, they became more frequent and less painful, until I was experiencing at least one every day or two. Many times the scenes were similar to the first one I had at the supermarket. Many dealt with faces, though no one I recognized. These scenes often had a dreamlike quality, although I was conscious and awake in every instance. Drifting from one scene to another sometimes, I saw people in different clothing and styles. Some of these were vaguely familiar, perhaps historical, while some were completely unfamiliar.

About three months after the first vision, I had to fly down to Virginia on business. Finding myself with a half hour to kill at the airport, I lingered in the bookstore, looking for an interesting novel to read on the plane. I couldn't find anything, so I drifted out of the best-seller section and down another aisle. I heard an announcement that my flight was about to begin boarding and, in a panic, ran down the aisle, still wishing I had found something to read. A book tumbled off the shelf as I brushed past. I picked it up, and without thinking, took it to the counter and purchased it. Once safely in my seat on the airplane, I examined the book. It was titled, *The Sleeping Prophet*, and it was the biography of a man I had never heard of named Edgar Cayce. My flight was a couple of hours long, so I settled in to read my strange purchase. Opening the curious book before take-off, I was immediately swept up into the story of Cayce's life.

The similarities between Cayce's early experiences and what had happened to me in Florida were startling to me. Although there had been some indications of paranormal experience in his childhood, it was not until Edgar Cayce was twenty-one that he developed a gradual paralysis of the throat muscles, which in turn caused him to lose his voice. When doctors were unable to find a physical cause for this condition, and hypnosis had failed to have any permanent effect, Cayce reentered a trance-state similar to that which had enabled him to memorize his schoolbooks as a child. In this way, he was able to discover the cause and proper treatment of his own illness. He went on to record more than *fourteen thousand* clairvoyant statements over a period of forty-three years. These documents apparently constitute one of the largest and most impressive records of psychic perception ever to emanate from a single individual, and they included many premonitions which were nearly identical to the visions I had recently experienced.[1]

I didn't stop reading until I had devoured the book from beginning to end. As I finished the last page, I became aware that we had landed and the last passengers were straggling out at the front exit, leaving only me on the plane. As I gathered my belongings and disembarked, I kept ruminating about the book I had just read. "I know it's all true," I thought. "The experiences that Cayce had, how he did it, why he did it ... I know all about him." I just knew. Everything I'd read rang of the truth.

Since that time I have talked to literally thousands of people who have had experiences of being directed to a particular book that had a profound impact on their lives. In my case, it was almost as if I'd been guided in a direction that, somewhere along the line, I would come to understand. While I understood the truth of the book, I still understood very little about myself, and I was afraid of the changes that were happening to me.

I spent the next several months processing what I had read. I didn't run out to buy any more books, nor did I look anywhere else for more information. In context, my visions no

---

[1] The biographical information on Edgar Cayce referred to here is from the book Edgar Cayce on Reincarnation, by Noel Langley, under the editorship of Hugh Lynn Cayce. (New York: Warner Books, Inc., 1967), pp. 8-9.

longer seemed so outstanding; they simply occurred.

Looking back on it, I see that I had started the first of what would be numerous learning cycles, struggling with and completing one lesson, then beginning another, each with a whole new set of obstacles to overcome, each building on the lessons learned previously. I was embarking on a completely new way of viewing myself in relation to the world. As I slowly learned to trust my inner knowing — that intuitive answer-book that resides in each of us — I became less dependent on collecting the external data I had most often used to make decisions. Slowly, I lost the feeling that comes from trying desperately to corroborate parental influences, popular opinion, perceived facts and various unfounded notions, all in order to figure out the next right thing to spend time on, where to live, what to wear, or who to associate with. Fear, I began to discover, has more to do with making decisions than anything else.

Bombarded by a flood of external data, each of us, moment by moment, attempts to filter all the information correctly and then make good decisions. What we are afraid of is that the data might be wrong, or that we might interpret it wrong, or a combination thereof. Denial is simply the candy-coating we use to make the fear palatable. Without denial, many of us might take root at the doorstep of our homes, never venturing out, or back in, again. Denial allows us to take many perceptions at face value, unquestioningly, so that we are able to continue about our business. Still, this is merely fear in disguise, and the fear is felt from within, an often unnamed dread, and we continue to look for authority figures who will tell us what is right.

What I began to discover as I looked inside myself for answers, is that the confusion of data that proliferates on the outside was simply not there. Trusting my intuition, I began to understand certain truths; and these were indeed certain, because there was no conflicting information to corroborate. I learned to ask questions and answer them all within myself, where it was safe. Taking these answers back out into the world to use, I felt sure and clear. As I strengthened my faith in my own intuitive abilities, fear and denial gradually subsided. No longer so afraid of the changes that were happening in my life, I was beginning to embrace the process of learning wholeheartedly.

My life lessons continued, and the visions I'd started to see at the periphery of my vision began to appear in my dreams. This was unusual in itself, because up until then I had been sure that I was a person who simply didn't dream. Before that point I couldn't tell you about a single dream I had ever had. Suddenly, though, I became aware of many of my dreams. Now I was having multiple dreams each night, vivid and detailed, and remembering them all when I awoke each morning.

Although I was having these fascinating dream scenarios now, and learning to trust my intuitive abilities more fully, I still had a long way to go. In many ways, I was not making any conscious improvements in my life, letting these changes happen to me or at me, rather than taking responsibility for the new course of my life. I had made a choice that day at the supermarket, and made a huge leap forward on my path, yet progress often came in fits and starts. I was eating food more suitable for a rabbit than a human, having given up much of my "old" diet while ignoring the need to learn more about what to eat instead. Also, my financial resources were dwindling rapidly. I'd begun to find it very difficult to do anything vocationally. Letting the physical and mental changes happen, rather than harnessing my will to the power of those changes, my productivity had suffered greatly. More and more I was being drawn to find out the *why* of all this. One more experience was needed, however, to tap me on the shoulder with a two-by-four (I now refer to this in my seminars as "the two-by-four effect"), before I would commit myself to seeking and studying more helpful materials.

On a morning in late 1981, I awoke feeling a tingling sensation throughout my body. The sensation itself was not uncommon, as I often slept with an arm or foot in a contorted position and would awake needing to massage the limb to get circulation going again. This particular morning I looked down to find that both of my big toenails had turned black. As I stared down at my toes, the tingling started moving as if it were a mild electric current. Actually, it was more as if my skin was being dissolved or touched by mild acid, not painful, but prickling. This sensation moved slowly up to my ankles, then up to my knees. I was struck by terror, because it was a physical experience that came from nowhere, again very much like losing my voice. Fearful and helpless, I lay motionless as the feeling spread rapidly up to my chest. I reached for my chest with both hands as if to pull the sensation back down, crying aloud, "No, I'm not ready yet!"

With the word "yet" still echoing in the air around me, the sensation subsided the way it had come, as if it were peeled away by an invisible hand. I can't explain why I said those words. I was now fully awake, alert and sitting up in bed. I didn't know what to think, nor did I have any ideas on what to do about it. Over the next few weeks, this experience happened several more times. Each time was more subtle than those previous, but I was no longer quite so terrified, and the tingling never proceeded past my throat. The sensation grew fainter, and without my speaking, it stopped each time and receded.

During the same time this was occurring, I began to see full-scale visions when I met people for the first time, or when I met up with someone I already knew. To the left of where they were standing, I would see scenarios of the person engaged in some activity. To the right would appear another "screen" of them doing something else. Often my visions were divided into three, rather than two, moving pictures — sort of a split-screen projection — following the subject and appearing to me as if part of a ghostly stage set behind them. Through experimentation (subtle questions when I had the opportunity to ask them) I realized that I was viewing probable future events in the lives of people I came in contact with. Seeing the possible applications of what I was experiencing now, I was ready to do some serious learning. I thought this might be a new career direction for me, and now that I had a practical application to focus on, I was no longer merely scared or annoyed by the changes that were happening to me, but fascinated.

I went out and bought books and books and books, everything that dealt with anything out of the ordinary. I had no friends who were into this sort of thing, so I didn't have any idea what I was buying. I read more Cayce material because I had had such a good experience with my introduction to him.

Reading all manner of books on unexplained phenomena, I found numerous contradictions among them, sometimes within the same text, and this frustrated me. I was looking for consistency, not hearsay from one author to the next. I wanted to know what was happening to me, and I wanted to know definitively, preferably without psychiatric influences telling me to "snap out of it." On the road towards uncovering my intuitive-self, I had come far enough to know that something real was happening to me and that it deserved my attention and nurturing. I didn't want to pay someone to tell me it was "all in my head," as if by knowing that, one could begin ignoring an experience and return to normalcy. The instinct to veer away from the therapists' couch was for me a positive one, but I still had a long way to go in terms of looking for answers inside rather than outside. I wanted information, but I wanted it to be handed over complete, with all the pieces of the puzzle already neatly fitted together. There was little of this type of information to be had in my reading, though there was plenty of the kind that left me with more questions than answers.

Then, bingo, a breakthrough! I came across a book that talked about meditation, and this sounded like a safe way to search for some answers, inwardly. Meditation seemed a gentle, solitary concept, and it didn't evoke in me the kind of fear that reading about occultism, possession or poltergeists did. My childhood was, as you may remember, steeped in Roman Catholicism, and attending church daily for many years had instilled in me a strong fear of tampering with things the devil might control. Meditation, unlike the occult, seemed more like a spiritual experience, like prayer. Indeed, the book talked about praying to God before meditation, and that seemed right and proper and very protective. Having read about meditation to the point where I felt I understood it, I decided I was ready to experience it, preferably in the company of others. I was ready for my first meditation class.

Lo and behold, twenty-four hours later I was directed (through a chance meeting) to someone who taught meditation. Since my funds were at an all-time low, I figured that after expenses I was left with about five dollars each week for frivolities. Naturally, that's exactly how much the meditation classes cost. Ten people were signed up to take it, and I looked forward to the first meeting with anticipation, hoping perhaps, that this would connect me not only with my inner-self, but possibly some people who were on the same path as me. The first night, I was the only one who showed up. The teacher was standing there alone, and I said, "Obviously, this is not what I'm supposed to do."

She said, "No, no. I want you to sit down. You have the aura of someone who knows about prophecy."

"Oh God!" I thought, and tried desperately for a few moments to figure out a graceful way to leave. But there was something kind, and ultimately, very professional about this woman, so I hesitated.

Then she said, "Now sit down, I'm going to light the candle." I looked across the room and saw that she had a small picture of Jesus on the cross, and she had a Bible out. This comforted me somewhat, because these were things I felt I understood. I sat down, and she explained that we would go through a short, fifteen-minute exercise which would relax my body and allow me to become more calm and at ease, so that I could better appreciate who I was and who I could become. That, too, seemed comforting, and I felt safe.

She instructed me to close my eyes, and led me into a deep-breathing exercise. That's the last thing I remember. I blacked out, and when I opened my eyes I found that I could not see. All that appeared in my vision was a bright pair of lights, seemingly an inch away from my eyeballs. Wild thoughts raged through my mind, and I was filled with fear.

After about fifteen minutes my eyesight came back into focus and the lights disappeared. The meditation teacher asked if I was aware of what had happened.

"No," I said. I was dazed and confused. "I need to leave."

She said, "Well, you had better take this tape. It's a tape of you talking for an hour." She took all of this quite calmly.

I said, "Look, I don't want a tape," but she insisted.

"No, take it."

I took the tape and left. I don't remember if I even paid my five dollars; I never went back. When I got home, I put the tape in a drawer and closed it. I didn't want to listen to it, or even acknowledge what had happened.

For the next three months I had no visions at all. No strange events occurred, and I stopped all my reading about the paranormal. It's almost as if that time didn't exist. Then early one morning I woke up and knew I had to play the tape. Nervously, I did. What I heard was the sound of my own voice, speaking very rapidly, very authoritatively. I was speaking English, but using the language in a way that sounded completely foreign to me. It seemed to be devoid of emotion, detached, and it spoke about me in the third person, referring to what had happened to me in the hospital, where I was going, and what I would be doing in the future. I say "it" because although it was my voice on the tape, I couldn't identify with it at all. The knowledge of the entity that was speaking was far beyond what I knew at that time, or what I know now. It was as if someone else, some other entity, was speaking through me.

CHAPTER THREE

Opening Up to Change

THE SOURCE

I sat and listened to the cassette tape from my meditation session, sixty minutes of my own voice describing who I really was, have been and would become.

It should be mentioned here that the voice speaking on the tape has since become known to me as my "higher-self," who I sometimes refer to as my Source. This is a portion of me, another part of myself that resides on a different continuum, and who has different knowledge from me, the Gordon-Michael that lives here and now. We all have these other parts of what we simplistically refer to as "ourselves." What I have learned in the fifteen-odd years since my first altered-state experience has explained to me the intricate, perfectly inter-connected motion of the cosmos in a way that science or religion alone have never been fully able to do, because they each tend to consider only part of the puzzle. We are all existing on many levels simultaneously. Time, space and consciousness are interwoven with each other in such a way that the word "simultaneous" even becomes somewhat inaccurate; however, my Source has explained that neither time nor space express themselves in the linear way we tend to look at them, but rather in cyclical configurations, or layers. These we might interpret as different times — history or the future — or different places on Earth or in space. Each consciousness exists at many junctures all at once ... try to imagine an individual consciousness as if it were a needle piercing an onion to its core, the layers of the onion composed of different times, places, or "lives" for that consciousness. Each "needle" is in contact with all of the many layers of the onion at once. We can learn to be aware of our whole selves, the whole "needle" of which this life is merely one juncture, to gain insight into our very reason for being. By accessing my Source on a regular basis, I have found that there is much to learn from communing with the "selves" which reside at these other layers. It is also an opportunity to give something back, and to be of service, to the greater Oneness of the cosmos.

For right now, the important thing to make clear is that *all of us* have these multiple selves that exist simultaneously in the past, present and future. We get glimpses of these other selves in our dreams and through other altered states of consciousness. Through the development of intuitive abilities, anyone can gain control of these experiences.

Although it is possible to communicate with other entities who are not parts of ourselves, as is the case with Ouija board, seance or channeling exercises, I have come to the personal conclusion that the most beneficial information we can access is often that which comes from within ourselves. Our intrinsic understanding of messages that come from inside us is always much greater than that which comes through, for example, channeling another entity.

At the time that I was listening to my tape, though, I knew

none of this. I had a million questions that I wanted to ask, the foremost in my mind being, "Who are you?" Amazingly, as I sat ruminating on the contents of the monologue I'd just listened to, and as I asked that very question inside my head, the response came to me clearly, also inside my head. In the same style and tone of voice, and with the same direct, unemotional personality as I'd heard on the tape, the voice (my inner voice) answered, *"We are all that you are, have been, or will be. We are you."* The response left me more puzzled and confused than ever; nevertheless, I went back to the tape.

My Source spoke of Earth's history, and the natural cycles it goes through. It stated that the Earth has been populated with intelligent beings for over fifteen million years!

Fifteen million years? I thought, what happened to the Creation and the Garden of Eden, only six thousand years ago? It seemed that, somewhere along the line, the recorded history of a rather enormous period of civilization had gone missing. This idea intrigued me, and later it became a major area of study for me. At the moment, though, it just seemed like one more weird, unverifiable theory with which my confused psyche seemed to be trying to send me over the edge. I didn't know what to make of it.

The author of this information — my own higher self — spoke of a concept called "Earth consciousness." I learned that in many cases the collapse of great civilizations had been brought on as a result of mankind's interaction with Earth consciousness. This was news to me, having had no experience of this now common concept at the time, but obviously I had accessed someone who knew better.

The idea that we humans control our own fate both individually and collectively is not a new one; what this idea of Earth consciousness states, however, is that our human collective consciousness is actually *interconnected* with the Earth and all its other realms of consciousness. The Earth, if we understand it in the context of the Gaia model, is an organism unto itself, and as such, seeks to exist in a state of health or balance at all

times.² As we have trampled on that health, in our dysfunc-
tional relationship as "abusers" of the Earth-entity, so can we
make amends or help to heal it through a shift in our collective human consciousness. The Earth changes that we, as
dependent life forms on the surface of Earth, see as disastrous
to our own survival, are merely the Earth seeking its own
recovery; just as coughing, sneezing or fever are our bodies'
ways of fighting off the imbalance of disease or stress. The
most important thing we can do to maintain the most stable
environment possible for ourselves is to recognize that what
we do and *think* as a species does, in fact, affect the health of
the Earth, and this translates directly into volcanic and seismic
activity, weather patterning and the fertility of the land itself.
Although there are certainly external influences which also
affect the Earth in these ways, such as planetary alignments
and universal electromagnetic activity, we are in a position of
great influence ourselves, and by taking responsibility for our
own power to interact with the Earth, we can make enormous
shifts in our environment.

I had no comprehension of these alternative approaches as I
played that tape, however, and I was unable to fully grasp this
idea of collective consciousness. I was still looking at the
world of humans as a very mortal group of individuals, who,
as best as I understood what I was being told, now needed to
all get together immediately and shift our thoughts to good-
will and peace, so that we might avert disaster, save the
world, and live happily ever after. The thought that kept
creeping back into my mind was that this was a totally futile
proposition. How could we possibly get the four billion
human inhabitants of the planet to agree on anything?
Everything I knew of history showed this to be impossible; it

---

² The notion that the Earth is not simply a place where life exists, but that it is a complex organism unto itself, "alive" in its own right, has developed in some form or another within nearly every culture throughout history. It was James Lovelock, the author of
several books on the subject, who first named this living Earth entity "Gaia," after the
Greek goddess of the Earth. His hypothesis: that the Earth is a single, immense, living
organism, which is self-regulating and self-changing, meaning that it is able to act on its
own behalf, in order to keep itself fit, healthy and in balance.

seemed to be an intrinsic part of human nature to fight, to have enemies, to disagree. Frustrated with what seemed to be conflicting concepts, I shut the tape off.

THE LEARNING CENTER

Things were moving very quickly now, in 1982. I rented a house, and moved in with all of my worldly possessions, which had dwindled to include little more than a box-spring/mattress set, a microwave oven, one frying pan, a coffee maker, a large terrarium lovingly crafted by an ex-girlfriend, and a very expensive stereo system. I had decided to open a learning center for holistic and metaphysical studies, and this house would give me the space I thought it needed. I hoped to somehow draw people to the center who had some knowledge in these areas, so that I could perhaps better understand what was happening to me. I wanted to create a space where others could learn and benefit from any knowledge we might collect there, and where I might make some discoveries of my own. Then, new phenomena began.

The first night I went to sleep in my new bedroom, I was startled awake a few hours later by the sudden intrusion of music playing loudly on the stereo downstairs. This was not unusual in itself, as I was prone to absentmindedly forget such things as shutting the door of the refrigerator, saying good-night to people, or eating meals, especially when I was absorbed in some interesting project, like solving an electronics problem. I proceeded downstairs without much thought on the matter. Shutting the stereo off, I headed back upstairs. But before I got even halfway, it went on again.

Now, since my background was in electronics, I knew right away that this could have been caused by a defective switch or some other malfunctioning component. I thought I might have only half-actuated the power switch, leaving it at the threshold of on/off, so I went downstairs and shut it off again. This time I got to the top of the staircase before it went on for the third time. I was exhausted after a day of moving, so I did not want to have to deal with the intermittent problem — a term used in electronics repair to describe an unidentified problem (one that usually disappears "mysteriously" after enough parts have been replaced) — until I'd had a good night's sleep. I pulled the plug from the socket, dropped it on the carpet, and headed for bed.

I half-expected the stereo to come back on at this point. It did not. What did happen was that as I went to open the bedroom door a violent push, almost as if a gust of terrific wind or air pressure was holding it against me, pushed back. Finally, after several tries, I got the door open and crashed for the night. I slept like a rock.

The next day I began to think about people who might want to get involved with my new learning center. My inner guidance told me that people would simply appear, but I found that hard to believe. Later that day, I answered a knock on my door. It was a man who said he'd noticed someone moving in, and had thought he'd come by to introduce himself and say hello, since he lived in the neighborhood. I invited him in, and as we talked, I told him about my plans for the learning center. It turned out that he had an interest in astrology, and he knew several people he thought would be interested in metaphysics. I tentatively planned to hold an informal meeting on an evening later in the week. My new friend said he'd pass the word along.

That evening the strange phenomenon of the stereo began again. Having tinkered with it throughout the day and finding nothing amiss, I promptly attributed it to an "intermittent problem," unplugged it and went back to bed. This time, the set came on even with the plug clearly laying on the floor, about a foot away from the wall socket. "Whoa," I thought, "we are into some uncharted waters here!" I quickly dashed through some books on strange phenomena, and fell upon a chapter about poltergeist activity. Aha! This was clearly the problem. Some poor misplaced, misdirected spirit — playful, of course, not harmful — was trapped in my house, and in need of salvation. Of course, this theory did have a few flaws, not the least of which was that almost all reported poltergeist activity occurs when there is a child or teenager present in the dwelling. Since I found so much conflicting information in my books, however, my thought was still that it might be a jovial spirit trying to make contact with me.

That night I stared into the darkness, drifting towards sleep, but unable to release consciousness. With eyes wide open, I observed a large form take shape at the foot of my bed — seven feet high, human in contour, but without gender or detail. It seemed to consist of a milky white substance, faint and still. Needless to say, I did not go to sleep that night, though I stayed just where I was, afraid to move, but also strangely calm. The form stayed at the foot of my bed until daybreak. With the first daylight, the presence gradually became invisible, although I felt an energy that remained. In fact, this energy remained for the entire time I resided in that house — a period of nine months.

A few days later, Friday, I had an "open house" meeting to introduce my new learning center. Surprisingly, some thirty to forty people showed up, although I'd done almost nothing to get the word out other than mentioning my intentions to a few people and putting out a small sign, announcing the date and time. Once again, my inner guidance proved to be correct, and people found me. The downstairs living room was crowded, and the stereo, which now appeared to be working normally, didn't seem to be giving anyone the willies. It was probably just an "intermittent problem," after all.

So, with the stereo playing softly in the background, the meeting began. During the course of our opening dialogue and conversation, a young man appeared at the door. He was a slender, quiet-spoken man in his early twenties, and he said his name was David. We welcomed the latecomer, but rather than taking a seat, he entered and said simply, "I am looking for Gordon Scallion." His pronunciation of my name was strangely garbled, but it was clear he meant to speak with me. He approached me and asked, "Are you Gordon Scallion?"

"Yes," I said, "how can I help you?" I expected this slightly dazed young man had heard about the center and had come for the meeting. He had a sad, lost look in his eyes, and I was filled with compassion and a willingness to welcome him to the group.

David appeared nervous as he approached me and said, "I have a message for you, Gordon Scallion, from the group." He continued, "You are not going to be doing what you think you are. Your destiny lies in another area. You will have many difficulties and eventually what you are now doing will cease to be. But it will help you learn what you need to learn so that those on the other side will be able to work more effectively with you."

The group this messenger belonged to turned out to be a spiritualist church that was in the area. He was telling me that my hopes and dreams of creating a learning center were going to fail, but that somehow I would come out of the experience somewhat whole, and that I was going to learn something in the process. A strange message, delivered by a strange person. I wasn't about to take any of it too seriously, yet there was something so odd and compelling about the whole experience that I filed it away in my mind. Suddenly, as quickly as he had come, the young man left, and I, along with the somewhat baffled participants of my first learning center group, got back to business.

SYNCHRONICITY

Interestingly enough, the meeting participants took the bizarre interruption in stride, and we went on discussing the possibilities for the learning center for many hours. Later in the evening, the group began to break up. Some left, but most stayed, separating into smaller conversation groups.

It was then that I noticed the lady who was to become my final partner in this life. It was her large brown eyes that immediately caught my attention, from the place where she'd been listening to me speak, a little ways across the room. Later on, she came over with a mutual friend, who introduced her to me. Her name was Cynthia. I had recognized the need to find someone with a financial background to help guide the planning of my learning center, and had put the word out that I needed an accountant, someone also attuned to — or at least open to — metaphysics, and concerned about the planet and its inhabitants. Cynthia was an accountant, concerned about the planet and its inhabitants, and ready for a change from her job. It seemed a perfect fit.

We discovered that both of our families had left the south end of Hartford at the same time, both of us going in different directions, neither knowing the other. She went on to private Catholic schools, while I had stayed in the public system, along with regular summer school to make up for the many sick days due to my asthma. My Catholic instruction had come in the form of after-school instruction several times each week, in addition to daily Mass. In spite of such close proximity and similar religious upbringings, miraculously, our paths had not crossed.

Synchronous with my own experiences of recent years, we discovered that Cynthia had recently endured a physical crisis which had become a turning point in her life, as well. Several months before, she had been hospitalized suddenly for severe pain on the right side of her body. After doing all the necessary tests, the doctors were unable to determine any cause for her illness, and suggested exploratory surgery. While in the hospital, she lost considerable weight, became very weak, and went into shock. She became convinced that if she stayed and had the surgery in the condition she was in, that she might not survive, so she searched for an outside solution. A holistic practitioner advised her to check out of the hospital, and for the next three months helped guide Cynthia's return to health through diet, herbs, and other alternative therapies. I could imagine how difficult that decision must have been for her to make. On the one hand you're already in a high-tech hospital with a qualified medical staff there to preserve your health and protect your life. On the other hand your inner guidance is saying that this is not going to work. Whom do you trust?

Having made the decision to leave the hospital, her family had to come and literally carry Cynthia out of the hospital to her home. Over the next three months she followed the holistic advice she'd received and did indeed cure herself. Since that time, we have found out through my guides that the condition she'd encountered was due to failure of her liver to remove toxins from her system, the effects of which had been compounded by the removal of her tonsils at a young age. The tonsils had in fact grown back after being removed a first time, and had been taken out again! That says a lot about the body's innate knowledge of what it needs to maintain its own health. As humans, we often insist that our minds — only one small part of ourselves — know best, when what we must do, for our very survival, is to begin listening closely to the intelligence of our whole selves.

Later on, Cynthia and I discovered yet another similarity between us. It turned out that although we didn't remember each other at all, as children we had lived across the street from one another. In fact, her brother and I used to play together, and — as Cynthia related in her introduction to *Notes From the Cosmos* — a particular incident had occurred which caused her mother to remember me immediately when Cynthia introduced us for the first time. As a child, I'd definitely made a lasting impression on her mother and sibling, if not on Cynthia herself.

Suddenly I had found myself in a joyful new place in my life. Here she was, the-girl-next-door whom I had not known, whose life now seemed to be intertwining with mine, just as earlier we had somehow missed each other completely. Now she was in a position similar to mine, searching for answers, and sensing for the first time that there was more going on in the universe than what at first appears. Our personal relationship developed quickly, and eventually Cynthia became my business partner with the learning center, as well as my friend.

CHAPTER FOUR

Following Intuition

FINDING THE RIGHT PATH

During the next several months the learning center hummed with activity. I had finally found people of like mind, and I absorbed everything taught at the center, from healing to astral travel.

In my free time, I would return to my first Source audio tape and play it over and over. It was as if I were looking for some clue as to how all of the new phenomena in my life were possible. The tape seemed like the right place to begin searching for answers. It sounded somewhat like me, and supposedly it wasn't a discarnate spirit, but merely a portion of myself which referred to itself as my Monad. After a dozen times or more of running through the recording, I found that I started to feel a tingling sensation running up and down my spine whenever I listened to it. I began to hear statements on the tape that I had not heard before. Clearly these phrases had been there all along, but somehow my conscious mind had blocked out certain portions of the tape. In the very near future, the Source said, I would be able to access the same altered state I was now listening to, and that I would then be able to have another person — a "conductor" — interact with the Source, and ask questions. Since I'd been in denial about so many things on my path thus far, it made sense to me that I might have disallowed this part of the message to be conveyed to my conscious mind until I was ready to hear it. Even understanding that, however, a full month went by, and still I was unable to take the next step in my initiation. But then, a strange event occurred to help me overcome my fears.

It was the spring, and weekends were filled with classes and counselors working with clients at the center. The mornings were always quiet, with no activity occurring until mid-afternoon. Most of the teachers and counselors had either full- or part-time jobs, and worked at the center only on evenings or weekends. One morning while I was reading, I heard a knock on the door. I got up to answer it, and was greeted by two elderly men in business suits. My first impression was that they were a part of a religious organization of some type. One of the men asked if I was Gordon Scallion. I responded that I was. The next thing he said caught me totally off guard. "We have been sent to see you about a matter of the most importance," he said.

"Sent to me?" I asked.

"Yes, you are the spiritual healer aren't you?"

"No," I said, "I am not a healer, but we may have someone here at the center who might be able to help."

"No," he insisted. "We were told to see you." Once again he asked if they might come in and talk about it. Since the center was open to the public, I felt obligated to ask them in, but I was feeling a sense of uneasiness around these men. Just at that moment tiny blue lights or sparks started to appear at the corner of my peripheral vision, just as it had that time in the supermarket when I was shopping for Easter dinner. I closed my eyes firmly for a second or two, took a deep breath, and hoped it would go away. Thankfully, it did, and I asked them in.

One man did all the talking, describing how the other man was his life-long friend, and that he was dying of liver failure. I felt compassion for them, and sadness at their story, but I explained there was nothing I could do — I wasn't a healer. I asked who had sent them, and the man answered with another question.

"Do you believe in the power of spirit?" he inquired. I was not sure exactly what he meant. I'd never heard the term, and I hadn't yet come across it in my reading. He explained that guides and angels had been speaking to him since he was five years old. These spirits were powerful helpers to him, and to other people throughout his life. I wondered why he was here with me, if this was true. Couldn't these angels or guides help him now? Perhaps they had left him, having moved on to other duties, I thought.

This stranger looked straight into my eyes and responded directly to my thoughts. "Sometimes my guides only direct me to a source to solve a problem. This is such a time." He continued, "My guides have explained to me your encounter in the hospital in 1979, and told me of the woman guide who came to you." I was astonished, since only a few people knew about the incident. My surprise must have shown on my face.

"Don't be alarmed, son," he said. "Spirit only comes to those who are ready, even if you don't think you are." With that he reached gently over and took my right palm and placed it on his partner's left hand. I withdrew my arm with a jerk. Calmly, he said, "Don't worry, you have the gift," and once again took my hand, placing it over the other man's. He looked straight into my eyes again and said in a firm voice, "What is wrong with my friend?" I coughed a few times, feeling out of control. I replied that I had no idea.

"Close your eyes and tell me what you see," he said. For some reason, I did what he asked. Upon doing so, I realized that I *did* see something. Again, the man saw the truth in my facial expression. "You see something don't you?" he murmured, urgently.

"Yes I do, but I don't understand it."

"Tell me. Tell me," he repeated.

"Well," I said, "I see a man in a long, white lab coat. I see equipment in the room. It looks like 1930s-vintage styling."

"What is the equipment for?" he asked, again with a firm voice.

"I'm not sure. It looks like grinding wheels and dust vents of some type; however, I see sets of false teeth on the table, I think. Isn't that strange?"

"No," he said with a slight laugh. "Now, tell me what the teeth have to do with my friend here."

As I focused on the teeth, my viewpoint in the vision suddenly changed. Now I could see small beakers of mercury and a white, powdery substance, labeled "porcelain." I explained what my new vision was showing me and added, "This is all very strange. I don't think I can continue ... maybe this is a mistake."

Abruptly, he placed his hand on my shoulder and said, "God doesn't make mistakes, only man does. He has given you something very precious! Please bear with this for a few more minutes."

I suppose his earnestness got my attention. I settled down, and simply let the answers flow through me. I completely relinquished the fear that I might give this man wrong or useless information, allowing myself to speak about anything that came into my mind.

I told him I felt that mercury was somehow related to his friend's disease, possibly mercury poisoning. I didn't know how this could be possible or why, only that I felt it was true.

"Please ask your inner God-essence for the correct curative, son."

Perplexed, I did as he asked. I closed my eyes, and was shown a series of herbs — pictures, although somehow the names came to me as well. I opened my mouth to speak, and instructions for the cure came pouring out, as if I were an opened faucet. My conscious mind was alert, but somehow standing aside, so that I could hear what was being said, aware that it was not coming from my own knowledge or thoughts. I explained how to prepare a poultice, and that it should be applied to the liver-region several times a day, and which results to watch for in the healing process.

When I opened my eyes, I felt extremely disoriented. Everything looked far away and warped, as if I were looking backwards through a pair of binoculars. I immediately recalled the experience at the meditation class, and began to breathe heavily, anxious at once again finding myself in unfamiliar territory. The man placed his hand gently on my shoulder, and a calmness washed over me. Within a few minutes my vision returned to normal.

"I'm sorry I couldn't help you," I said. "I'm sure what I said is just some part of my imagination. What you need to do is see a doctor."

Smiling, he said, "I am a doctor." He went on to explain that his friend had worked in a dental lab for over thirty years, and after retiring recently, had grown quite ill. Tests had shown his liver was failing, but the cause had remained a mystery, and so far there had not seemed to be a cure. The herbal treatment I'd dictated did not seem so far-fetched to the doctor as it had to me. The two men thanked me, and went away.

* * * * *

Over the next two months others seemed to appear at the center constantly, seeking me out. I was seeing several people each day, and still more were requesting appointments with me. Whenever I pushed myself to receive more clients, I would be stopped in my tracks by a monstrous headache, which would not disappear until I'd succumbed to at least fourteen hours of sleep in a darkened room. But within the limits of what I seemed allowed to do, I found that the more I did, the easier it got. As I stepped my ego out of the way and let the information come through me — acting not as an expert on healing, but as a conduit — I found that I could easily answer questions about health, past lives, or relationship difficulties. There seemed to be no limit to the information my Source could provide, and I can only imagine that it was somehow accurate and helpful, because people continued to come.

Gradually, my headaches became more frequent, however, and I was forced to curtail my activities involving clients. Visions were now occurring to me during full consciousness. I had started to see auras again — as I'd done when first walking out of the hospital in Florida — and these became such a hindrance that I spent much of my time and energy attempting to control my clairvoyant sight and shut it down. I enjoyed the idea of helping people, but my life felt out of control. I wasn't me anymore; I was becoming an automaton.

As that summer drew to a close, I answered an unexpected knock at the door one day, as was not uncommon. Upon opening the door, I viewed the same two elderly gentlemen that had first sought me out several months earlier. They were just stopping by to thank me, they told me. It was obvious that the sick man's health had returned, for the color had come back into his face, and he seemed animated and at ease. It seemed that the herbs and treatment I'd offered had been successful, and his disease was in full remission. The two men were retiring to Europe together, they said, to enjoy to the fullest life's later years. I felt warm and fulfilled, realizing such a choice might not have been possible for them, had a cure not been found for the one man's disease. I was a little wistful, as I said good-bye and wished them well. I also wanted to take some time off, "to enjoy life to the fullest." But it was not to be.

*   *   *   *   *

One day I received a call from one of the center's facilitators, which once again altered the course of my life's path forever. The instructor had contracted a bad case of the flu, and asked me to find a substitute to teach his class on past lives. I said I would, and proceeded to call all the resources I had. By six o'clock, though, an hour before class was to begin, I had still not succeeded in finding a replacement for the evening. I decided to cancel the class, but there was no contact list available, so I waited until people arrived to tell them. Promptly at seven, about twenty people — ranging in age from eighteen to seventy, or so it seemed — arrived at the learning center. I greeted them, and explained that the teacher was ill and unable to be present that night. A silence came over the class. Some students had driven for more than an hour to attend, and obviously they felt disappointed. To break the silence, I suggested that although a make-up session would be offered at a later date, perhaps the time now could be used as a forum of some type. It was then that one of the students asked me to give a talk about past lives and reincarnation. I was somewhat stunned, and explained that I knew very little about the subject myself at this point, being a relative newcomer to the study of metaphysics. With that, however, a discussion had been put in motion, and I soon found myself offering up insights as they came to me on the concept of reincarnation. The entire class stayed, and before long I had drifted into the altered state I used with people when they came to me with questions. By the end of two hours, I had completed the exact lesson the regular teacher would have conducted.

It was so strange to me, this experience. I could hear myself talking, in a tempo close to my regular speech, but with a knowledge I surely did not have. My inner voice could even make comments about things "I" was lecturing about. It was like I had split myself into two entities, each with their own personality, both able to interact with the outside world, although the more knowledgeable half definitely remained at center stage. At the end of the class, I simply stopped and said, "Well, that's all." There was total silence for a few beats. Then, rhythmically, everyone in the class rose to their feet and clapped for what seemed like minutes. I had entered a new phase in my journey. I had become "more than I was," just as my Source had said was possible for all us. It was electrifying.

From that point forward I conducted classes on a wide variety of subjects: from ancient civilizations, to the existence of life in outer space, from health and healing, to my favorite subject, intuitive development. Throughout the eighties, I conducted thousands of private intuitive sessions and presented hundreds of seminars, despite the occasional headache, which I correctly interpreted as a not-so-subtle hint to slow down and take care of myself through all of this activity. Somehow, with a little prodding from the spirit world, I had entered the Twilight Zone, and returned from it, better off than I had ever been in my life.

THE DREAM TEACHERS

During the period after my spiritual awakening, I had many vivid dreams. Of all of them, one recurring theme stands out, in that it became the major pathway by which I could gain access to the guiding forces I'd first encountered in my trance state. Today, in fact, this lucid dreaming is one of the most frequent methods I use to enter the realms of higher consciousness. In these early days, the dream scenario was set for all of my future mind voyages.

In this particular dream I would find myself in the presence of a distinct pair of entities, although they took on varied forms, depending upon the dreamscape. Sometimes they would appear as two bright lights (the same bright lights that I first encountered during my extremely upsetting meditation session, but thankfully, at enough of a distance that I could see them in full perspective!) At other times, the two entities would appear as priest-like individuals in long, white robes.

Using the dream state as a writing tablet, our whole-consciousness describes things symbolically for us, and in this way communicates with us. Sometimes the symbols are chosen to be comfortable for us, so that we can absorb information that we may be turning away from in our wakeful lives.

At other times, the symbols might be ambiguous and confus-
ing — spurring us to think hard or wonder about the dream
— providing resistance to "exercise" our conscious mind
with. Or perhaps the message requires strong emotional
impact — nightmare scenes that act as wake-up calls when
we have been sleepwalking through our days, ignoring the
signals and warning signs all around us. Always, the realm of
higher consciousness seeks to remind us of change. Change is
the natural state of the cosmos, and to deny that is to deny the
reality of our place here on Earth.

So although the tactics of communication depend greatly on
the individual, and on what the individual needs at that time,
the message itself could be looked upon as a universal pulse
— to be open to change, to growth, to learning, and to see this
as a cyclical, rather than linear, progression. In my case, the
message came in the form of these entities, these holy men or
" beings of light," for a reason. At the time, I desperately needed my teachers to impart the sense of comfort and guidance
that these icons could bring. I found myself with plenty to
learn simply in coming to an understanding of the teachers
and classroom themselves.

My lessons took place in a granite hall, which my teachers
called the Hall of Wisdom. I would begin the dream by feeling
myself come awake in my own bedroom. The teachers would
be waiting for me, and I would sit up, feeling the pop as I left
my sleeping body behind. Then the robed figures would join
hands with each other, reaching their free hands out to me in
welcome. Although I could never really see these figures'
faces, the hoods of the robes shadowing their features, I
always had the sense that they were benevolent and supreme-
ly caring mentors. Joining hands with my teachers, they
instructed me — telepathically — to close my eyes. When I
would open them, seconds later, we'd no longer be in my
moonlit room, but standing in the Hall of Wisdom.

For many months, upon awakening I would remember the
feeling — not the details — that indicated I had taken
another class. This education continued nightly for a full year,

then tapered off, as I became more adept at accessing the lucid dream state purposefully. Even now, when I need to pay attention to some bit of life that I am resisting awareness of, my guides will come back to me in sleep and gently point the way in this manner. Now I understand that these are not dreams, but out-of-body experiences in which the various vibratory levels of my consciousness cooperate and communicate with one another, and with other consciousnesses in the cosmos. These guides may come from some other planet, continuum, or time on Earth, or they may embody pieces of consciousness from all of these realms. I still don't have a definitive answer to these possibilities, but I have come to believe that the origins of my dream teachers are not nearly so important as my ability to accept them, to learn from them, and to trust what they have to tell me.

GOING THE DISTANCE

During 1983, I received a series of early-morning communications from my dream teachers, urging me to go to Los Angeles immediately. I mentioned this to Cynthia, and she was very supportive, encouraging me to follow my instincts. Early on, Cynthia, extremely intuitive herself, was often more willing than I was to put trust in my burgeoning intuitive process, and her presence in my life helped a great deal as I came to accept my inner knowing.

Going to Los Angeles was far from being a rational decision for me. I knew no one in Los Angeles, and there was nothing there that I knew of to which I felt drawn. Nevertheless, I obtained a ticket and boarded a non-stop flight which, many hours later, deposited me at LAX. I stood in the terminal, looking around expectantly and keeping one untrusting hand firmly placed on the small carry-on bag hanging from my shoulder. I half hoped to see some sort of guide, spiritual or otherwise, who would be awaiting my arrival, and would now take over and show me the way to whatever it was that I needed to do here.

Nothing. No translucent, winged companions, nobody holding a sign with my name on it. Just a busy, international airport filled with thousands of hurrying people, none of whom threw so much as a smile in my direction. Panicking, I dashed to the nearest cluster of phones, telephoned Cynthia, and told her I was at the airport and freaking out. Obviously, I had acted on a bad instinct; there was nothing for me here, and I had no idea what I was supposed to do next.

Cynthia said, "Why don't you check into a motel on the water someplace, and get some sleep." The nurturing quality of her voice and soothing words placed me at ease temporarily. I rented a car and followed the flow of automobiles streaming away from the airport. Soon I was driving on a five-lane California freeway and the sky was growing dark. The headlights of the on-coming lanes poured past on my left, while red tail lights blinked and seemed to merge with one another ahead of me, the massive expanse of road curving away into the distance. I had no idea where I was going, so I drove and drove, allowing the darkness and the rivers of light to soothe me.

By 10 p.m., exhaustion from the trip, jet lag, frustration, and disappointment at not finding a clear mission waiting for me upon arrival, all crashed in on my consciousness at once. I pulled off the highway and stopped at the first motel I could find, not even knowing where I was. Thirty dollars and thirty minutes later I was in a room, sound asleep.

When daylight woke me, I could hear children laughing and the muffled roar of what sounded like surf, though I assumed it must be wind or the highway that accounted for the noise, and a motel swimming pool full of traveling youngsters, since I could not conceive of being near the ocean. But upon leaving the room I found myself facing miles of blue, active water, the coast stretching away to the south, and bending towards low, rocky crags to the north. I walked down to the beach and with my bare feet stepped into the Pacific ocean for the first time, realizing that I had crossed some three thousand miles in a matter of hours, and was touching this new terrain for the first time. As I walked on the beach, the anxiety that had been with me since my arrival in Southern California eased, as I felt a sense of peace and well-being flood through me.

Rather than lingering to enjoy the morning-cool sand and salt air, however, I packed up and moved on. I was driven to drive, endlessly, it seemed. I half hoped to observe a parting of the clouds, an emerging shaft of light, and the voice of a Supreme Intelligence booming out to say, *"Gordon, this is why you are here."*

It is important to note, once again, that the information given to me by my teachers — especially when it concerned me directly — was always vague, at best. In hindsight I understand their reasons, and the clarity of the simple words they used to tell me simple truths. It has been only the intrusion of my ego that has kept me from understanding information which was presented so concisely and lovingly, for my own benefit, to enrich my life and the lives of others. Here I was, driving up and down the coast of California. No beams of light, no silver disks in the sky, no booming voice, no voice at all even, since the radio was broken in the rental car.

Then I saw a sign that said Malibu. I turned off the main, two-lane highway and headed into the high country. The winding roads through the hills of Malibu were breathtaking. As I rounded one corner, a loud voice rang out in my mind, with a clear directive, for once. *"Gordon,"* it said, *"turn up this driveway."*

I turned onto a long, tree-shaded drive, ascending some two hundred feet to a clearing at the top of a hill. A low ranch house with a nice view of the surrounding hills nestled here. In the distance, the ocean could be seen at the horizon, a couple of miles away. At the end of the drive I observed a little sign that read, "The Aquarian Center," but other than this, there was nothing to suggest anything other than a large, perfectly normal, private home. I was more than a bit nervous about going up to the door, afraid of seeming odd, but determined to follow my instincts in the hopes of getting some answers.

But as destiny would have it, the person who came to the door was a pleasant lady who asked simply, "Can I help you?"

"Excuse me, but, what do you do here?" I stuttered hesitantly. She invited me in and showed me volumes and volumes of books written by a man named Torkum Saraydarian. The name had a kind of mystical ring to it, I thought.

She said, "He wrote all these books, you know, but he's only here one or two days out of the month. He spends the rest of the time at his Arizona center." I felt the weight of disappointment come down on me. Apparently, I had been guided to this location only to be left hanging once more. She continued, "Fortunately, he's here today." But then more disappointment. "He has sessions scheduled all day. I'm afraid he probably can't see you."

The woman left me in the foyer, and I stood looking at the case of books, some twenty or thirty in number, all authored by this one man. The subject matter ranged from reincarnation to how to achieve spiritual bliss, to other even more esoteric subjects. Here was a man, I thought to myself, who appeared knowledgeable in the ways of metaphysics. A true wise man. Perhaps he was to be my teacher.

A few minutes later, a small, dark man came out from a side room, saying good-bye to his current student or counselee. The lady who had met me at the door intercepted him and spoke quietly to the man, gesturing slightly at me. He beckoned me to come forward, and I entered his private study. This delightful, loving man looked into my eyes, and I felt suddenly as if I were disappearing into the depths of myself.

"Why are you here?" he asked in an Armenian accent. Without thought I responded, "I don't know."

"Gooood," he said. He told me a little of what he did, and said that he spent most of his time at his center in Sedona, Arizona. "Have you been there?" he asked.

"No," I said, "I've never been to Arizona." Nor had I heard of Sedona.

"You will be there," he said. "I will see you in Sedona, in one year's time. Now, go with my blessings."

And with that, the meeting was over. I left, disappointed that my hopes of having found a teacher were not to be realized. Was that not the purpose of my trip?

I couldn't believe that this simple meeting had been the purpose of a three thousand mile flight, a car rental, and hours of driving aimlessly all along the coast of south California. But it felt like there was nothing left to do now except to go home. Only time would tell whether my instincts had been wrong.

I returned to New England at once. Although discussing the trip with Cynthia helped some, I was still left with the feeling that once again I had been following my inner voice blindly, and probably misinterpreting what I was supposed to be doing. It was a disappointing time. If following my intuition was the right thing to do, then why weren't the signals clearer? And if I was doing the "right" things in my life — possibly for the first time — then why did I feel so unsure?

CHAPTER FIVE

The Magic of Sedona

One year later, Cynthia and I found ourselves working in Phoenix, Arizona. My dream teachers had directed me to move there for the time being, and I had followed their guidance. Business was bad, and emotionally things were even worse — disastrous would be a more apt description — but I decided to stick it out until the next step was clear. While I was there, I asked Cynthia to come visit for a few weeks. I needed her help on a project I was working on, and I missed her terribly, too. She agreed to fly out and stay with me for a while.

Then, a very special event occurred. Cynthia and I decided to marry. Each of us had been married before, so although we both felt that it was the absolute right thing to do, we were somewhat nervous. It was almost as if we were both characters or actors in a play — knowing the script by heart at some deep level, moving through the various scenes as if they were written for us alone.

Cynthia was a single parent of four daughters. The three older girls were mostly away at school, but the youngest, Cissy, had been just eleven when Cynthia and I started seeing each other, and had somewhat resented my presence in her mother's life at first. After a while, she seemed to tolerate me well enough, although she continued to be concerned that I might "act weird" in front of her friends. But I remember clearly the moment when I knew I'd made a breakthrough with her. Cissy had come to me one day, and said, very seriously, that she had something to tell me. "You can marry my mother if you want to." At the time, I was quite taken aback, since Cynthia and I hadn't been seeing each other for that long, and had not even discussed the possibility of marriage.

I suspect I muttered something like, "Okay, Cis, thanks. I'll talk to your mother about it," but somewhere deep inside, I think I felt pleased. Cynthia had been just as surprised as I was to hear that Cissy had given us her "blessing," so to speak. But while we had no plans for marriage at the time, thanks to Cissy, the seed had been planted. In Arizona, the decision finally seemed clear.

It was while we were in Phoenix that we first heard of a magical place called Sedona. I had not searched for it, because the events at Malibu had been almost entirely forgotten; I'd looked at that trip as another dead end in my search for answers. But then someone told us about the magical properties of Sedona — its beautiful red canyon walls, and its vortexes. We had to see it.

My dream teachers instructed me that vortexes are abnormalities which occur within the Earth, becoming more pronounced at different times, depending on planetary and solar conditions. They are most likely to affect the surface of the Earth near a volcanic area — either a current one or a past one. They are created by particulars in the composition of the soil, and in various minerals present in the magma that exists in the Earth's upper crust. These cause what the teachers termed "standing-wave eddies" that could be enhanced, depending on longitude and latitude, and relationship to the positions of various stars and planets. As I understood it, vortexes act as powerful junctures in the space-time continuum, and Sedona was one of the places where this occurs.

We found Sedona to be indeed magical, with its red-rock canyon walls standing stark and tall against the clear, blue sky. There were photographers everywhere. Sedona is probably one of the most photographed places in the world. You've no doubt seen it pictured in dozens of magazine ads and TV commercials.

Cynthia and I so enjoyed Sedona that we decided to go back and visit it on the full moon, just prior to the time the sun comes over the horizon, which turned out to be about 4:30 a.m. We brought a bottle of water and a glass bowl, to be filled and left in the open, allowing the energies of the moon — and the sun — to permeate it. We then drank the water. I don't know whether it was something psychological, or something more physical, but that water tasted sweeter than any water I'd ever tasted previously, or have tasted since. This was such a powerful experience for us that not only did we decide to get married at that time, but we chose Sedona as the place for the ceremony. Cynthia made plans to stay on while we planned the wedding, and Cissy joined us as well.

We decided to marry on a special day — April twenty-second. In numerology, "22" is considered a power number. It was also Earth Day, and Easter Sunday that particular year, all of which felt very symbolic and spiritual. But it was also very close. We had two weeks to go, nobody to perform the ceremony, and no license; just a desire to marry. We searched for anyone in the area who might perform the ceremony, but no one could do it because it was Easter, and they had other commitments. With only four days to go before our chosen day, we still didn't have anyone to perform the ceremony. We had calls out all over Phoenix, so we simply sat back and hoped for the best.

That night we got a call from one of the people we had been

referred to. She said she couldn't do it, but that she could give us the name of someone who might be persuaded to perform the ceremony, although she doubted it, as his schedule was usually filled up months in advance. His name was Torkum Saraydarian.

I realized with a start that it had been just one year before when I first met Torkum. I remembered his parting words: "I will see you in Sedona, in one year's time."

I thought back to that seemingly uneventful trip to L.A. and said to Cynthia, "Perhaps it had a purpose, after all." And as it happened, Torkum was free to perform our marriage ceremony on Easter Sunday.

*   *   *   *   *

Friends and family arrived from New England, California, and other places in between. Torkum was to take us to a secluded place that was very beautiful and, according to him, very special. Along with our small group of guests, we followed him along a narrow trail through shadowy woods and across a narrow stream. In our wedding finery, we made our way from stepping stone to stepping stone in the clear running creek, and I wondered just where Torkum was taking us. We continued on the path for awhile more, when all of a sudden we found ourselves in an opening in the woods. The sight was breathtaking. A massive, red canyon wall was before us, which seemed to appear at the edge of this clearing as if from nowhere. At the foot of the wall was a beautiful lagoon of crystal-clear water. Here in this place of perfect beauty, Torkum performed our wedding ceremony, which incorporated, symbolically, all the people, ideas and things that were meaningful to us. We asked Lightbear, our friend from New England whose ancestry was Lakota Sioux, to perform the owl purification ritual, which involved burning sage in a conch shell and fanning the smoke with large owl feathers into each of our faces. (Cissy, thirteen by then and very much the skeptical non-believer, gagged on the smoke, coughing and waving it away with great flourishes. I'm sure she felt that her mother and new step-parent had taken up permanent residence in the Twilight Zone, and worse yet, didn't even know it.) Another friend, Cyril, who likes to refer to himself as a "French refugee" and who is a gifted musician, brought along a three-foot gong, which he played as part of the ritual. With this transcendent mix of cultures, spirit, friends and loved ones gathered around us, in this mystical locale full of powerful Earth energies, we had everything going for us. The spiritual energy of the group was high, placing everyone in what could only be described as an altered state of being.

Gathered beside the small lagoon, the ceremony began. As Cyril struck the gong over and over, building the pulsing beat until it resonated throughout the canyon, a warm wind picked up and rustled the leaves, causing the birds and other forest creatures to compete with the sound. This was a box canyon, three sides composed of two-hundred-foot walls of sheer, red rock, and the wind seemed to come from nowhere. Periodically, the gong would decrease in intensity, echoing away into nothingness. The wind and the singing of birds would stop too, creating total stillness, utter silence, and then begin again as the gong sounded once more. This continued throughout the ceremony, which lasted for half an hour.

We felt numerous presences. They were not describable as spirits, but simply presences, unseen and yet clearly a part of the group. Without discussing it earlier, everyone voiced this feeling immediately after the ceremony. Several people reported seeing large birds — eagles — circling above us in the canyon. But when we all looked, most of us were unable to see any movement in the sky, although a couple of people kept insisting they were still there, pointing up excitedly at the unending canopy of blue above us. Somehow, this was not eerie, but sacred and comforting. Perhaps we felt blessed, or protected, whatever the presences were. Slowly, peacefully, we made our way back down through the canyon, woods and streams, back to the main road and our cars.

As Cynthia and I began to drive away, a huge bird suddenly

appeared from above, some twenty to thirty feet in front of us, slowly flapping his wings. We were moving slowly, perhaps fifteen miles per hour, and keeping pace with the bird. With us were Cynthia's daughter, Jackie, and her husband, who had spent several years in the forestry service and was knowledge-able about wildlife and the identification of birds. He commented that it was, indeed, a very large eagle. For some distance the great bird continued to lead us around curves and bends, until he eventually soared up towards the sun, and we lost him. It seemed to be some form of interconnection with another kingdom, bidding us good-bye for now, and somehow blessing the event. It doesn't take much to read all kinds of things into experiences! But perhaps, perception is just as much a part of reality as anything else in the cosmos. We all agreed that it had been a magical, special day, and an experience that we'd remember always.

One month later we returned to New England. It was as if we had come to this place to discover the unique energies residing here, to work with them, and to allow them to assist us in our life lessons. The ceremony of our marriage in Sedona seemed to represent the culmination of these lessons, and it was now time to graduate and move on. Upon leaving, I felt a great clarity of spirit, as if I had been cleansed. My time in the desert had made me keenly aware of Gaia's powers — earth, air, wind and fire — as well as the unseen presences which are all around us, binding together this Earth, this reality, and our own humanness into a Oneness that is beyond our under-standing, although seeking to understand it is certainly one of life's greatest joys.

What lay ahead for me and Cynthia was unknown. Our intuitive guides seemed to supply us only with enough information to keep us moving forward. All we could do was to trust, and be patient.

CHAPTER SIX

The Right Place to Live

Upon returning to Connecticut, my consultation work fell back into place so seamlessly, it was as if the difficulties in Arizona had never existed. Or more accurately, as if the Arizona chapter of my life had been written to explore another kind of experience — a subplot — and now I'd returned to the flow of the main storyline. Almost before we had settled in, businesses began to approach me as an "intuitive consultant," and I found this to be a rewarding way to use my abilities for the good of others, although I sometimes still saw clients on an individual basis as well. Eventually, Cynthia and I knew that Connecticut wasn't the right place for us to be, but as a temporary place for us to get our bearings and make some more long-term decisions about where we were going, coming back to this home territory made sense. The ease with which we were able to fall into some kind of a pattern of existence there simply made it all the more practical.

It was 1984, and we'd been back in New England for perhaps six months when I received the first in a series of dream scenarios which would eventually point the way — quite literally — to the area where we would make our permanent home. In the first dream, I found myself guided to fly higher and higher until, looking down, I could see New England spread out below me like a map. As the scenario unfolded, a bright red arrow appeared (sometimes my dream symbolism can be surprisingly simple), and zoomed in to point at a little Vermont town called Brattleboro. The dream ended abruptly at that point, and I woke up. I went back to sleep, but when I got up the next morning I recorded the experience in my journal, hoping the next night's dreams would give me additional insights.

Months passed, with no apparent links to provide clarity regarding my dream. It stayed in my mind, though, and finally I let my curiosity get the better of me. I decided to check a map to see just where Brattleboro was located. Because I'd occasionally heard the unusual name come up, I knew such a town existed. I'd never visited it and knew nothing about it, however, other than that it was somewhere in the state of Vermont, perhaps a hundred miles north of where we lived. As I scanned the map, a red arrow appeared in my field of vision and quickly drew my eyes to Brattleboro. Startled, I closed my eyes and then slowly opened them, hoping the red arrow was gone. It was. I sat back and took a couple of deep breaths, slowly folding the map.

I put the whole issue out of my mind and went about business as usual. Another three months went by, and I had another dream vision. In this one, the terrain once again unfolded below me, and the arrow swept in, pointing to Brattleboro. Then a voice came to me as well. It said, *"You will eventually move to within ten miles of this town."* Nothing mystical about that!

Again, the dream ended abruptly, and I recall waking up with a jolt and searching in the darkness for my dream journal. I knew this dream was important, and I didn't want to trust that I would remember the specifics when I awoke the next morning.

At sunrise, I found myself at our kitchen table, blearily scanning the Vermont map for clues. Cynthia and I discussed the dream, and the urgency of my feelings about it, and decided it was time to take a trip up to Vermont. After a pleasant two-hour drive, the highway banked by the rolling, green hills of New England in the summertime, Cynthia, Cissy, and I found ourselves in Brattleboro. It was a quaint town, with a population of about eleven thousand people. Brattleboro had grown up as a typical mill town around the turn of the century, although later on in the early 1900s the addition of a sanatorium (which later became the Brattleboro Retreat) brought about a distinctive "healing" element to the flavor of the community, which has remained to this day.

To me it appeared as if time had stopped here, and we'd suddenly stepped back into the sixties. There was a proliferation of bookstores, coffeehouses, health food restaurants, and merchants specializing in beads, pottery, crafts and textiles. As we walked around the small downtown area, everyone we met seemed friendly; the lifestyle looked pleasant enough, and the pace appeared to be slower than what we were used to. It was charming, certainly, but I could not figure out why my dream guides were saying I would live within ten miles of this town. Cynthia and I both enjoyed life in the city, and most of our family and friends were in Connecticut. We knew no one in the Brattleboro area at all. Agreeing the dream must somehow be symbolic, we decided that what I was experiencing might be some type of message for us — perhaps a reminder to slow down and return to a lifestyle more like what we'd found in Vermont. Returning to Connecticut that same day, we went back to our normal activities.

My dreams over the next several months dealt with other subjects in my life, most of which related to my intuitive development, ancient worlds, and day-to-day problems. In the winter of that year, another dream occurred which would change my life forever. It was the same scenario: the map-like landscape, the red arrow, and the voice, this time with a new message.

"Environment establishes the resonance in which you will find new development in mind. Study stones, and their effects on the body, mind and spirit," it said.

Somehow I knew it was time to move, but I couldn't bring myself to move further north when all of my desires pointed to the warmer climates of the south, perhaps back to Florida, or maybe even one of the islands in the Caribbean. We took several trips south, but they produced no additional clarity. On pure instinct, we'd gone ahead and put our home on the market. It had sold, and time was now running out, since we had to be out within two months, and we had yet to make a decision on where to go. It was a frustrating time in our lives. A battle seemed to be going on between our personal desires — to leave New England for warmer climes — and our subconscious knowing, which was being amplified (probably because we were trying so hard not to listen) through the nagging questions brought up and left for me by my dream guides.

With only a few weeks to go before we would be forced to seek refuge in motels, or worse, we took one last trip to Vermont. This time, however, we decided to cross the river and check out New Hampshire, since it was only a few miles from Brattleboro. As fate would have it, we passed a small farm with a house situated on a hill, and a barn next to a running stream. It was picturesque, even in the dead of winter. We rounded the corner and were about to pass by, when we noticed a sign by the edge of the road. It read simply, "For Sale," and included a phone number.

We drove around for an hour or so, and decided to return to Connecticut. As we drove past the farm on our way back, a loud voice rang out in my head saying, *"Call!"* We stopped for lunch later, and I made the call. The long and short of it is that we bought the farm. Its location? *Exactly* ten miles from the center of Brattleboro.

So here was a dream sequence that lasted for many months. Its purpose was to slowly point me in a direction that was correct for my spiritual development, not necessarily my ego development.

Much has changed in our lives since that time. I now appreciate country life more than I could ever have imagined. We no longer live in that first house we found — or which found us — but we are still in the same area of New Hampshire, across the river from the thriving little town of Brattleboro, Vermont. We have llamas, gardens and ponds on our land, and enjoy views of the Green Mountains, while living in an ecology-conscious neighborhood. This environment has allowed me and Cynthia to move our intuitive work in a direction we might never have taken, had we not heeded the gentle prodding of my dream guides.

* * * * *

Once in our new home, I experienced a series of dreams that explained how various minerals from the Earth can benefit us, and further illuminating the final message I'd received which prompted us to reconsider the move to upper New England. The dream relayed to me a long list of substances and their related uses, but there was one that jumped out at me which pertained to crystalline substances. In the dream I had a mentor, a man who looked like he could have played Merlin in a movie about the days of good King Arthur. He spoke in great detail about crystals, and about minerals containing crystalline substances.

"Crystalline substances have many purposes," he told me. *"But it will be found that their highest purpose relates to inner-world psychic communication. The key to this will be found in common, ordinary granite."*

He then looked directly at me and nodded, continuing, *"And you, Gordon, should now be aware of why you truly came to live in the Granite State."*

Making the move from our little mini-farm to the larger

property we now inhabit, a few miles up the road, a funny thing occurred. Just after moving in, we were digging around the foundation of the barn, and found that we were hitting stone ledge everywhere we dug. I called in a local excavator. He remembered our new house very well, as he had done the blasting work for the original foundation many years earlier. "Solid granite," he said. "Your home sits on solid granite."

* * * * *

Throughout my travels in the dream world, I have learned the importance of working with all dreams, no matter how elusive, simple or just plain silly they may at first seem. Dream time is structured differently than the linear time we currently base our "real" lives on. Based on our spiritual needs, dreams are rooted in a cyclical time structure, and often don't configure easily when we wake, remember, and then try to translate them into our more familiar linear format. This does not mean that our dreams never deal with day-to-day needs, or give lessons that pertain to everyday life. They do. But most of the time we confuse "everyday" needs with our strongest emotional needs of the moment, which are seldom speaking out on behalf of our cyclical, eternal, or karmic best interests. Often, what we *truly* need becomes suppressed, imprisoned in our subconscious mind. One of the only ways our deepest-knowing, intuitive self (the higher part of us that is concerned with the whole cycle, or the "Big Picture," rather than the linear tangent we currently rest on) gets to communicate with our everyday self, is by sending us messages through the dream state.

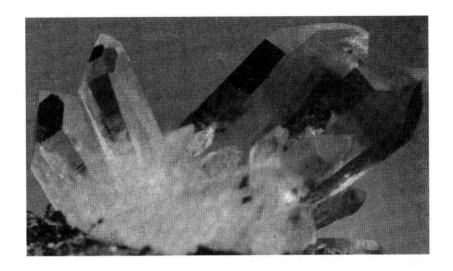

CHAPTER SEVEN

The Psychic Power of Gem Stones & Color

THE RING

My teachers had spoken to me about the powerful energies of vortexes, and had alluded to the fact that there were minerals — other than granite — that could assist me in increasing my level of awareness. The idea of working with these natural forces intrigued me, and I set out to learn as much as possible about this subject from my Source. With Cynthia's help, I underwent several trance sessions with the intent of getting specific information about minerals and gem stones. We devised a list of questions ahead of time, and with Cynthia present, I entered an altered state of consciousness. She was then able to "interview" my Source, asking the questions we needed to answer.

In one of the earlier sessions, my teacher had specified gem stones and minerals as especially powerful in relation to the individual. This led us to further inquiry. What we both wanted to know was whether there was a particular mineral or gem stone that would be helpful for Cynthia. What would be the best "power stone" for her? The following is a word-for-word transcript of the response we received from my Source.

For self, this stone would be the garnet. This would have the greater vibratory forces for the work of self's life. And by this we refer to those soul forces within that desire expression. Self in this sojourn is desirous of bringing in, or making known to those of a larger family, knowledge that would go beyond the normal senses; an understanding, a knowing that all needs to be in balance. And so the garnet for self tends to enhance, through its vibrational structure, those unique patterns imprinted at birth. The force that the garnet exerts simply amplifies the desire for outward expression. It can be thought of as a catalyst.

The symbol for self, we feel here, would be that of one taken from the Akasha — the universal library. This symbol would be one of ancient times, taken from the time period in Og, when self was attuned to same, for in many incarnations self has worked with one form or another of various objects that would have symbolic form, whether it be of the pottery, stonework, gems, tapestry, tile, or mosaics. Self has worked often with these, so it will be a natural tendency for self to create or use same in self's life-work. This we find to be true whether it be symbolic or thorough color — and color is a symbol, make no mistake about this!

For self, a ring would be best. This would be worn on the second finger of the right hand of the entity proper, and cast in that of what you would call white gold, platinum, or silver. Self should always use that of white metals near the body, for the resonance will bring a closer attunement with all parts of self. Although self can wear the yellow gold, we find that the white metals will be of benefit, and will have a more calming effect upon same.

As to specific design, we feel it would be one that would be circular — moving to a spiral, as a coiled serpent. This symbol, transferred into the physical reality of the snake being coiled, has many connotations. It is a spiral which is indicative of the energy rising within self. Those kundalini forces rising up through the spinal column — the antenna system for the physical vehicle — are tuned to the pilot frequency of the Earth core. It is here that the energy rises up. So the stone should be mounted in that of a spiral, with the garnet mounted in a bridge upon the top of the coil, extending from the ring band proper. Coil the band also, making the complete ring open. We feel herein the darker hues of the ruby color would be the more appropriate. The gem could also be inscribed, but this would affect the transmission of light and limit other benefits of this force. The symbolic denotation of the snake in its coiled position carries for self a reminder to continue moving from the smaller to the larger, encompassing all. This symbolizes the higher consciousness of self, the springing forth or the expansion of energy, the moving outward of the greater soul force. These, we find, would be best for the entity in this life, as it pertains, as we said, to the outward expansion of self.

A year was to pass before any action would be taken on this advice. As was often the case when we conducted readings of a personal nature, much time for reflection seemed to be required before an opportunity would present itself. Although we'd considered having a ring custom-made to my Source's specifications, somehow other priorities had kept us from acting on this. The suggestion that Cynthia needed to have this item was not forgotten, but it was certainly relegated to the back-burner.

Then one day, while browsing in a jewelry shop in a small town we were visiting in Massachusetts, Cynthia noticed a large terra cotta bowl in a floor display. The bowl was low and wide-mouthed, filled with sand, and decorated with a Native American motif. As she went closer, she saw a brightly colored stone peeking out of the sand in the bowl. Drawn to the color, she pulled it out, uncovering a ring which had been mostly buried. Yes, it was the exact ring she had been told would be best for her — a deep-red garnet in a silver setting which was shaped like a serpent, in an open coil.

The Mineral World

The following is a summary of all the information I've received on this subject of the power of stones. Through my Source and my dream teachers, I have gotten consistent answers to my questions. In the process of strengthening our intuitive abilities, I believe this information, as well as the exercise described here, are crucial building-blocks in our quest for greater understanding. In our culture, we have been taught many things about the natural world which are simply not true. It takes hard work and an open mind to rediscover the knowledge that has been lost to us. Be willing to experience these things, and I believe you will find the process fruitful.

As we begin to reconnect with the Earth realms of minerals and crystals, the first thing we need to do is to realize that a mineral — a gem stone, for example — is an actual "consciousness" unto itself. It is a consciousness very different from man's, but it is connected to — and as such, in communication with — the collective consciousness at all times. Like a pulse — a heartbeat — of the Earth, like the music made by the motions of water and air, it is always there, speaking to us. The mineral world has a language; it is alive. We may laugh at this, or find it hard to conceive of, but it is only our limited understanding of sentience that limits us. After all, doesn't the human body contain all the same elements and minerals that are contained in the Earth? It is a fact not open to conjecture that life as we know it is built from the elements of Earth. Perhaps one of the reasons we can barely understand the workings of our own human consciousness is that we have ignored (for several millennia) the subtler nuances of "consciousness" which are not embodied in the complex biology of the brain.

Secondly, we need to realize that just as the conscious life of the mineral world profoundly affects us, so does the conscious life of humanity affect minerals. On a large scale, the shifting and quaking of the Earth is an example of this. Although it is true that earthquakes and volcanic activity are a natural part of the Earth's living process, the actions of man upon the face of the Earth significantly alter, sometimes severely, the size and direction of seismic upheavals. This mutual interaction can best be thought of as a vibratory force, an oscillation, which can be interpreted as a language. Each and every element vibrates at its own frequency — speaking in its own "dialect," if you will — and these different mineral vibrations seek to synchronize, to become resonant with other life forces of like vibration.

The human vibration rate varies, depending on the time of day, the lunar cycle, and the Earth's position in the solar year. On an individual basis, one can alter his or her energy frequency by making changes in diet, geographic location, or consciousness (such as through prayer, or meditation), or by focusing energy through the use of bodily adornment, such as in the case of Cynthia's ring. As a collective consciousness, humans are actually capable of attunement with the "pilot" frequency generated by the core of the Earth — approximately 7.8 cycles per second. It is only during brief, actively Earth-conscious phases in mankind's development that this has been achieved, at least on a global level. The individual, however, can indeed attune to the Earth — become "one" with it — by establishing a connection with the pilot frequency of the core. It is when our personal energy frequency is synchronized and operating properly that we can detect movements or disturbances within the Earth before they reach the surface, in the form of volcanoes or earthquakes. Animals are naturally attuned to this frequency, because their consciousness does not limit this ability, and we too, can rediscover this sensitivity in ourselves. Only man limits himself!

To learn more about attunement, and eventually, to bring yourself into sync with the pilot frequency of the Earth, it is helpful to start by concentrating on a specific stone or mineral. Different stones have different vibrations, so some stones will be better suited to the resonance of a particular individual. According to my teachers, the mineral's frequency depends upon its atomic structure, the geological structure at the site of formation, and by the positions of astrological bodies at the time of its formation.

If we suppose for a moment that this accurately describes the nature of minerals, we can look at it from a purely scientific standpoint to see that, as a hypothesis, it makes a great deal of sense. We know that all minerals are composed of elements which are made up of atoms. Each atom is formed by a central nucleus orbited by particles called electrons, each of which carries a tiny charge of electricity. In its normal state, each atom has a neutral electrical charge, because the positive charge of the nucleus is balanced by the negative charge of the electrons. If an atom gains or loses one or more electrons, however, it becomes charged, and is then called an ion. Each of these ions has a certain "frequency," depending upon its charge and its atomic weight. The frequency of an entire structure — such as a gem stone — depends upon the overall electrical charge or vibration of the stone. You can think of a stone's vibratory frequency as the sum total of all factors which created, or have since affected, that particular stone. These include, among other things: the ratio of ionized particles in the stone's make-up, and where the particles appear within the crystalline structure of that mineral's composition.

Once the correct mineral for an individual has been determined, healing of the physical body or of the psyche can be enhanced by finding a stone composed of the required elements, and using it to focus on and interact with. Many stones that have commonly sought-after healing properties are sold in stores these days, often in the form of polished pebbles. These work fine, but so do stones that are in their raw state.

When determining which stones will work best for you, simply keep in mind that the stone's frequency is made up of the accumulated energy of its "life." In your search for the "right" stones to use, it matters not whether they have been cut, polished, or remain in the rough; what is important is that they speak to you in some way. Trust your intuition.

As my teachers have told me over and over, *"All healing stems from the willingness of those persons who request healing, attuning them to the creative forces inherent in Earth."* Gems and other mineral combinations simply act as tuning devices, which can help us access the greater healing power of the whole Earth through a process of induction. Learning about stones and their elemental properties, handling stones on a regular basis, and fine-tuning our affinity for those that are most harmonious with our own energy, are practices which eventually allow us to enhance our well-being, and to maintain a state of balance once we have attained it.

Induction is a term my teachers have used to explain the modes of interconnection that tie together the various realms of consciousness that exist. It can refer to an electrical process wherein a conductor is "charged" by another nearby object by momentarily grounding the conducting object. It also describes a biochemical phenomenon wherein the body's glandular production can be increased at the genetic level. My Source has suggested the following example — an individual with a thyroid imbalance — to show how induction works, within the greater scheme of the cosmos:

> *To achieve a balancing, or tuning, of the thyroid gland, the vibration of the element copper may be required. By bringing some copper close to the one in need of healing, an induction occurs in which the person's inner crystalline structures attune to the element through consciousness. The process is similar to what happens when a tuning fork is struck at a particular note and the vibration is felt by another fork several feet away, which then resonates with the same frequency.*

How do you begin to know which gems or stones you need to seek out? First, you must spend some time with the question, perhaps through meditation, or by writing in a journal about your feelings regarding the issue. In this way you establish your intent, and you attune your conscious mind to the energies required by your whole self, your higher consciousness. Think about what you need. What feels lacking, overwhelming, or out of balance for you, either physically, mentally or spiritually? This step sets up a great rapport between the conscious self and the energies of higher consciousness. Having done it — even if the exercise felt very "normal" and undramatic — you will find the stone selection process goes very quickly, almost as if guided by unseen forces. Which, of course, it is.

EXERCISE ONE

As you enter into the step of determining the correct stones to use for your unique energy frequencies, use this step-by-step exercise as a guide:

1. Pick a stone, any stone — either faceted, polished, or in the raw state. Pick one with a color that is pleasing to you; however, keep in mind that color is not purely visual, but that it is an energy force which can be sensed in other ways as well. Trust your feelings when choosing a stone, more than your eyes.

2. Place the stone in front of you, either on a table or on the floor. It should be about twelve to eighteen inches in front of you. Close your eyes, and spend at least five minutes getting into a state of relaxation.

3. Place your palms three to six inches from the stone, as if shielding it, and slowly move your hands around in the energy field which surrounds the stone.

4. With your eyes still closed, practice using your natural

attuning abilities to sense and perceive the stone. Be aware of any physical sensations of energy, thoughts that seem important or relevant, and feelings or emotions that come up for you.

5. As you begin directing your consciousness in this manner, your own crystalline structure becomes more active and begins to build up its electromagnetic field, which actually moves outward from your body as its power increases. When your field encompasses the stone, you will probably feel a tingling, a pulsation or a vibration, beginning in your hands and possibly moving to other parts of your body, and in the area around the stone. This is the frequency of the stone interacting with your own frequency. Some other experiences this exercise might bring about are mental pictures of colors or energy fields, or sensations of heat or cold.

6. When you have gotten to this point, you may stop at any time. You might want to rest, write about the experience, or try again with a different stone. When you are just starting out, however, it is not recommended to attempt this with more than three or four stones in a sitting. Give yourself a few days between sittings, as well, especially if you are working with multiple stones. These are powerful energies, and sometimes enthusiasm can obscure our common sense. Remember, the key to attunement — and to health — is relaxation. Practice patience as you practice these exercises.

At this stage, it is not as important to detect a particular frequency as it is to detect *something*, anything at all. Specifically, you will sense a coupling with the stone when one of the endocrine gland systems in your body begins to respond to its frequency. After you have practiced with many different stones, you will begin to sense that one or several are "right" for you. Sensations such as tingling, heat or coolness will be accompanied by intuitive feelings. You have already called upon your higher consciousness to guide you in this exercise by completing the first step in the attunement process. Your instincts — as you work with different stones — will prove to be remarkably accurate. As you become more experienced in the use of gems and stones, it will take you less and less time to know which stone is the most appropriate to use for a particular healing purpose. Eventually, you will just *know*.

PSYCHOMETRY

Another example my Source spoke to me about was how objects, such as stones, develop added memory. This also holds true for any object, whether natural or man-made, including furniture, jewelry, clothes or other belongings. The following is a transcript of information I received on this topic.

A stone in its raw state, taken from the Earth, will have its own vibratory force. If it is passed from the finder to another recipient, the vibratory force of the stone's environment is coupled with the consciousness of the individual who found the stone. That vibratory force is then transferred to the new owner — whose own vibration will be added to the vibration of the stone. That is how psychometry works — by perceiving from the vibrations emanating from objects or picturing the feelings or knowledge contained in them.

Then you have to add another element, that of the consciousness of the person who carves or facets the stone, for his or her consciousness becomes part of the stone's vibration. If the carver is one of love and compassion, much of that vibration will be programmed into the gem, for instance.

When a stone is being active — when it is being held — it transfers its consciousness, which is now a collective consciousness, to the person holding it.

The symbols that might be etched or carved into a stone add even more in the way of vibration. There exists a universal library of symbols, recorded and updated since the beginning of time, which can be accessed through the dream state,

*or the realm of the subconscious mind. When carved into a
stone in a certain fashion, through consciousness, symbols
can bring forth good luck, safety, healing, psychic attunement, and so forth. The same is true with faceting, for
faceting involves angles, and angles involve numerology. All
this brings in other vibratory rates, as does refraction of light
through crystals.*

*Once you have decided on a particular stone, the place to
wear it on the body depends on the endocrine system and
which center or chakra would be the most receptive.*

*To determine this, simply place a stone above each of the
chakras and see which one gives you the greatest sense of
attunement. Notice, also, if there is any negative reaction —
a sense of discomfort. These feelings will be subtle sensations
within you. The bio-electrical field of the body is made up of
thousands of electrical sensors of various polarities, and
these act as detectors sending information to the brain,
which causes you to feel the various sensations.*

*The settings into which you place a stone in jewelry may
change, by the way, over time, depending on the changes that
occur in your own life. You may be drawn to one gem and
setting at one time in your life and to another at another
time.*

THE ENERGY OF COLOR

In another session, my Source explained the power of color. It
seems that each of us comes into the Earth on a particular
color ray, unique and individual to us alone, although the
individual color rays do meld into groupings, defined as soul
groups. Souls choose to enter the Earth plane for specific
lessons at specific times in history. It is here on Earth that they
become part of the collective consciousness of human beings.
Souls enter on different color rays at different times, most
often shifting from one ray to another between Earth lives, but
occasionally making the jump from one group to another dur-

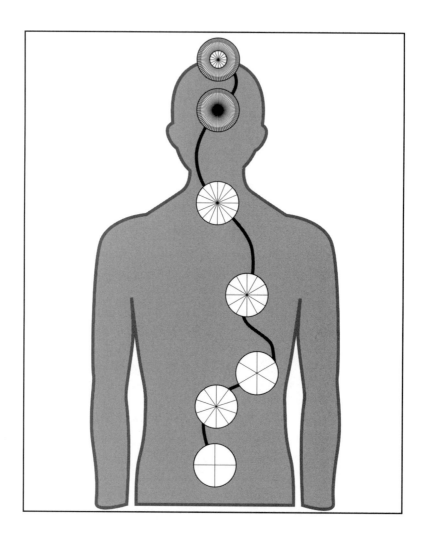

The Chakra System of the Human Body

There are seven energy centers, or chakras (a Sanskrit word meaning wheel) in the body, each corresponding to one of the endocrine glands. Each chakra vibrates at a different rate, following the visible light spectrum. The base, or lowest chakra, is associated with the color red; the sacral chakra, orange; the chakra located near the solar plexus, yellow; the heart chakra, green; the throat chakra, blue; the brow chakra, indigo; and the highest chakra, the crown chakra (located at the top of the head) is associated with the color violet. A person who is clairvoyant is able to see these colors emanating from the chakras, the totality of which make up the human aura.

ing a single lifetime. All souls are capable of moving from one group to another whenever the need arises.

The lowest color realms are in the red range — this is where much learning is required even to gain awareness of the soul as part of the greater Oneness of soul force — and the graduating levels are arranged to correspond with the spectral, or prismatic, arrangement we are familiar with. Red moves into orange, which moves into yellow, which moves into green, which moves into blue, and so on. As we move into the realms of indigo and violet, the soul is at a point in its growth where it is concentrating on lessons of spiritual service and selfless love. I was surprised to be told that I am — like Cynthia and many others with whom we were to become associated along our paths — a part of the Indigo Ray group. Since I was still at a point in my transformative process where I didn't see myself as very spiritually enlightened, I found this difficult to accept. But my Source told me that this view of myself was only because I was focusing on the present-life me, not the multi-dimensional me that resides in all the layers of reality simultaneously. By becoming aware of the significance of colors — and by learning to use them to soothe, to heal, or to create places for action and rest — we can actually guide our present consciousness to harmonically attune itself to those higher levels we are constantly moving towards. As we practice intuitive awareness, communication with our whole, multi-dimensional self becomes not only possible, but certain.

EXERCISE TWO

My Source suggested that an individual's color ray might be determined through an experiment with colors. The explicit directions given to me can be used by anyone, right at home. To do so, get large panels of poster board — panels that are at least two by three feet works best — in the seven colors of the prismatic spectrum. Try to find the truest colors you can, especially for the primary colors: red, yellow and blue. You can also expand the experiment by getting more colors than just the basics, so that you can really zero-in on your specific color frequency. For example, try doing this experiment using three or four shades in each color range of the spectrum: red, orange, yellow, green, blue, and violet.

With eyes closed, spend time with each color panel, recording your feelings and sensations as you touch it, hold your hands over it, and even put your face near it. Remember that you are focusing on your personal response to the energy of color, not your visual preference for a particular one, so don't use your eyes as a gauge. You can also test how strongly the color affects you from a distance, by starting up close and then slowly moving away from each panel, noting any perceived shifts in energy. The best way to do all of this is with someone else present, because you can then talk about impressions freely, while the other person handles the panels for you, and either tape-records or transcribes your perceptions for you.

Despite what we have been taught, all of our senses are able to respond to color; vision is only one of the many ways to perceive the energy waves that we identify as "color." As a species, we have become so dependent on vision, and so out of touch with our more subtle senses, that we think of color only in terms of what we can see. Using the above experiment, we can learn a lot about the power of colors, beyond the visible realm. When we did it, Cynthia felt herself drawn towards violet colors — they felt more stimulating for her than any of the others. For me, it was more of the deep purples, and sometimes the blues. I had more of a feeling of restfulness and peace when I came in contact with these hues. Since that time, I have changed most of my wardrobe over to blues, grays and whites, whereas before I tended to wear earth tones. I find that it has indeed changed my consciousness, and my overall sense of well-being.

Wherever *your* strongest feelings fall in this spectral analysis, however, it is important to keep in mind that we are all moving from red towards blue, and that you can enhance your own progress — and acquire an increased sense of peace — by incorporating colors like mauve, indigo or violet into your surroundings. Try experimenting with these colors near your bed, in the place where you meditate, or by wearing them on your body, or carrying something with you. Over time, the benefits received by taking this small action can be profound.

* * * * *

We have experimented with the information presented here in various workshops, and have found it to be useful to anyone truly desiring to make a shift in consciousness. For me, the greatest benefit from these exercises was in becoming more aware of the Earth as a sentient being. Years ago, I would have laughed at such an idea, but today it seems so clear to me that I have trouble understanding why everyone doesn't realize it as so. As my Source continually reminds me, however, even to this day, *"Awareness comes to each in his own time. It is not being correct all along, but the journey that matters most. The end result — awareness — is but the memory of the journey."*

I feel strongly that the information I have received about the applications of color, gems and minerals could hardly have come at a better time. Humankind has developed technology in the last decade that far surpasses anything we had ever previously imagined, even as recently as a few decades ago. We have gone far beyond sending men to the moon and back, and have developed real technologies which allow us to move towards exploring the farthest reaches of our universe. We have built computers that talk, walk and emulate the functions of the human brain. Daily, and without even thinking about it, many of us use chemicals to help us get started in the morning, to relax at night, to cure our diseases (or our symptoms), and to grow and preserve our food and the products that we use. And the list goes on. It is true that we have, as a civilization, accomplished many positive and wonderful feats with our technology — expanding our abilities to travel around our own world and beyond, prolonging the productive part of our life spans, exchanging information and knowledge between individuals and cultures in ways never before possible. Yet, along with all of these advances in mass communication, speed and apparent efficiency, there has come a regression in our overall quality of life that equals and perhaps surpasses the benefits of our technological progress. As individuals, we have grown further and further away from our roots — spiritually, emotionally and sometimes even physically — separating ourselves from and thereby neglecting our planet. Our Earth, which we are dependent on for our very lives and sustenance, has become a stranger, a force to be reckoned with, rather than a part of who we are.

The advanced civilizations of ancient history viewed man's connection with Earth — the Great Mother — as sacred. When we understood the power of our Earth, and understood our Oneness with it, we had a truer sense of our own power. Nowadays, we have lost our connection with the very rock beneath our feet, and with it, our access to the most powerful source of energy that exists for us, besides the sun. The Earth's energy, and the sun's, are here for the benefit of humans — not to use up and plunder as we have, but to *interact* with — so that all of creation benefits from the process.

Our society has gotten horribly out of balance; as individuals, we must direct our efforts towards rebalancing. The energy of our minds is the gift we have to offer the Great Mother in return for her energy and nourishment. Unfortunately, what we have done of late is to spend all of our collective mind-power on ourselves. However, we can learn from this and move on in a new direction. The first step, as individuals, is to begin redirecting our focus back to the Earth. The information I have received on colors, gems and minerals seems to me to be an important reminder of what the ancients knew to be true. Quite simply, that we must honor the Earth, respect it, and attune to all its various forms to the best of our abilities. In return, the Earth supports, nourishes and protects us, providing a place for all conscious entities to come learn, grow and live as human beings.

According to my Source, the psychic uses of gem stones and minerals were common knowledge in the days before the last flood, taught to every child in those ancient times, just as we now teach our own children to tie their shoes or to read. This knowledge is being rediscovered today, as the need to re-attune ourselves to the Earth's elements makes itself known to more and more people through visions and dreams. Each of us must trust that we are part of the greater whole, and that we are all a part of the creative force that makes up the cosmos. When you make a conscious effort to attune to a stone, you are reestablishing your connection with that wholeness, Oneness, creative force, or whatever you feel comfortable calling it. With diligent practice, you can begin to discover that each of us, like stones and everything else in creation, radiates a subtle energy, and that you yourself have the sensitivity to perceive it. With this awareness, it soon becomes apparent that all of us — all things — are interconnected.

CHAPTER EIGHT

Crisis in the Borderland

THE VISION

Since the mid-eighties, I've had visions of strange energies coming into the Earth realm from somewhere else. When they began, I understood little about the energy patterns I was seeing, and since so much else was happening to me, I didn't spend very much time exploring just what these forces were about. Then I had an extremely powerful dream vision, that clarified the scenario for me. And of course, led to more questions.

As it begins, I observe clouds floating in over a valley. The clouds are dark and threatening, like thunderheads. As I continue to observe them, they seem to expand to cover cities and villages. The vision continues, with strange lights emanating from the clouds. I can see threads or fibers of red light streaming down to Earth.

Slowly, the vision becomes more expansive, and I'm able to see larger areas, as if I've been pulled back by some force, and can now view hundreds of miles instead of only a few. From this perspective I can see multiple streams of these red lights coming down. There seem to be more of them going into cities than into the rural areas. A few more seconds go by, and I then I am able to see even farther — the West Coast and the East Coast. Now there appear to be hundreds, if not thousands, of these red streams.

If I follow the red streams down with my eyes, I see that there seem to be more of them in areas where there is heavier pollution, such as Los Angeles. I observe Chicago, New York, and Washington. All of these places appear to have more of the threads, which seem to move in a snake-like fashion back to where they first entered the Earth.

Next, I find that I am actually inside one of these clouds, and I cannot see the Earth. It appears almost as if there is a cloud below me and a cloud above me. The one above me seems to be blue in color, and there are no streams coming from it, but rather a bulge which grows downward.

As I look down, I see the beginnings of the red streams that lead toward the Earth. When I look around in this area, I feel a sense of darkness and discomfort. My physical body reacts violently. It isn't fear — more like dread. I only know that I want to leave. I am extremely uncomfortable.

I observe that there are groupings of red balls or spheres of light. Some of these are as large as buildings, yet others appear smaller, perhaps the size of tennis balls. There are literally tens of thousands of these spheres! They are everywhere I look, yet none of them are near enough to touch, and I can't get to them. I can only see them.

I see smaller spheres mingling with some of the larger ones, trying to become part of them. Indeed, in some cases they succeed. I observe that the largest spheres seemed to discharge static electricity. I watch various forms of lightning-like action occurring.

After the lightning begins, I see that it is causing a break or tear in the cloud. While I am observing this, I suddenly find myself on the Earth once again, looking up at the tear to see how it is getting through the clouds. Indeed, the fibers of red light are coming from the large red spheres that were up on the top side of the cloud. As soon as I see this, I find myself immediately catapulted back to the red layer.

Slowly, as I turn around, I feel a great sadness, and I sense this is a place where people are lost. I call them "people," because up to this point I had thought that it was simply a visual phenomenon, but now I am beginning to sense that there is a consciousness to these lights. The consciousness contains a sadness. There is anger, frustration, and bitterness, too; but most of all, there is confusion everywhere.

My attention is then drawn up to the top layer of the cloud, where I'd seen the blue bulge earlier. It is an electric blue color, with a bulging depression like you might see if you were inside a balloon that a great hand was pressing on from the outside. I find myself moving around to where I can see other bulges. There are no lightning-like actions moving through, just depressions of blue coming into the space. I am moving toward the bulges, and eventually I get to the point where I am engulfed in a blue gelatin-like material. As I look down, I can see that there is a large build-up of this blue material that is pushing down on the red cloud layer.

I realize that these are not clouds at all! Rather, they are levels, or separations — similar to pouring oil and vinegar into a vessel of water and seeing the layers of separation. This blue level has a feeling different from the red, more of a calming influence. I feel as if there is a presence that is aware of what exists below, down in the red layer, and that it is exerting a force, a form of assistance, in that direction.

I see that there is a layer above this blue one which is yellow. I somehow know that it isn't my time to move to that area. I try anyway, but I am gently pushed back by some force. I drift back into the red realm. I observe that wherever the blue electric matter is bulging, the red matter — the spheres — move away from it. I also observe that directly beneath the blue bulges, the red penetration through the clouds, the red streams, are not present. It's almost as if the blue force somehow provides an energy that keeps the red force from penetrating down to the Earth.

I find myself slowly drifting back to the Earth. When I wonder to myself where the red streams are going, the vision clearly shows me large areas where there is heavy smog. In those areas, the streams are flowing in by the hundreds, moving and dancing almost as if they are searching for something. They seem to be building in strength as they attach themselves to this smog area, almost as if they are feeding on the pollution.

The lights, once they get strong enough, penetrated through the smog. I watch as several of these lights enter into the necks of two or three people. Wherever there is a grouping of people, particularly around school areas, I observe these lights coming in numbers. I observe that along highways, these streams are attaching themselves to the cars.

As the movement continues, I look up once again, only to observe that the lights have doubled in number. They seem to be getting stronger and seeking out, with some intelligence, certain life forms. They seem to enter more in some countries than in others. I see them hovering around certain streams of water. Once they attach themselves to something, they seem to draw more light streams to join with them. Now I observe them entering two individuals. Within a few minutes I noticed that other individuals have come into the area, and they have the same threads. Almost as if there is a kind of meeting going on.

The overall feeling I have is that the lights are a kind of intelligence, seeking out similar energy to their own. When that happens, they become stronger, and the lights from the red borderland flow more freely, in larger numbers. Once that occurs, the blue borderland has to work much harder to impress its force into the area.

Slowly, the vision becomes dimmer, and I notice that the lights are starting to extinguish themselves. Not that I feel them going away, but more like it is time now for me to withdraw from this vision. I try to pull myself back into it several times, wanting to know more. I still want to know what is beyond the yellow border, and to know more about the blue border, too.

The cloud I am in becomes darker and darker, until I find myself in total darkness. As I look around, the darkness slowly dissipates. Finally, I can see the sun, white puffy clouds, and the green valleys once again.

INTERVIEW WITH CYNTHIA KEYES

CK: Gordon, while you were describing your vision, many questions came to my mind. One of the first things that I was wondering about was: Is this a single vision, or is it part of a series of visions?

GMS: The first vision of this type occurred in 1987. I remember specifically because it was a time when I was beginning to have multiple visions and writing them down. Previously, the visions would come once or maybe twice a year. Now they were coming frequently, as often as twice a month, sometimes twice a week. The early visions were fragments of what later built into a much fuller vision.

CK: My first impression while hearing you describe your vision was of storm clouds forming on the horizon as if we were in for a disturbing time. Was that how you felt at the time?

GMS: In later visions, I clearly understood that these clouds represented levels, or separations from the Earth. It was something not physical, yet the visions were showing me physical clouds.

There was a very uneasy feeling. It was a difficult time for the entities which were part of that borderland. I felt discomfort for them, and I also felt that there was somehow going to be discomfort for a lot of people. The feeling was like a warning that things were going to become troubled, as dark clouds may warn of a thunderstorm, cyclone or hurricane. Those feelings, I remember, were clearly present.

CK: Could you describe the consciousness of the lower level with the red flashes of light?

GMS: This first borderland, which has other names now such as the astral realm, clearly is a place in the time-space continuum. It is not physical, yet it interacts with the physical. It is a place where one's consciousness, one's soul, if you will, passes through just after death. The way we have lived our lives on the Earth determines how quickly we move through the various borderlands, or layers.

One life, for example, may have been full of bitterness, drug addictions, killing, violence, or extreme fear. These energies or vibrations find a home in the first borderland, the red area. Most of the entities there are troubled, confused and unaware of their own presence. This borderland is a level where you spend time until your consciousness awakens to a higher vibration, in which case you can move to the next level.

CK: You describe streams of red light emanating from the clouds and reaching down to areas of high density, like cities or other areas of high pollution. It seems that they are feeding on pollution. Is that what draws the red streams into those areas?

GMS: I believe so. I believe the energy and the consciousness from this borderland, this astral realm, comes from entities who only know one thing. They only know a specific energy. The energies of certain places are in harmony with them, such as areas that have heavy positive ionization, like smog, for example. Or areas where there is a lot of negativity, such as a city with all of the commotion, vehicles moving around with their generators and alternators, air conditioners, and people moving about. This positive ionization is like a food for them, and they are drawn to it.

These entities desire to return to the Earth, yet they can't. They will become companions to people of similar energy. People who, for example, are chronically depressed, contemplating suicide, on drugs, or who are very negative or angry. These conditions can allow a type of possession, if you will. The borderland entity attaches itself to the person's etheric or astral body. This is how many of the entities in the borderland are expressing themselves and modifying the personalities of the people they are involved with.

CK: There seems to have been an increase in random, senseless acts of violence. Do you sense that this could have anything to do with what you have seen in this vision?

GMS: My sense was, and is, that these things do interplay. There is such a large body of these astral forms pushing down on the physical Earth, the numbers would be measured in the billions. We have as many entities in the astral realm as we have people in the physical world today. Therefore, the percentages are such that the negative energy will affect more people.

I have also observed that violence begins by the patterns established in a person's life. These include their home life, their experiences in life, their personality, as well as the influence of the soul's continuation through reincarnation.

You also have to consider the totality of this negative consciousness. Just the thought of doing a negative thing is enough to draw an entity to a person. Then the thought of doing it becomes so real that the act becomes second nature. There is no remorse once the act is done because, to this person, it is just a continuation of the thought pattern that has been developing throughout life, and perhaps over many lives.

CK: So for people who are already on the edge, if you will, this attachment is all they need to maybe, push them over that edge?

GMS: If they are not working toward a healing process, they are at high risk. Once they have the desire to move toward a better life, toward being a better person, the negative energy will decrease. The only thing that is required is the thought, the desire. Changing your vibration, even if you are on that fine edge, will repel any negative entities that may be drawn to you. These include the red thread from the astral realm, but also negative people who might be drawn to you. It is a case of energies attracting or repulsing.

CK: Could you explain the nature of the blue level, which you saw above the red borderland level?

GMS: There are eight levels in all, including the physical Earth. Each realm becomes lighter in vibration until we reach what we might call the Logos, the Christ Consciousness, or the Universal Mind. Each religion and each culture has its own name for this realm.

The consciousness of the blue level is trying very hard to

awaken more of the souls in the level below, to reduce the burden of that level. Many entities from the blue level are in contact with people on the Earth through dream states and other levels of consciousness.

As we live our lives, we establish vibrations of our own, which attract people of similar vibrations. Any vibration we create is also sensed by one of the levels of consciousness.

CK: How can we join forces with the upper level of consciousness, the blue level? This level seemed to be trying to heal what was going on in the lower levels.

GMS: You can make a conscious effort to connect to the blue level by using certain shades of blue, electric blue, I would call them. Healing work, whether through a mental process or a physical process, will also change your energy and attract positive forces such as those of the blue level. Groups of people have additional power in these endeavors, especially groups of three or multiples of three. For example, this can be accomplished through group meditation, by two people coming together to help a third person who is depressed, or by several people concentrating on positive thoughts together.

One of the most positive things that you can do is increase your awareness. Appreciate what you have, get out and experience nature, and try to be open to new concepts. Become aware that the physical world is much more than we think it is, and the non-physical world is literally a whole new universe.

* * * * *

As a result of the dream visions I have received about these borderland energies, I have become aware of how crucial it is for each of us to try to live in a state of balance whenever possible. This is more true of the times we now live in than it has ever been before (at least, that is, within the current cycle we know as recorded history). My sense is that the vibratory speed of our current society is moving faster and faster, and as this continues, the negative borderland effects will become increasingly pronounced. Eventually, however, the same ener-gy that now enables borderland forces to operate here on Earth will experience a major shift in polarity. This, in turn, will create a conduit by which more benevolent energies will be activated in each and every one of us.

CHAPTER NINE

Reincarnation

Occasionally I venture into uncharted waters by having specific questions asked of me while I am in an altered state of consciousness. A subject I have found interesting that seems to come up over and over is the concept of karma and reincarnation. While this is not a subject I was taught about in catechism class and, in fact, tends to go against all the religious teachings I've been raised with, it has always held a certain fascination for me. In readings with clients, karma came up time and again as the reason for an illness or a particular difficulty in this lifetime. Some clients were told by my Source that they were a senator in Rome, a king in Atlantis, or a famous scientist at the turn of the twentieth century. Of course, I was curious to discover what great historical figure I might have been in another century, but I was so busy doing sessions for other people that I never made the time to explore my own past lives. A rare turn of events changed all of this. Indeed, it changed my understanding of the concept of reincarnation completely, establishing it as a new part of my belief system, and my view of the cosmos, forevermore.

Past-Life Dreams

Earlier this particular day, I had been thinking a lot about the mind and healing, wondering just how much our daily thoughts affect the state of our general health. My dream guides were continually speaking of the power of mind — how we are what we think — whether past, present, or probable future. I was never quite sure what all of this meant, but trusted clarity would come some day, as they often told me it would, "When the time is right." I did not expect, however, that this would be the day.

Often, I take cat naps during the day, after lunch. They only last for a few minutes, but somehow this rest seems to rejuvenate me. Perhaps this is because my work days are very long, typically lasting for ten to twelve hours, not including my night-school work when I'm dreaming.

As I closed my eyes to take one of my "power" naps this day, I drifted off, and found my thoughts turning to the cold weather outside my living room window. It was winter in New England, and about twenty degrees at the time, with a heavy snow falling. It's usually during this type of weather that my chronic asthma kicks in. The last conscious thought I can recall was musing about whether or not it would ever be possible to cure the asthma which had continued to plague me, off and on, since childhood.

The next thing I can remember is that I entered a lucid dream state. I was totally aware, and all of my physical senses were operating. Yet, I was no longer on the living room couch. Suddenly, I could hear the sound of water against shore, taste and smell salt on the breeze, and feel a warm wind blowing on my face. I opened my eyes and found myself outdoors, looking out at the ocean.

I turned, and from my vantage point in this dream world, I found myself looking down on a seaport, which was surrounded by a large city. A long channel led from the circular harbor out to the ocean, creating a keyhole-shaped cutout in the land. The port itself was enclosed by a huge man-made seawall, comprised of megalithic blocks of stone. The wall was a hundred feet wide at the top, its height obscured by the lapping water below. This massive retaining wall surrounded the mile-wide harbor, providing docking space for the boats.

Strange-looking ships, such as I'd never seen before, were tied up everywhere in the bay. Some were moving in or away, through the channel leading out to the sea, which I could see in the distance, perhaps three miles from the docks. I could hear many voices around me, speaking in an unrecognizable foreign tongue. How the boats were propelled was a mystery. No sails or motors were evident. Just the slow, silent movement of those few ships entering and leaving the harbor.

My viewpoint shifted then, and I found myself hovering above one of the ships in the harbor. I seemed to be flying. This vessel was perhaps a hundred feet long, the huge prow shaped into the likeness of a woman's head, her hair circled by a wreath of stars.

On the deck were many men, all with bronze-colored skin. Several of these men had whips and chains in hand, and they were shouting down into one of the cargo holds of the ship. I willed myself closer, and found that I could control my actions in this dreamscape by directing my thoughts to where I wanted to go. I floated closer to the main deck. I now had a clear view into the cargo hold. Hundreds of young men and women were crammed together there, packed so tightly that they could barely move. It reminded me of a cattle yard.

As I continued to look, I thought I saw movement — the flick of a tail — that was not human. I watched closely, and could not believe what I was seeing. In amongst the people in the cargo hold were apparently animals of all different types, some of which looked like nothing I'd ever seen. The stench, as I moved closer, was appalling. Then I realized something shocking — these were not animals and humans being held together in the hold, as I had first thought. The ship's hold was filled to bursting with creatures that were half animal, half human! Some had long tails, but otherwise human bodies, others had scales or fur all over; all seemed to have two arms and two legs.

A loud voice cried out, startling me. I thought for a moment that he was yelling at me, even though I did not understand the language. It was clear that this was the captain of the vessel. At his command, the creatures were pulled from the dark hold, one by one, and chained at the foot and neck. They were then dragged to the dock area, where perhaps fifty poles topped with large rings were mounted, apparently for attaching to the creatures' chains.

After the last man-beast had been taken out and the cargo hold was silent, one of the crew members leaned far down into the hold, checking to see if any were left. I willed myself around behind him, moving in directly over his head to gain a clearer vantage point into the hold. What I saw there filled me with sick horror. In the darkness at the far end of the hold I could see dozens of creatures lying motionless, eyes and mouths fixed open, their all too human faces frozen into an expression that could only be described as panic. I knew they were all dead.

I closed my eyes, feeling such remorse that I thought I could not bear it.

Then, with a jolt, I found myself back in our living room, my eyes wide open, looking all around to see where I was and what had happened.

My head was pounding and my eyes were blurry. I felt like I had fallen from the top of a twenty-story building. The next thing I remember was hearing a voice in my head, which said, *"While you may search for lifetimes where you have achieved greatness, it is the lifetimes where you have fallen that will be the greater focus in this life."*

In my thoughts I responded, "But what does this experience I've just had have to do with me?"

Instantly, the voice answered, *"Your inner world journey has taken you back to a time period some eighteen thousand years ago, to a place where you once dwelled. In this land you were captain of the vessel* **Star Maiden,** *out of the port city of Alta-Nuune in the greater land known then as Atlantis. You were a highly successful trader in what was then known as servant-class mixtures. These were beings containing both human and animal qualities — human form with tails, fur, scales, horns, or combinations of any of these features. Some creatures contained vestiges of the plant kingdoms as well. For at that time creatures such as these were still on the Earth, a result of genetic experimentations with nature by those early souls who came to the Earth millions of years earlier.*

"These beings, while containing the original spiritual spark of the Creation, were looked upon as beasts of burden. Some had language capability, and these were more valued as home-workers rather than field hands. Your name then was Bu-te-nam. You were the captain of this ship you saw.

"In your dream you were witnessing an actual past-life event — your life. Though more than past-life recall, you have actually time-traveled in this dream — the you in the twentieth century has traveled to meet the you eighteen thousand years ago. A simultaneous reality experience."

Completely overwhelmed by what I was hearing, I nevertheless continued to listen to all that the voice had to tell me.

My guide continued, *"From this life as Bu-te-nam, you lost in soul growth, creating karma which lasts to this day. To you, and to most people at that time, these beings of God were less than cattle. To increase your profits, you packed as many of them into the hold of your ship as could fit. Through your actions over the years, many hundreds lost their lives through suffocation. This brought to you the karma that directly impedes you in this life now, and has affected your health adversely since birth."*

I knew what my guide was referring to — my asthma.

"The suffocation you meted out during that life, you have brought back to yourself in other lives, as well as this one. Asthma for you is a result of karma, and is truly a disease of the soul force. It affects your lungs in this life, to remind you — with each breath — of the

suffering you caused to others. The misuse of your spiritual gift of life and your unfeeling treatment of other spiritual beings is the karma you now have."

With that I broke down, sobbing uncontrollably. How could I have done such a thing? I am so careful not to hurt anyone or anything ... I will go to great lengths even to let a spider or bee out of the house, so it can continue its life. The character of this lifetime as Bu-te-nam was so foreign to me, I couldn't believe that it could be a part of me, that it could have been me.

My teacher continued, *"Your soul has worked on this for many lifetimes. This karma last caused death in 1745, in Virginia, when you died of consumption. The soul then realized that the only way to rid itself of this karma was to suffer each day a fate similar to those it once destroyed, and to gradually turn its focus towards helping others to realize the importance of thoughts and actions."*

Rather than sounding mysterious and strange, I understood what was being said to me all too well. Every cell in my body felt the truth of it, and I was in agony. For how many lives more would I have to endure the suffering that would right the wrongs of that lifetime?

Answering this thought, my guide continued, *"As stated, suffering was the soul's first action. Now it is in aiding others that it becomes aware. Thus in helping others, the self is repaired."*

"But what else can I do?" I thought.

"As with all karma, the end comes when self realizes, balances its soul force through long suffering, and finally forgives self for the deed. When all are realized, the karma is paid."

Throughout all of this, I felt great remorse. "I am so sorry," I now repeated aloud, over and over.

Suddenly, I was thrown off the couch, violently. My body flew across the room, striking the fireplace wall and landing on the hearth. My head throbbing, I stood up, and felt a trickle of blood running down my face. I went and looked in the hall mirror. There was a cut on my forehead.

It was snowing hard outside, and as I opened the front door, cold air rushed in. I went outside a few steps and looked up at the sky. The cold, falling snow felt refreshing on my face. I scooped up some snow from the porch railing and held it to my head. It calmed me down, and the throbbing subsided.

Still shaken, I went back into the house and sat down. It was then that I realized I wasn't coughing, as I usually did when I went outside in this kind of cold, for even a few minutes. Typically, I'd be hit immediately if I went out without covering my face, the resulting attack lasting anywhere from fifteen minutes to several hours. Now, there was nothing. Was my karma on this issue over? Had I truly forgiven myself, as my guide had said I must do? Only time would tell.

* * * * *

More than ten years have passed since this experience, and I have yet to suffer another attack of my childhood disease. Even now I have flashbacks to the memory of those poor creatures, laying in the cargo hold of a ship called the *Star Maiden*, and a deep sadness comes over me.

One time, my Source addressed these feelings. It said, *"Once karma is addressed, those energies driving it are neutralized, balanced. This does not mean forgotten, for the soul always seeks to use all experiences in its journey towards perfection, and reunion with its Creator."*

In other words, my teacher was saying that I would forever carry the memory of this karma, through life after life, but that it would no longer be a negative force. Transformed by acceptance, and finally, forgiveness, the worst mistakes can always be turned toward the good; the soul gains strength through its own learning, eventually using such experiences so that we may aid each other, even as we have harmed each other in the past. It reminds me of a lesson from the Catholic teachings of my childhood. Perhaps we are our brothers' keepers, after all.

Civil War Incarnation

After the experience with my Atlantean past-life karma, I rarely ventured into that subject willingly. However, similar events were to become part of my lessons, regardless of my desire to explore further in this direction.

It was spring when I began to have a series of spontaneous visions. The first began when I was working in our office-studio one afternoon. The window near my desk looks out into our back yard. Occasionally I will stop and look out the window for minutes at a time, taking a mental break and appreciating the tranquility of the trees and grass rustling in the breeze.

This particular day, while working at my word processor, I heard a distant voice. It was definitely a young person, perhaps ten or twelve years old. It wasn't uncommon for me to hear this, since there are children who live on our street. I paid no attention at first, but the voice seemed to get progressively louder, and it seemed to be coming from our back yard, rather than from the direction of the street. I turned and looked out the window. There was no one there, and the voice stopped instantly. The rest of that day was pretty normal.

A week later I was at my word processor again, and once more I heard the voice. Looking out the window, I saw a boy standing in our yard. He was perhaps fourteen or fifteen, and dressed in a gray jacket and gray trousers. I turned away towards the computer screen for just a second, and when I looked back he was gone.

I continued working. After perhaps fifteen minutes, I again heard voices. I couldn't make out what they were saying, but I turned, and once more caught a glimpse of the young man out the window. This time he had a cap on. His attire looked like a uniform, perhaps something from the Civil War. I got up from my computer and went to the back door, wanting to see who this person was. When I got outside, there was no one there. I searched around the house, walked up and down the road, and finally returned to the studio.

A week later, I heard voices again. I looked up, and this time there was a girl, with the same teen-age boy. She wore a frilled dress with a full, wide skirt, and her hair was braided and pulled up in an old-fashioned way. She appeared to be twelve or thirteen. They could see me through the window, apparently, and they were both looking at me. The girl pointed right at me. I jumped up, went to the door of the studio and opened it, only to find no one outside. I went up our road to the dead end, and down to the corner, but there was no one around.

I thought no more about it, until about a week later, when they again appeared. This time I decided that I wasn't going to move. I would simply freeze. As I did so, I thought, "Who are you?"

Immediately the girl responded, "He has heard us ... he's heard us!"

"Yes, he has," the boy replied.

Another girl appeared, and then another, both dressed in the same full skirts, one wearing an apron with a red cross on it. They seemed to appear from out of nowhere. First there was nothing but grass, and the next second there was a person standing there, apparently solid and real. Another boy in his teens appeared then, wearing a blue uniform and cap. Clearly, these were people from some other time and place.

Over the next fifteen minutes about twelve of them appeared, all standing in a circle together, holding hands. I sat and watched, motionless. I thought, "What were those voices I heard?"

The boy spoke clearly. "It was the prayer we were doing, hoping you would hear us."

"What do you want?" I asked.

"There are so many of us here, and we need you to come down to the wilderness," he said.

With that, the vision dissolved. I sat back and wondered what this was all about, but I had no clues to work with. For the next several weeks I continued to work in my office, uninterrupted by further incidents.

As spring turned to summer, I began to dream at night of Civil War battles. These were vivid dreams, with none of the inconsistencies usually involved in dreaming. They seemed very real. One particular scene kept repeating — I saw a young man charging up a hill, only to have a cannon-shell explode in front of him. That vision repeated itself dozens of times in my dreams, and I sensed that perhaps the young man was me, from another time period.

These dreams of battles always gave way to scenes of a cemetery. In one of the dreams, the voice of my Source came to me. It said, *"Your presence is required in the wilderness. Visit the cemeteries."*

"What cemeteries?" I replied, in the dream.

My Source said, *"Go to the one where both North and South are buried."* And the dream ended.

Weeks went by, and the image of my Civil War visitors remained deeply embedded in my consciousness. I spoke with Cynthia about it, and we agreed that we should drive down South, to see what would happen. We had no plan, we simply knew that we ought to go.

Conducting no research in advance, we simply got into the car and drove. In Virginia, we suddenly found ourselves getting off the highway at a particular exit. We drove on for awhile, and then Cynthia said she thought we'd passed a sign on the road that might be important. "Let's go back and look at it," she suggested. Whizzing by on the road it had appeared to be nothing — a small brown and white sign of the type used to denote state parks and facilities — but we went back anyway. We turned in, and found ourselves at the historic site of the "Battle of the Wilderness."

We spent several hours there, went through the tour, and finally left. Both of us felt very somber and reflective, mulling over what had happened there. In one day, thousands of young people had given their lives in a great battle. We had both read about such things in school, and even seen them in movies, but it had never made as much of an impression as being at the spot where it actually happened.

As we drove away from the site, following our intuition, we soon found ourselves at another Civil War site, the Fredericksburg National Cemetery. It was getting late in the afternoon, but the gates were still open. As I looked up the hill, I could see a cemetery. It was the same cemetery from my dreams.

The man at the desk in the little tour building asked, "Would you like to go in? The guided tours are over, but you can still walk around on your own."

"Who is buried here?" I inquired.

"Soldiers from both the North and the South," he said, "after a very bloody battle."

It was almost closing time, but we drove up, parked, and walked through the nearest gate into the cemetery. Cynthia gravitated towards the far end of the cemetery, but I found myself moving directly to a large marker, close to where we'd entered the graveyard. I knew that I needed to be there. I sat down on a stone bench next to the marker, and began to meditate, praying for guidance, so that I might understand why I had experienced my visions about this place, and what I needed to do now that I had come here.

I sensed a presence, and looked up from my meditation, only to find the first youngster — the boy — who I had seen back in New Hampshire. He said, "Thank you for coming, sir. Private Jemison, sir." He gave a small, formal salute as he announced his name, and stood quite still. At ease, but with the alert air of a soldier about him.

I could see other forms starting to solidify, grouped around Private Jemison.

He said, "We've called for you, and we are glad you came."

All of a sudden, I realized that there were figures everywhere, all over this area of the cemetery. I could see soldiers in Northern uniforms, and soldiers from the South, as well. They were sitting in groups. There were also young women, girls really, aged twelve, sixteen, and seventeen. They all seemed to be mixed together, male and female, North and South. Taking sides did not seem to matter to them at all, as if the war had never happened.

The young man named Jemison said, "From our perspective, we are seeing great changes in the borderlands — we see that the Earth is about to change. We must remain here until we can go on to other levels, and we are concerned because we believe that in a few years the Earth will have erupted, and these battlegrounds of which we are a part will be lost, buried for thousands of years."

"How can I help?" I asked.

He said, "Please share with us what you have seen, and explain the other levels that exist beyond the physical level. Explain to us the level that we are at, so that we may understand what we are to do."

I sat in the cemetery for the next hour, doing my best to respond to the young man's plea. I explained the levels of consciousness as I understood them: our transitions through death, our movement through the alternate vibrational levels that make up the cosmos, and how we can use rebirth as a tool to facilitate this movement, this path that we are meant to follow. I explained how human souls learn by moving through the levels, always seeking perfection, always seeking a higher spiritual level, and how sometimes we choose to return to Earth for further lessons. I explained that in order to move on to the higher vibrational levels, there must be a peace within the soul, and an awareness of the forces which guide us, and of which we are all a part.

As I spoke, I noticed that some of the forms were waving to me, as if to say good-bye. Slowly, they dissolved. Within the next ten or fifteen minutes, I looked up again to find that many more had disappeared as well.

Private Jemison, standing nearest to me, said, "More need to know about these changes. There are many of us — several hundred thousand — who are caught. We were so young at death. We knew so little. Our lives were gone before we had time to prepare for this transition, and we were caught off-guard. Many at this level are in shock, continuing to replay the battles that took their lives, and those of brothers, friends and lovers. This war forced us to choose sides, and did not leave us time to make choices for ourselves. Your words have helped many here today. Perhaps others will come to help at other gravesites."

He stood back then, came to attention, and gave me a sharp salute. Then, he slowly dissolved into nothing. One by one, the remaining figures around me faded. I realized that nightfall had come, and now it was almost dusk.

I joined Cynthia, who had been praying and meditating in another portion of the cemetery. As we talked with each other, we found that our experiences in the cemetery were amazingly parallel. In the darkened grounds, we made our way out to the gate, which was still open, and found our way back to where we had parked our car. Somehow, despite the strangeness of what had just occurred, Cynthia and I both felt remarkably at peace.

Later on, we read some historical accounts of the Battle of the Wilderness. Waged in Fredericksburg, Virginia, from the fifth of May to the seventh in the year 1864, it was a part of General Ulysses S. Grant's overland campaign. Tactically, it was considered a draw. The Union forces in this battle numbered just short of one hundred and two thousand, with estimated casualties of over eighteen thousand. Confederate forces numbered only sixty-one thousand, and their casualties were estimated at eleven thousand four hundred persons. Those who died in the battle are buried at the Fredericksburg National Cemetery and the Fredericksburg Confederate Cemetery.

Upon returning home, we realized that we still had many questions regarding our Civil War experience which had been left unaddressed. I decided to try to enter my trance state, so that I might gain some intuitive insights which might help answer these questions.

Cynthia and I sat down together, and I began the process I'd developed by then. It took about seven to ten minutes to achieve the open link between the sub-conscious and higher-consciousness that we were looking for. I waited for the familiar spiraling of lights to occur in my mind, behind my closed eyes, a signal that I had reached a connection point. Cynthia had prepared a list of questions in advance for this exercise, and had not shown the list to me, to help ensure that my personal knowledge would not enter into the outcome. In this session, I was both lucid and accessing intuitive information at the same time. It was not a trance dialogue with my Source, so much as a trance state of completely opened mind, wherein the greater knowledge of my higher consciousness was available and fully accessible. This session proceeded as follows:

CK: What kind of help did the Civil War children need from you?

GMS: Where you have massive loss of lives in a few hours, that creates an amazing release of souls. Often there are not enough angels — guides — to help.

These young people needed to have some hope that there is a continuation. It was almost as if they were caught in a rerun of their last battle. I was able to add to their awareness that, just as in the physical world, we go through changes in the borderland. That understanding was like opening a door — it allowed the angels and spirits to come in. I believe that the few who were aware became the spokespeople for the many who were not aware.

There are other battlegrounds — not only of the Civil War era — where we have the same situation. Thousands, in some cases tens or hundreds of thousands of people, are caught between levels of worlds, and other people will be called to be of service.

CK: That was one of my questions. There are other places where wars have occurred and where there has been massive loss of life. Are there similar conditions in those places when there are great numbers of lost souls trapped?

GMS: The greater losses are not in recent time. Though there is a period where the loss was very high in the twentieth century, the greater losses are over ten thousand years old. Let me speak on both of these levels.

During World War II, there were atomic attacks on the huge

civilian populations of Hiroshima and Nagasaki. Suddenly, we had tens of thousands of people instantly pushed into the borderland without warning. At the same time, something new occurred. The bomb altered the matrix, or the energy pattern, between the physical Earth and the borderland. It established a hybrid between the borderland and the physical Earth which wasn't there before. It was a brand new level of consciousness that had no structure, no spiritual guides. So those who were in that space had to create links to others at the higher levels of consciousness. This is still being worked out. It is not anywhere near complete.

If we look back over ten thousand years we find that there were major geophysical cataclysms, massive sinking of land and loss of life in twenty-four hours or less. We are talking of losses of a hundred million people or more, just in Atlantis. Most of them are still trapped. The reason is that the survivors of the cataclysm were focused on survival. So all of that mental thought was going into pure survival.

Even today there are literally millions of them entrapped. I have had experiences with them by visiting ancient sites and allowing visions to unfold. From their perspective, ten thousand years has not passed. They are reliving an event, and that is where their consciousness is.

Whether we are talking about the Civil War, World War II or the sinking of Atlantis, a percentage are trapped.

CK: In your previous vision, which we have referred to as "Crisis in the Borderland," you talked about souls in the borderland being helped by those from higher spiritual levels. But in this case you seem to be helping them from what would appear to be a lower level. Is this unusual?

GMS: Right now I see pretty much an equal balance between those in the spirit world that are assisting and those in the physical world. I see almost an equal number who are working at a very focused level. Those who have been on the Earth many times through the reincarnation cycle, moving higher and higher in vibrations, are closer to the creative forces. In other words, they have learned patience, compassion, suffering, all of the things that the Earth can teach. The next natural process is to serve others. We have different names for them, such as guides or angels. We have many words. Each culture has a different viewpoint of this, but the commonality is that there are spiritual beings that aid and assist.

Now, in conjunction with that, service often comes from one in physical form. Especially today, when we are not taking as much time as we should to reflect and to enter into a state of meditation or prayer, it's often difficult for these guides to get through.

So, many of the teachers who have worked through the levels of consciousness have come back to the Earth as teachers. Right now on the physical Earth we have the largest concentration of teachers and speakers that we have ever had. They express themselves through many different disciplines; it's not just through religion or spiritual movements, it's through television, children's books, even the Internet. We'll find these everywhere.

CK: Gordon, what was happening to the soldiers as they dissolved towards the end of your experience in the cemetery?

GMS: I perceived that they were leaving this reality and moving toward the upper spirit realm. There were teachers who were going to meet them at the other end of that thread. They understood, by our dialogue, how it would occur, what it would be like when they were met, and how they would move on.

CK: It would appear, then, that you were of some help to them. Do you feel that other people can do similar things?

GMS: I believe that there are many people doing these things today. Most do it quietly through their own thought processes. Just praying for a friend who has passed over is enough to make a difference. You have added a bit of your own essence; you are able to share a spark of your strength. So prayers, thoughts, your compassion, your love, just your awareness, aid these people.

THE FRUITLESSNESS OF WAR

At this point I was ready to disconnect from the altered consciousness state. Usually I see the spiraling lights fade, and slowly I come back into a conscious state. This time, however, the colors became even more vivid, and the spiraling moved faster until I found myself in another place, watching a Civil War battle. It was similar to my Atlantean voyage, because it was a sudden, very real vision, where I was clearly meant to be an observer. I could hear the voices calling out to each other, both Confederates and Union forces, as if I were at a juncture point in the battlegrounds. Cannons sounded out with an intensity of sound quite unfamiliar to me. Without intending to, my visual focus came to rest on one hill, which had a line of trees along the ridge, and a split-rail fence in front of the trees. The fence appeared to run for miles without break, finally disappearing into the distance. I could see soldiers in Union uniforms loading and firing the cannons that were in place behind the fence. As I looked to my left, hundreds, perhaps thousands, of Confederate soldiers came running towards the hill. By the hundreds they were falling, as shots from the cannons found their intended victims.

My vision then focused on a young Confederate soldier, his rifle and bayonet raised, approaching the railed fence. A loud roar sounded and a huge puff of smoke bellowed from the cannon directly in front of him. The young man had been no more than ten or fifteen feet from the cannon, and I watched in terror as his body was thrown back at least that far again, as if he were a leaf suddenly swept up in a gust of wind. I went to hover above him. He was quite motionless, laying face up. The left side of his face had been blown away, and the flesh from his cheekbone to just below his eye was completely gone. I gasped, not only in horror at the sight of him, but because of a sudden realization. I knew this boy, I thought. But how was this possible?

My inner voice called to me. It said, *"You are One. This is the battle of Antietam, at your passing. It was another life in which you chose to experience the role of warrior. It was in this life that you came close to realizing — at the soul level — the fruitlessness of war. To ensure that you would remember, you retain the interest in battles, which stems from this series of warrior lives. In this life you will be reminded, until your next passage, every time you look into the mirror."*

My Source was referring to my birthmark. From just below my left eye and down to my cheekbone I have a red, circular discoloration. As a youth, my parents had tried to have it removed, but the therapy had only succeeded in fading its color from raspberry red to light brown. To this day the mark remains, as my Source said, to remind me of the perils of war.

MARCONI

In the first chapter of this book, I mentioned the many sick days I spent at home during my childhood, and how I found some enjoyment in teaching myself Morse code, and in tinkering with electronics and my crystal radio set. I said that I *taught* myself Morse code, but perhaps it would have been more accurate to say that I *knew* Morse code, the first time I ever saw it. I recall flipping through a *Popular Electronics* magazine one day, and coming upon a Morse code chart in an article I was reading. Excited, I built a crystal radio the very next day, like so many other young boys did at that age. However, once I hooked it up and tuned in to a Morse code station, I found I could read the code! Somehow, I not only knew Morse code characters, I immediately understood and was able to read the encoded messages.

From that time forward, I was obsessed with wire antennas, building all types of large receiving apparatus, made from wire. I could not explain it, but the technology of radio seemed to be second nature to me, almost as if I had come into this world already programmed with the knowledge. I'm sure my neighbors often wondered what the strange sickly boy was doing next door, with all his towers and antennas.

Later in life, my interest in radiotelegraphy continued. As an adult, I found myself drawn to Cape Cod, where there is an old wireless site built by Guglielmo Marconi, the Italian engineer who won the Nobel Prize in 1909, along with Karl Ferdinand Braun, for their invention of wireless communications. I must have visited that site dozens of times over the years, though there is not much there to see, except old pictures of where the antennas and radio-shack were once located. Parts of the base are still present, but most of it has been lost to the sea as the coastline has changed over the years.

In 1996, Cynthia and I needed to take a break from our hectic schedule, and planned a brief trip to Nova Scotia and Cape Breton Island. Nova Scotia was my father's original home, and Halifax is only a few miles from his old homestead. Halifax is a marvelous city, and we spent a few days there, before moving on to Cape Breton and the Cabot Trail. The scenery in this region is breathtaking, and many tourists pass through Cape Breton, on their way to admire the views. Once night comes, however, the town closes up until the next day, when tourists once again descend on the little community. Cynthia and I decided to stay for the weekend. Walking around after dinner, we came upon a small bookstore, and with little to do at night, we thought we'd curl up with a couple of good books. After scanning the shelves for twenty minutes, I still felt uninspired, and was ready to leave without anything to read for the evening. As I rounded the end of an aisle, I noticed one book which seemed ready to fall off the shelf. I went to push it back into its slot, and caught the title out of the corner of my eye, *Marconi and His Life in Cape Breton*. A coincidence? I scanned a few pages, and electrical sensations ran up and down my spine. I now know this occurs whenever I come across something to which I should be paying attention. It's my intuition letting me know physically what I already know subconsciously, although I probably haven't been paying attention. I purchased the book, and we left.

Back in our room, I read non-stop about the life of Marconi.

Not only was I reading and seeing some of the photos in the book, I was also seeing scenes, in movie-like fashion, appearing before my eyes. Pictures of Marconi, his boat, his mother and father. None of these pictures were in the book, nor had I seen them before in other places. I couldn't get over the parallels in our lives, strange little coincidences that affected me at a deep emotional level. Marconi's mother was a Jameson, of the "Jameson's Irish Whiskey" fame. While I am not a drinker, I will occasionally have a beer, or glass of wine with a meal. But whenever I'm offered a cocktail, I've always said, "Coffee with Jameson's, please." Since I was in my early twenties, this has been my drink of choice. "Jameson" is also hauntingly similar to "Jemison," the name of my young Civil War visitor. It does seem a strange coincidence, though I'm still not sure if it is a significant of one.

I also saw parallels in our families. The Irish side of my father's family originally came from the same region as the Jameson family. My mother's family, Italian, came from the same province as did Marconi's father. Does this experience of familiarity mean that I was Guglielmo Marconi in a past-life? Perhaps not. Seeing visions of information about people and places to which I've never been exposed does not necessarily mean that I took part in the original experience. But as I read the story of Marconi's life, written by his surviving daughter, I could see parallel after parallel between our lives. Time-wise, the possibility that I was once this man certainly exists. Marconi died in 1937. I was born in 1942. There are many times that I have thought of contacting his daughter, to share what I know about her father. But something keeps telling me that it is not yet the right time to do so.

*　*　*　*　*

Many people I speak to about the subjects of karma and reincarnation do not believe in them, even as they seem to find it fascinating to discuss the possibility of such cycles. A concept of life-after-death, in any form, is difficult for us to understand. Our ideas about it are always inextricably tied to our beliefs about ourselves, and to the choices we have made in this life that we are at least relatively certain does indeed exist.

We may never know for certain who we were and what we did in past-lives, or even if reincarnation is a true part of the way the universe works. The issue for me is not so much whether or not reincarnation exists; my question is, rather, this: What benefit or learning might come to those of us who allow ourselves to believe in the *possibility* of cyclical lives on Earth?

By opening my consciousness to dream voyages through time and space, and by exploring these realms from the viewpoint of one who was a *part of* that time and place — not just a visitor bearing witness — I am increasing my own sense of interconnectedness with humanity, the past and future of mankind, the Earth, and indeed, all of the cosmos. And if my past predictions about uncovering new evidence of ancient civilizations come true in this decade, then perhaps the dream voyages I've taken to my own past-lives may help to validate the reality of reincarnation, at least for me. Later on in this book, I will discuss a different type of past-life dream voyage — simultaneous reality — a kind of dream excursion during which I am able to meet with one of my past-life selves, and have a series of conversations with that individual. These interviews have greatly helped me to better understand my experiences living in the present world.

CHAPTER TEN

Simultaneous Realities

BERYL OF IRELAND

Throughout the eighties, I regularly experienced past-life dream visions. I also received an enormous amount of information regarding my past-life situations through my Source. After several years, all of this became somewhat overwhelming; nevertheless, the insights and clarity I was able to gain by opening to these opportunities seemed to justify the hardships, and for a long time I maintained a positive attitude, although much of what I saw was painful to address. Just about the time I was feeling as if I never wanted to experience or know about another past life, however, I encountered a new and rather pleasant type of past-life experience, unlike any I'd had before.

One day my step-daughter Shari came to me for a private

reading. She requested that the session not be recorded. It was obviously very personal to her. Under normal circumstances, my conscious mind would have been present, listening to all that my Source would share. Something different happened this time, though. Without a taped recording of the session, as it turned out, Shari had a very personal and private reading indeed.

I entered into my usual meditative state, waiting for the slow spiral descent into a shower of light, from which my present self would drift away, allowing the consciousness of my Source to enter. This time, I experienced the spiraling light only to come back into myself immediately. Or so I thought. Shari had to explain what actually happened. Apparently, after my coughing fit subsided (normally a signal that the transition to my Source was complete) a new entity introduced himself. He had an Irish Gaelic accent, and identified himself as Beryl (pronounced beh-RILL, with the accent on the second syllable). He was a consciousness from the fifteenth century that, we found out later, was not a spirit. Rather, he was a portion of me — one of my past lives — that had travelled through time, or perhaps transcended it, to enter into my present-day consciousness and make contact. Beryl said that he was communicating directly from *his* unconscious mind. His own consciousness — the waking life of Beryl in fifteenth century Ireland — was not aware of these communications. If anything was remembered at all, they would only be perceived as dreams.

Beryl was an entertaining, comical personality. Later, we conducted many more sessions which we were able to record, always with Shari or another young person present. We asked why Beryl had chosen that particular session to first make contact. He said that he had come to assist my present personality, which needed to become "lighter." He felt called to remind me of my more humorous side, to help me not take everything so literally and seriously, but rather to enjoy my days, and to see the fun parts of life. He never directly answered why he had chosen Shari's private session to appear. But in the time since we last encountered Beryl, we have hypothesized that he was drawn to her youth, and perhaps by her own ability to see the humor in things, continually applying it to life's most difficult situations.

Beryl's visit was short, lasting only three months from the first session to the last. Early on, he explained that the "portal" — the mode by which he was able to transcend his own time period and come directly to me — operated cyclically, and that his visits would be limited by this. He said he hoped he would be able to accomplish what he had set out to do, before the cycle passed. The gist of his personal message to me was quite simple, if only I could catch on. *"Lighten up!"* he said. For the others we invited to question Beryl, he willingly answered any and all inquiries, about all manner of topics.

Below is a compilation of excerpts from the many transcriptions we accumulated during Beryl's visit, touching on several key issues that I sense have universal application. For myself, I only hope I learned from his wisdom as well as he would have liked. Here, I trust ye'll agree he has a bit of the Irish wit about him!

MH: This is M.H., and I would like to ask about the relative influences of the moon and stars, as far as human beings are concerned. In the effort to send out vibrations, or to absorb the energies that are in the cosmos around us, how can the influence of these bodies enable us to do things in a stronger way, if I may put it that way? Is the influence as great as astrologers would have us believe, and if so, does the moon itself have the greatest immediate effect on the human body, mind, or spirit?
Beryl: *We feel you'd be a very good reporter.*
MH: Thank you, thank you!
Beryl: *You've developed a way of getting about four or five questions into one!*
MH: Well, I value your answers greatly, so ...
Beryl: (interrupting) *Well, we are going to do the same thing. We are going to wrap them into one for you.*

MH: I'll do my best to unravel it later!

Beryl: *We wish to tell you first that the power of the spheres is very real. It is more than you would ever imagine, but we also wish to tell you that no matter what the astrological or numerological configuration, no matter what the cards say, none of these things can override that of the free will of the soul energies.*

The Creator gave you the power to choose. What you have in the spheres and in the environment which you live in, and in the locations that you dwell in, is that it sets up the conditions for learning. You chose your parents, you chose the location to develop your lessons, and we wish to tell you that it is not so much that the moon, for example, was over here (indicating one direction) *at your birth, when right now we see that it is over here* (indicating the new location). *It is only when these things are beaming on you that matters. We wish to tell you that astrology has lost its true understanding. This, since the time of the Persians. They truly did have the understanding — they had the understanding of where you must focus. Your knowledge now is geocentric. The heliocentric and the geocentric — you know about these things? We do not want to confuse the words here. One is viewed from the sun; one is viewed from Earth. That is the difference between the two. But we want to tell you that the reason the heavens affect you is not because they are here and here* (gestures) *now. It is because you were once there! That is the reason astrology truly works — because you spend time on the Moon, you spend time on the sun, you spend time on Mars, and on Venus, and so forth, and then on Earth. These are all lessons in the many cycles of life you lead — reincarnation. You spend time in each of these spheres, because they are part of your lessons. The powers of the spheres touch each other at all times, through all lifetimes, all the journeys of spirit. An example is that, if you have spent much time there, when the Venus configuration comes about in the heavens of this lifetime, it will have a greater effect on you. So, it has to do with the reincarnation process, and it does affect you tremendously.*

As we said before, we have had others that have come to us and who have said, "Oh, we've got this astrology chart, and it tells us that we're going to have a bad life, that we've got this very heavy karma." *We wish to tell you that it is a lot of chance, where the astral bodies are concerned. Truth comes from where you are in your heart, and is learned about when you make the heart connection to the Oneness. This truly is what the magic that we spoke of last time is about, because it supersedes all chance. Where you live on the Earth, and everything that connects with it, are simply your tools, they are part of the lessons. Because whether you are in Boston or in Antwerp, it makes no difference. You always have an opportunity to share. And we feel that you are moving more and more in the direction of sharing. So we may have got a bit off your question here, but we think we've lumped it all into one, and we are going to move on.*

Sometimes Beryl gave very practical advice:

Questioner: On the subject of planting. Some say that seeds should be planted on the rising rather than the waning moon. Is there any sense to this? Is it an old wives' tale, or what?
Beryl: *We wish you to know that the farmers, particularly the older ones, truly know this and have abundant crops. But the rule you want to use is right after the new moon. Anywhere between the third and ninth day. These would be the best times to plant. Where this would seem a bit strange, it is better to do this late in the day rather than in the sunlight of the day. You'll find this gives them a bit of time to work at night.*

As it pertains to the abundance of this crop, also, you'll find that the seeds themselves can be super-charged, so to speak, before you put them in the ground. And what you want to do with this is to take the seeds themselves and expose them the month before to the rays of the full moon directly. This only needs to be done for perhaps an hour or so. So you can kind of spread them out on a canvas or forms of burlap. These would be good. And you will find when you wrap them back up and plant them in the times we told you, you will have a fertile and very dynamic crop.

At other times, Beryl provided rather surprising insights into the physical problems of the questioner:

Questioner: For four years I've been trying to solve a weakness in my neck and back. Are my efforts going to work?

Beryl: *We don't think so. Because you still have the doubt in you. We wish you to know where it is coming from. Then you can deal with it. You are familiar with the meridians of the body? Okay. We wish you to take your right hand now. Reach up on your neck, across your body. Find the artery. We're going to point to it right here* (identifies location of the artery in the neck). *Apply a bit of pressure there. Aye! Hold it here. A little bit harder, please. Okay. You've got it now. The tension you've been feeling there — that is going through your body — where that's coming from is karma. It is where you took the fatal blow when you passed over from your last incarnation. What you need to do is to apply a bit of pressure there. You do this about five times a day, and you'll find after about, oh, perhaps two to four weeks, you will get rid of the pain. You will also take care of that karma you do not need. Get rid of it, and get on to the good stuff!*

Nor did Beryl shrink from the more esoteric questions we posed:

Questioner: Is it possible for the soul to have several lives in the same time frame?

Beryl: *Conditions did exist. We will give you an example. It could be done with those at the causal level, or above. It cannot be done by those who have not reached that level of evolution in the soul's life. That of the Jesus, when he was upon the planet, we wish you to know that was a duality soul. That of Mary and of himself was of the same soul. Or a division, and a separation of the soul. All souls at one time were without sex. It was only at some time in evolution on the planet that they divided the sexes. As such the soul can divide itself into two, and dwell in two realms of consciousness. But it takes an evolved soul.*

Sometimes questioners wanted to know about how they had spent their most recent incarnations. Beryl would oblige:

Questioner: Can you tell me about my most recent past life?

Beryl: *Aye! But it was not the most important one. That one would take much detail to explain, and it was done many thousands of years ago. But we are going to tell you of one almost as powerful. And it was a recent one.*

One of your last contacts with the Earth was in the Victorian era. So you are drawn this time to that very architecture, aren't you? You will find the clothing, too, is very familiar to you. You almost have a fantasy, you kind o' drift into it, eh?

We wish you to know about the area that you were a part of. It was not in the North, but in the South, so you have an affinity for that part of the world, as well. There you were what you'd call a school-marm. You were very much a teacher, a gifted teacher, but you were a bit of a rebel.

You were looked upon by the community as a bit of a strange one, because you would take the children out of the schoolhouse and bring them out into the fields. You would sit in the fields, full of daisies in spring and summer. So in this life you like the daisies, and you like the clover and the grass. You knew back then that this was more important to them than much of what they would learn in the schoolhouse. You believed in teaching through environment, and you are going to do this again, we wish you to know. You are going to be involved in a community and you are going to have an opportunity — like others — to be a part of this. Your work will involve music, or the manipulation of sounds. You don't have to do anything. It will just come by your way. It is a ways off yet, but it will come to you.

Your name at that time was Lu Ellen. You were a very attractive lass, and there were many suitors. Again, you were a bit of a rebel, for you would go out after dark without an escort. That was considered a negative. You would do it to get the goat of many of the people in the town. You have a bit of that in this life, don't ye now? Aye! It's healthy for you, because you speak your mind. It is good that you do not hold it in. If you do, it brings about a bit of disease with you.

So, in that life you learned much. You gained an appreciation of children. You came to appreciate the power of environment in telling a story. This is why when you go to do your work with sound, it is going to be great. Because you are going to add things in the back-

ground, such as breeze, and things of this nature. You have a real gift for this. We wish you to know that, so you can apply that in this life.

You did well in that life. You gained. Although your mother — once again the same mother you have today — she had some difficulty with you. She still does a bit, doesn't she? Aye! She's a good lass, we wish you to know that.

Other questioners took the opportunity to seek advice on how to improve aspects of their spiritual life, such as meditation:

Questioner: Could you give some advice, or some suggestions, on quieting the mind? I find it very difficult.
Beryl: *We were hoping you could give us a bit of advice on that one! But seriously, we feel here that what happens is that when you become lighter in spirit, you have more vitality, so the thought process becomes quicker. We talked to you before about the meditation, and how up through the seventies of your century it was beneficial for many. And we still say that it may be for many. But we are seeing now that there are perhaps different ways for this to be applied. We feel that the best way to quiet the mind is by not trying to do so.*

We feel that for you, in particular — you resonate so well to colors — that we feel you need to find your color. Each person has his or her own color-tone. You have a tone that you resonate with. There is a primary tone, and there are other tones or harmonics in support of these tones. Where we last come from in the life cycles will determine the predominant tone. This is why sometimes, if you are out at night, when it is quiet, you will actually hear a tone in your head. In particular, during the harvest moon you will find this. What you are doing is you're listening to your primary tone.

This tone, which can be audible on the interior, if we listen closely, also resonates with color. You must find the color, and this is very simple to do. You simply quiet yourself down some day, and get some color swatches and close your eyes. Do not look at them, 'cause the eyes will deceive you. Simply allow your fingers to move across the colors. Mix them up, so you cannot tell, because the body and the brain are very clever — they try to trick you many times. When you feel the color that is right, then open the eyes and that will be your color. Trust that it will be. Then, by simply taking this color and glancing at it, you will find that it brings to your mind a quiet, and you will find this even as you are busy and doing things. It is not necessary to quiet the mind so that you see nothing, and hear nothing. It is how you interact with the thoughts in mind that truly counts.

The use of color also came up in response to a seemingly unrelated question:

Questioner: You mentioned earlier the negative influence of drugs and alcohol on children. What is the most effective means of dealing with — working with — addicted young people?

Beryl: *We feel that there are many variables. You can work from many levels. You can very much work from the level of getting involved in the child's life, taking part in the discovery process of finding what went wrong, and so forth and so on. We also wish to tell you there are much easier ways to do this than is thought. We wish to tell you that when an irritant has reached the point of the physical — where it is either bothering the body, or where there is some sign of psychological change within the body — that it has already worked through the self at two other levels.*

Do you remember that we talked about how things begin in spirit form, move then to the mind form, and finally, to the physical? We suggest herein that the easiest way to help is to completely alter the environment of the child. Because to do it the other way, there are not enough people out there. Truly the people who need the help do not get it. It is only when a crisis occurs that the problem is recognized, and action is taken. People in your present do not go to an attorney to say, "Hi, how are you today? I wish to talk to you about, you know, things in general." You do not seek that advisor unless you have been sued, or if you have had an accident, or some other matter. How many times do you go to a counselor to say, "It's a nice day, and I thought I would stop by to let you know that I am feeling quite well this afternoon. Here is fifty dollars for your time. Thank you!" Your culture does not use advisors, except in crisis. There is no such entity. So when things seem okay for you, you do not question whether or not this is the true state of things. You hope that it is true. Then the problem comes, and it must be worked with from that point on.

So, we suggest that one of the ways of dealing with this is by changing the environment. By changing the environment, we mean the direction they are moving in, either in the home or at the school, the classroom or its surroundings. You can do some very subtle things. The easiest thing to do is to add music and add color. It takes a bit longer to see results, but it works, and it will work continuously. When you find someone struggling with drugs, you move them into the colors of blue. In particular, put near them the blues on the higher levels — toward the ultraviolets, that side of the spectrum. If you see them in an office, and your office is that color, you will find that this changes the results as well.

You will also find that there is disruption in much of the music today. Truly, it is as some have said: the harshest vibrations of the music called rock are harmful. Not all music of this name is hurtful, but much of it is. The effects can be seen. It disrupts the resonance, and those who are most susceptible — those especially who are already struggling with addiction — go over the edge. Other music — all that comes through the higher source of creation — can be of benefit in these cases. So if you do these two things, adding colors of ultraviolet and music of beauty and substance — even if just barely audible — to the environment, and if you can then bring those troubled ones into your sphere, then you have set in motion a great healing. It will unfold automatically from there.

EC-KAR OF ATLANTIS

After Beryl came and went, it seemed to open the door — the portal, as he had called it — for other past-life personalities to enter my present consciousness in the same manner. This is the specific phenomenon I refer to as "simultaneous reality," because my past-life selves are actually existing in their own time, living their own life, at the same time that they are communicating with me now, even though that time is hundreds, perhaps thousands of years in the past or future. While the conscious mind sleeps, the unconscious mind travels through time and space, gathering much more knowledge than the waking self ever realizes. By opening myself to this unconscious level through the trance state, I can meet these other parts of myself, while they are engaging in their own dream voyages. As Albert Einstein theorized, time is not linear at all, but elastic. My simultaneous reality experiences prove to me that this is true, beyond a shadow of a doubt.

One interesting past-life entity that visited me in this manner was a man named Ec-Kar. He referred to himself as a fifth-level initiate, dwelling in the city of Poseidia, Atlantis. The time, he told me, was some sixteen thousand fifty-two years before the present in which I now dwell.

When I lived as Ec-Kar, I was a teacher in Poseidia's great Hall of Wisdom, which was a part of the city's university. Ec-Kar taught in the field of "interplanetary energies." There is no corresponding discipline today, but it could be described as a combination of what we would now call philosophy, spirituality, astrophysics and biophysics. In Ec-Kar's time, the general understanding of all these subjects seems to have far surpassed what we know in the present. He explained that he was able to effectively bridge the time-span by accessing certain astro-energies that overlap our two time periods. In Ec-Kar's case, unlike Beryl, he was consciously aware of the communications between us, because his attempt to do so was purposeful. It was as if Ec-Kar and I were both entering trance states, moving into the realms of higher consciousness, and then meeting there to talk and fill each other in on what we'd been doing. I imagined it was sort of like two friends leaving their respective homes and meeting downtown at a coffee shop, only on the larger astral scale of time and space.

It was Ec-Kar's intention, he said, to assist me in my present work by sharing the technology, concepts and philosophies of his time, the evidence of which has largely been destroyed. His insights have helped me, my friends, and many others, by making us aware of a time period in history which has been almost completely lost to us — the civilization of Atlantis, which thrived for some two hundred twenty-thousand years, before great seismic upheavals sank the land, burying all that they had built at the bottom of the sea. In our sessions, many of which were attended by groups of people, Ec-Kar described life in his present, discussed the history of his society, and utilized his own intuitive abilities to project into his own future, theorizing on the time period up to the last days of Atlantis, some eleven thousand five hundred years ago. Later in this chapter, transcriptions of some of these sessions are included, allowing me to share the more complex details of Ec-Kar's stories.

The procedure for communication with Ec-Kar was similar to that for Beryl and others. Although his personality and vocal patterns were distinct — as was that of each entity — I am able also to see clear similarities between myself and the past-life personalities I communicate with. I assume that "they-I-we," being a part of the same whole-consciousness, have parallel patterns to start with, and that the others must use my current memory, brain, and voice in order to communicate verbally. Both Ec-Kar and Beryl made clear that they were not separate entities from my "self," but rather a past-version — or aspect — of who I now am.

While discussing past-lives and karma one time, Ec-Kar made a surprising statement. He explained that there were also future realities which existed simultaneously with my present, and that I would undoubtedly make contact with one of these personalities very soon.

Multiple lives, and the lessons they teach, do not really happen sequentially, Ec-Kar said, though our present view makes them difficult to think about otherwise. Lives are not built upon lives, taking lessons learned in the past and applying them to the future. Rather, it is circular, he said. Each of our lives meld with one another; they are parts of a whole essence

of being, which in turn, intersects with the collective consciousness at each time-place, or juncture. (The model is simple, really, he told me. But it takes more than three-dimensions
to show it, because it does not translate easily into our three-
dimensional viewpoint, and it is difficult to draw a metaphor.
The onion, pierced through with thousands of needles, which
was mentioned as an example in Chapter 3, is the closest we
seem to be able to get.) It is the *focus* of the present life that is
most important.

For example, sometimes our lessons involve communication
with other lives — other parts of self — and sometimes they
do not. Just as we sometimes need solitude to work out problems in daily living, while other times it is better to seek out
the company or advice of others. Our whole-consciousness
seeks times, places and lessons that interest it, that nurture the
whole being and help its overall growth. This may not always
appear to be so for a particular version of self, however. A perfect example of this, Ec-Kar reminded me, was my incarnation
as Bu-te-nam, the slave trader. Bu-te-nam committed the original destructive action. The act of inflicting suffering during
that lifetime created karma that would have to be overcome in
other lives. But this karma could just as easily have occurred
in the future, with the lessons to be worked on occurring at an
earlier time in history.

What Ec-Kar was trying to tell me was that although the
greater self is constantly moving from a less enlightened to a
more enlightened state, we do not necessarily move through
our lives — through history — in a linear manner, each time
progressing to a more enlightened state (or getting knocked
back a few pegs because we were "bad"). The whole-self
exists outside of time. Perhaps rather than judging ourselves
or other people, we really do need to just look inside ourselves, and try to figure out what *we* are here to do. No matter
what it is, we can be sure it is for a reason, and that ultimately,
that reason is good.

Ec-Kar continued to say that although we may choose not to
interact with our past-life entities, we can do so at any time.

We can even find out about a particular karmic situation, contact that entity, and influence them to modify their behavior, thus affecting the overall balance of karmic debt and repayment. It seems that the cosmos is very pliable, constantly moving, changing and becoming. "Reality" is simply an instant of focus. A moment later, it has become memory, and we have become something else, though we are always a part of the universal structure, the cosmos itself. Whether we choose to spend a given second of reality in the darkness, or in the light, we are still and always a part of the whole.

* * * * *

Listening to all of this completely destroyed my concepts of Saint Peter standing at the pearly gates, heaven, hell, and purgatory. Ec-Kar was saying that there is no judgement in the universe, other than that judgement which we inflict upon ourselves. We create our own karma, forgiving our own "sins" when we are ready to do so. My next question was the obvious one. How did the structure of the cosmos come into being in the first place?

In response, Ec-Kar wove an incredible story for me. In the beginning, he said, the infinity of space and time was uniform in consistency. Never a void, it was rather composed of the same substance that now exists — that has always existed — though in the beginning (of this cycle in the cosmos, as we know it) all matter and energy filled the expanse in equal portions, with no definition whatsoever, throughout all that was. He said that this uniform expanse, this great collectiveness, this Oneness, began to stir within itself, and as it did so, lost its uniformity and began to experience awareness. Islands and realms of collective consciousness were gradually formed, over more "time" than we can imagine, as this great expanse of matter and energy began to move towards a new form of being. The great collectiveness, the Oneness, is never-ending and always changing. Movement — change — is what the cosmos is.

Of all the realms of consciousness, Ec-Kar went on to say, Earth and its system are unique, containing multiple levels of reality, both physical and non-physical. It is ours. We are a part of it, and it is, in turn, all that we are made of, all that we have come from. And all of this — our conscious realm — is part of the greater Oneness of the cosmos.

Existing within this realm of consciousness are individual expressions of the Oneness. These are the soul groups of which each human life is a part. These are the original souls that were first created — created *by themselves*, out of their own movement, change and growth — from the substance of the Oneness.

As Ec-Kar explained it, the cosmos was indeed created, but not by an outside entity. The *stuff* of the cosmos has existed throughout all eternity. The universe as we perceive it is merely one step in an unending process of motion. Each spark of life, of consciousness, beauty, energy, or substance, has been created out of the motion itself, the coming together of the right "ingredients." And once consciousness is born of this motion, it continues to create — through thought, choice, action, and procreation — perpetuating that endless movement of the stuff of the cosmos.

The original souls that make up the conscious Earth realm exist at many levels simultaneously. The best way to describe them is that they are omnipresent, for although our own collective consciousness in this moment is but one layer of their being, they also embody the consciousness of the sentient Earth itself, and exist, at the very same time, separate from us, separate from our reality. Because of this omnipresence, these originals were able to "project" themselves onto the Earth as the first human consciousness, even though the Earth had already been created as an earlier expression of their same conscious realm. And all of this, remember, is yet still only one part of the great Oneness that encompasses everything, including that which exists at other levels entirely, never involving us at all.

I could sense how difficult it was for Ec-Kar to express these concepts in words, in a language that I could understand. I suspect that even this complex explanation is, in fact, an extreme oversimplification. To really understand these concepts, Ec-Kar hinted, one must be existing at — or at least traveling through — a higher level of reality than the one we currently live in. The mind must leave language behind, and move in the realm of images and intuitive knowing. This description he was giving, in answer to my question, was more of a pictorial expression, a very rough sketch, to help guide my conscious mind in the direction of understanding. Total comprehension at this level, I realized, was probably not possible. I tried to just let the pictures his words evoked sink into me.

His story continued. The original souls — millions in number — projected themselves onto Earth as part of what we might refer to as "the divine experiment." Once here, they mixed with, and began to modify, the nature of those life-forms which had already begun to multiply on the Earth. This all occurred some fifteen to eighteen million years ago. At this point, biological life had already emerged and progressed in its development upon the Earth's surface for several billion years. The projected entities reproduced on Earth, procreating through many millennia by combining with the various life-forms already established on Earth, both animals and plants. The descendants of these experiments became the race of mixed creatures that I had once abused during my lifetime as Bu-te-nam, in Atlantis. These creatures still existed in Ec-Kar's time, some two thousand years after my slave-trading days; however, he described these souls — half human, half animal — not as "servant-class mixtures," but as "the fallen angels."

Many millions of years had passed on the Earth from the time "the divine experiment" had begun, and the collective consciousness became aware that difficulties had arisen in the course of this process. Many souls that had mixed with the life-forms of Earth and stayed here, procreating, had become entrapped due to etheric forces and the effects of gravity. These souls found that they had lost their omnipresent connection, and were no longer able to enter and leave the Earth domain at will. Their vibrations had become so dense (although they were still very light by today's standards) that they were unable to access the other realms of consciousness to which they had previously been free to travel. Literally stranded on Earth, out of touch with their counterparts in other vibratory realms, these mixed-beings eventually forgot their origins completely. They continued to exist and biologically reproduce on the Earth plane, marooned on this island in time and space. It was here that the process of reincarnation began.

The omnipresent ones, of course, knew the plight of these lost souls, although the Earth-bound ones were no longer aware that those in the higher realms existed. To lend assistance, a group of these omni-souls chose to project themselves onto the Earth once again, marooning themselves as well, but this time not mixing with the other Earth-life. They came as the five races of man, and all at once throughout the world they appeared, all speaking one common language. Their job, it had been decided, was to help the trapped entities to regain the memory of their own origins, and to achieve the vibratory levels that would allow them to once again travel freely to and from the Earthly realm. Through a series of lives, opportunities would be presented so that they could learn who they were and where they came from, eventually rediscovering their full power within the greater whole, the Oneness. For many hundreds of thousands of years, these humans stayed on the Earth, until they too, to some extent, forgot their origins. The enslavement of the mixed-souls came, no doubt, long after the humans of Earth had forgotten their original mission here. But still the constant learning process of reincarnation and karma remained in play, slowly guiding the souls of Earth back to the higher vibratory realms. Indeed, the suffering of eons of slavery has taught many lessons, pushing at least a few lost souls back to where they once belonged.

In Ec-Kar's times, the fallen angels still existed on the Earth. The country of Atlantis was politically divided — yea or nay

— over slavery, a familiar description of times not so far gone as well. No wonder that slavery was once again confronted in an almost identical scenario, little more than a hundred years ago! This is karma at work. The whys and wherefores are not so important as the understanding that each life on this Earth, each singular experience of pain, joy, suffering or happiness, is part of a greater, magnificent pattern of learning for us all. Accepting this for oneself and applying one's own creative-intuitive abilities to the learning process can only help in reaching the highest levels of conscious to which we all seek to return.

I asked Ec-Kar what had happened to the mixed-creatures, the fallen angels, and why they no longer appear on the Earth, if returning them to "grace" was the original reason that the whole-consciousness came to Earth in human form to start with. And why, I asked, if they are gone now, are we humans still here?

About twelve thousand years before the present day, he explained to me, the vast majority of those original fallen ones began to be reborn, reincarnated in wholly human form. At least genetically and physically, they became indistinguishable from the five races of man, although emotionally and spiritually, many were still at a very low vibratory level. The negative karma which has been earned through the infliction of slavery and violence on our fellow humans, in addition to the fallen angels of Atlantean times, has created lower vibratory levels for much of the human realm. Now, though — through this process of reincarnation — all have the opportunity to raise their own vibratory level. As Ec-Kar said, *"this is the way of the cosmos."*

* * * * *

As a teacher in Poseidia's great Hall of Wisdom, Ec-Kar would regularly share with his students things that we would consider today to be mysterious, perhaps even beyond comprehension. But at that time, interplanetary energies were understood and accepted as a natural energy form, and the system of utilizing these energies of the Earth and the various suns in our realm was considered the common standard. Through exchanges of energy between the Earth and these suns — primarily the local solar-Earth exchange and the Arcturus-Earth exchange — a natural field of etheric energy has been established. This exists in space, and covers the surface of the Earth and other planets and bodies at all times. This energy can be received or collected and then used, simply by combining "tuned" crystals in various manners. In Ec-Kar's culture, these crystals were produced — manufactured, in our terminology — so as to capture the energy from this invisible field. These crystals transformed this energy internally — as a prism transforms a beam of white light into a visible spectrum — amplifying it, or perhaps focusing it would be a better description, so that it could then be used as a power source.

Of course, I asked Ec-Kar if he could give me the design of this system, thinking it would surely revolutionize our current modes of consumption, and perhaps put a halt to the ecological devastation we inflict on the planet in our never-ending quest for fossil fuels. To my amazement, Ec-Kar's response was, *"Three nations in your time now utilize this energy. It has been in use since 1959, both in the private and military sectors."*

I was alarmed to think that this knowledge of an alternative energy source could be here already, only to be guarded as a secret, rather than put to global use. I wondered why Ec-Kar couldn't simply share it with me, so that I could then share it with everyone. Wouldn't this be the best way to effect major changes in the way our civilization is conducting itself, before it's too late? Ec-Kar answered, *"It is only necessary for people to study cycles — politically, environmentally, socially, and spiritually — to have a better understanding of the marvelous workings of the Oneness. Do not seek to share answers, but questions. The only answer, that all must learn, is to trust, and look within. That is intuition."*

*   *   *   *   *

As a consciousness-raising exercise, I chose to enter into some of my communications with Ec-Kar in a group forum, so that those who were interested would have the opportunity to communicate with this amazing entity firsthand. As with Beryl, the portal was open for only a limited period, and I felt strongly the urge to share Ec-Kar's acquaintance with others. He agreed that this was the correct way to proceed. The following excerpts are taken from our group's conversations with Ec-Kar. As you will see, he provided us with electrifying information, right from the start:

> *Good evening and welcome. We are Ec-Kar. We thank you for the opportunity of being with you this evening.*
>
> *We at another time are in a school system that you would call a university. It is known in our time as the Hall of Wisdom. In this hall, students are chosen through the Council of Education to learn the applications of the Earth energy systems.*
>
> *We can tell you that the Earth itself is the greatest source of energy, as it exchanges energy with that of the solar body. Or properly, the sun itself emanates an energy field, which couples with that belonging to the Earth, meeting at the equator. Between the Tropic of Capricorn and the Tropic of Cancer is the coupling point of the fields. So, if you can visualize your infinity sign and visualize the sun and that of the Earth with the infinity sign passing between the two, you begin to understand the coupling energy that is available.*
>
> *This energy is a vibratory force that is low in frequency, rather than high. The body proper naturally attunes to this force most easily. So, we can share with you today what you can do to tap this energy. It is a matter of finding a correct location within your own dwelling — for therein, a vortex point resides. By this we mean that within any structure there are various lines of force that intersect. Where these do*

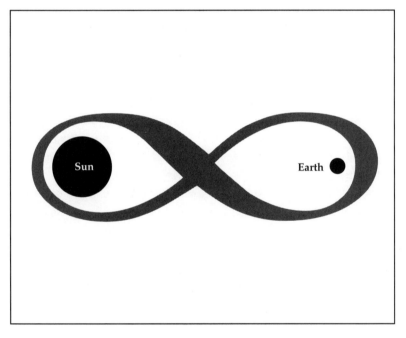

Energy exchange system between Earth and the sun.

intersect is the place where you should stand.

As to how to find this intersection, we would suggest that you begin first by practicing orientation — finding, with body awareness, the direction of magnetic north. Begin by closing the eyes. Turn slowly in one place, attuning the senses to the magnetic field. This will be your first experience in attuning to this force. Once you have determined north, and repositioned yourself several times so you can do it naturally without guesswork, you will find that you will then be able to move slowly through the dwelling until attuning to one of these vortexes. To check accuracy once this is achieved, you will find that these points will usually lie at right angles to the north, northeast quadrant of the structure. In a field no more than forty-five degrees from magnetic north would be the most natural place for these vortexes to occur.

Once you stand at the vortex, you will begin to sense — to feel — the energy therein. As such, you will feel upon the under part of your arms, and on the back part of the neck, just below the ears, a sensation, almost a tingling. This is the indication that you succeeded in tapping the energy source. This is part of what we teach the youth of our time. Bodies tuned to this force are highly resistant to disease, for disease cannot enter into the body easily when the body is protected by the greater force. Once tapped, only mind energies can disrupt this force. Until these disruptions occur, protection is assured. When the mind saps your field, you can reenter your vortex, rejuvenating the energy force, wherein this is necessary.

What we have relayed here tonight is but one aspect of the teachings that will come to your realm from the temples. If there are any questions in this room — on this subject or on others — we will pause for the time you call one minute, in silent thought, and then we will answer particular questions. For above all, we wish to be of service to those who seek to change themselves for the better, from within.

Questioner: We appreciate your coming to spend some time with us tonight, Ec-Kar. We haven't had the pleasure of your company before. What made you decide to come to our group on this night?

Ec-Kar: *These are as portals of opportunity that come. It is not that we are somewhere else and come to you, but rather, it is that we are here always. But there are those conditions, those configurations, that allow for this gateway. It is as if we shift aspects — or time, as you would determine it — to allow the energy to flow through. The group itself determines the entity that will speak forth. For this evening there is much interest in this subject matter. Thus, we are here.*

Questioner: These vortexes, how small are they? How many might there be in a room?

Ec-Kar: *Within each rectangular room, there will be a single vortex. It will always be in the quadrant that we have mentioned — in the forty-five degree angle east of magnetic north. There will always be one in each room, though junctures in the correct quadrant of the overall structure will provide the strongest energy.*

Depending also upon the geophysical location, the vortex will flux in vibratory force, or magnitude. Those vortexes that are closer to the equator will have a "lessening" effect. By this we mean less distortion than those vortexes that reside at greater than thirty degrees above or below the equatorial circumference. By distortion, we refer to planetary noise, internal in nature; also, that created by your present electrical lines and power networks. These networks also add to the distortion. Each transformer, indeed, adds further distortion, as do the generators in cars and other machinery. At the equator, this distortion is lessened.

Questioner: Can you tell us about the lifestyle in your time, in the lands of Atlantis?

Ec-Kar: *My city is known as Poseidia. As to the civilization and culture, the system operates in what would be termed a caste system — or levels of development — for there are mixed races of people that abound throughout the three remaining islands of Atlantis, and* this is not the sole determining factor. Rather, the vibrations at which the individual comes into this life dictate the caste. Some are brought forth and chosen through this system to become educators. Others are chosen to become workers who work in the fields. For each it is divined, at birth, what their life's caste will be.

Our technology has taken a different course than that of your current civilization. It is as if, given the choice between discovering electricity or discovering solar energy to accomplish the same goal, at our time we have chosen the sun and furthered our technology in that direction. Over time, much of our knowledge has led to simpler solutions than those required to support your scientific advances. This simplicity has perhaps allowed us to remain clearer — our minds closer to our spirits — than is possible in your day.

Our life span extends to approximately three hundred years. In an earlier time — during the first civilization of humanity, before the Atlantean period — it was three times again this span. These reductions were due to atmospheric changes, which continue to your present. So much so, that much of our technology, when it is found, will not be applicable to the present time period. For when the first of the three great cataclysms came to the Atlantean lands — some fifty-four thousand years before your present — the atmosphere of the planet was partially ripped away, and took several thousand years to rebuild. So severe was this cataclysm, in fact, that what had been a single landmass spanning all that you now know as the Atlantic Ocean was broken apart, leaving five large islands or subcontinents. A second cataclysm then occurred some twenty-six thousand years later, reducing Atlantis to the three islands, of which Poseidia is a part. This was caused primarily because of our own misuse of technology.

Those few that survived the first great cataclysm, and the second, adapted — first by applying what technology they could to their escape and to remaining alive, and then, through the generations, by becoming acclimated to the new environment. In the end, one more cataclysm will occur, and the land of all we know as Atlantis will pass away beneath the sea. Those remains that are left intact will be uncovered in your present day, as your technology for exploration of the seabeds increases. Remnants of our land will be found in your

Azores, your Bahamas, and your Canary Islands.

Questioner: I'd like to know how one can effectively heal another individual from a great distance.

Ec-Kar: *In order that you may all understand the process for this, we shall share with you what we teach our students, for this question is common during our day.*

First, it is important to realize that what you know as space, as distance between objects, truly does not exist. In the conscious mind, you must come to believe that space is an illusion of perception. This is the discipline that must occur, training the belief to follow the inner knowing and not the eyes. Then what you term telepathy exists, and a connection is made.

We were speaking earlier of the vortex energies that occur in rooms. We wish you also to realize that these are joined by "ley lines."[3] These you can visualize as an invisible network — or weaving — a kind of fishnet stretched across the surface of the entire Earth. If you can visualize the grid of this network, then you must next imagine the individual people moving about on the Earth, either coming in direct contact with the ley lines, or feeling the lesser energy in the areas between the grid lines. This energy may be felt — received — anywhere; however, by purposely tapping the power at any juncture, or intersection, in the grid, one may easily connect to all. You do not question telephone lines that carry the human voice across vast "spaces," nor do you question the fact that radio or television can be conveyed through the airwaves, although someone living two hundred years earlier in your culture would have thought these things impossible. This vortex grid is simply one other vibratory force that has not yet come into your common usage. It is much lower in magnitude and oscillations than that which you have dis-

---

[3] The term "ley lines" was first coined by Alfred Watkins, who used it to describe the energy alignments between ancient sacred sites throughout the world, which he felt were intuitively positioned based on a global infrastructure of energy. The term is now used more generally to refer to the energy grid which surrounds the Earth. For more information on Watkins, please refer to the book *The Ancient Science of Geomancy* by Nigel Pennick. (London: Thames and Hudson Ltd.,1979), p. 80.

The Earth Grid System

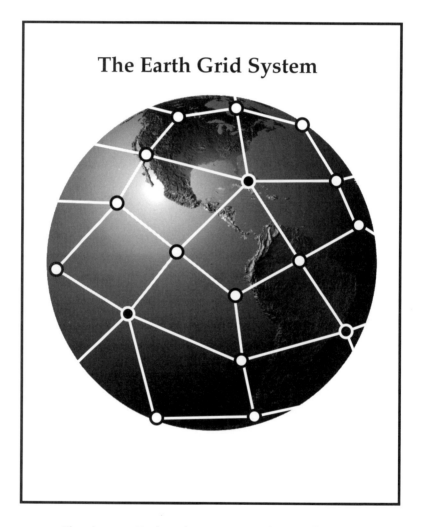

The planetary Earth grid — a system of energy lines that encircles the globe.

covered; nevertheless, it is a frequency that exists, and the human body is already naturally attuned to it.

So the process for healing is that you must seek this attunement. The correct cycle can be achieved by positioning oneself at a vortex, as mentioned earlier. This is easy to do, once you have developed sensitivity, because the net is very fine, and one never has far to go to find a pulse point. Listening to certain types of music — that music known as baroque, for one — may also help to set up within the body a proper pulse, enabling you to make connections with others on the Earth. These others need not be at a juncture as well, for the energy of the grid affects all areas on Earth — the ley lines, but also the spaces between. With practice, even the sender need not be at an intersection, but will find the proper cycle easily, at any place. But this takes practice.

Once you have the belief, and have practiced and achieved the connection you seek, it is only necessary to carry the thought of the individual. Now it may be said — it is said sometimes even in our time period — that other things are needed to make this connection, such as a picture, a belonging, or a piece of clothing. We wish to tell you that all of these are but focusing devices. They become necessary only if the belief system requires it. It is a matter of practice and discipline to evolve to a point where healing can be a common occurrence. So if you wish to heal at a distance, we will give you an exercise to use. By doing so, you will increase your belief system and thereby increase your facility to effect change from a distance.

EXERCISE THREE

(The following exercise has been adapted slightly from Ec-Kar's original terminology, for the sake of clarity.)

1. Find an individual who is open to doing an experiment with you. Someone across town, across the street, or across the planet will work just as well. It makes no difference.

2. Ask that person to take his or her temperature, at a specific time of day which has been prearranged. While he or she is

doing so at that specific time, enter into a visualization in which you see and feel yourself connected to the grid network of the Earth.

3. Visualize your partner in your mind's eye. See this individual surrounded by color. The correct color will come to you, and it will differ each time you try this.

4. Continue to visualize the color surrounding your partner, and see it increase with intensity as time goes by. Do this for about five minutes.

5. When you are done visualizing, call your friend and have him take his temperature again. You should find you have effected a change of approximately three-fourths of a degree. This will begin to strengthen your belief system, as you repeat the exercise, for you will find that time and time again you will achieve identical results.

Questioner: Would you tell me if the continent of Lemuria was in existence in your time?

Ec-Kar: *At our present time there is still a part of it which would be in the vicinity of your Hawaiian Islands, but this is to change shortly. The settling of the Lemurian land into the sea has been gradually occurring, and truly began some eighty-thousand years ago. In this time period, some sixteen thousand years before your own time, there are but small remnants left of the culture that once existed. Indeed, these have already been rediscovered in your present, though unidentified. The greater portion will begin to be excavated in your near future.*

The culture here was one of a spiritual community. The migrations of the survivors brought their culture to your Mexico, and also into the western part of your United States. They moved also to the north of that continent, by various land bridges. Those you term as Eskimo are descendants of a hybrid race, composed of Lemuria's off-spring, and native people. Those who became the Aztec race, and the Mayans, were also mixtures of those races that already existed, and the Lemurians who mixed with them, bringing much of their culture and knowledge. This land in our time is called Mu, and it is the last remaining continent to exist at our time period, besides our own. Although we do allow for communications between our two peoples, very little occurs, for though the Lemurians are not at our place technically — at our technological level — they are spiritually far beyond us. They have no taste for commerce with us, as they disagree with many of the principles of our social order. Likewise, Atlantean policy has tended to look down on their culture as what you would call barbaric, or unadvanced.

Questioner: What are some of the other differences between the two peoples?

Ec-Kar: *Their process of living is to live within the environment rather than to try to change it. This is the greatest difference between our cultures. In all of Lemuria, they choose to live mostly underground, for the beasts still roam their land freely, whereas in ours we have found ways to restrict the natural movement of animals, and to limit their activities upon our land.*

The Lemurians are also predominantly vegetarian, whereas Atlanteans eat equal portions of flesh and plant. This is not because they feel it is wrong to eat meat, for they believe that to survive, each animal — including human — must find sustenance in the life around it, and that is as it should be within the cycle of life and death on Earth. But the Lemurian view differs greatly from our predominant Atlantean view, in that they conserve all aspects of their environment meticulously, taking only what they need, wasting nothing. The consumption of meat is simply more wasteful than the harvest of plants for food, and so they choose not to seek out flesh as a part of their diet. They have done this for many ages, even when their land mass and population was far greater than now, for they are more attuned to the greater Earth being than we, even as we are in some ways more attuned to it than you are in your present culture.

In family structure, they are also different. Theirs is not a caste system, but rather they live in multi-generational groups, or what you would term tribes. The lifestyle and its structure are dedicated to strengthening the creative force and living forever in harmony with the nature of Earth. While Atlantis has developed technology that utilizes a certain attunement with the higher planes of consciousness, it is for the most part the domain of our master and teacher castes, with only the results of our special knowledge passed down to the lower caste members. The greater proportions of our population — especially in the cities of Atlantis — have no understanding of the interplanetary energies that power the technologies they use. All in Lemuria, though, have a mental affinity for communication with the higher realms, so as a people they are bound tightly to the Earth, and have mostly survived the slow, natural changes in their land, moving away far in advance of any catastrophic shifts. Regretfully, this is not true of our own culture, so that when the time comes for the final cataclysm, great and swift environmental devastation will occur, and very few will survive.

Questioner: Are there occasions in which the Lemurians live together in the same places as Atlanteans?

Ec-Kar: *There are exchanges. But you must realize that the Atlantean civilization is in all ways a parallel existence to your present United States. Most of those souls incarnated in the time period prior to our final destruction — this would be considered a span of some six thousand years — have only just returned to the Earth for the first time in your Western culture of present. This influx of souls spans only the last two hundred years prior to your present, with most incarnations occurring only within those fifty-odd years that are most recent. So your United States is, in effect, filled with those same souls that helped to bring an end to the civilization of Atlantis, through their own carelessness and disowning of their own spirituality.*

As in your time, the prejudices that do exist here dominate the political scheme. Isolation has been the desired situation for thousands of years here. Where we have created citadels and circular walls around our fairest cities, it is not only to keep the "beasts" out, but other men, as well. So it is as if we have created these technologies which we do not wish to share. For although we are proud of the bounties our forward-strides have brought to us, we are even less

*willing to share what we have with others than we were when we
had much less to offer. As the final days near, we become even more
of an isolationist country. The few ambassadors who do come from
these other areas to visit are shown special privileges, but tourism is
not encouraged. By the same standard, our citizens are allowed to
travel, but for the most part are kept too busy to do so. Only those of
the highest castes have opportunity to travel to other places, and
these are not interested in trading what they have here for what they
may see in other places.*

ROHAN FROM THE
TWENTY-FIRST CENTURY

I could probably devote half a book to exploring each of the
entities I've experienced through simultaneous reality, and
there have been many more than those I've explained here.
However, my interest here is primarily in getting across the
kind of information accessible through these mind journeys, so
that the possibilities of the experience itself becomes more of a
focus, rather than the description of my particular adventures.
Whether or not you agree with the information I've shared
with you, I would like to think that my experiences will spur
you to discover your own past- and future-life entities. If
nothing else, I hope I have stimulated your curiosity on the
subject. The world we see — the world we generally pay
attention to — is but a small fraction of what exists. Most
importantly, far more of what lies beyond what we have come
to accept as reality is accessible, if only we allow ourselves to
try.

That said, I thought it would be of interest to readers to
learn about one more entity I've encountered in my travels.
Rohan — a future aspect of me — who exists in a different
layer or realm than the one we know. He still belongs to this
Earth system, but in a time frame that exists parallel to the
twenty-first century.

Rohan came through in a time period when I found myself

also being drawn to study UFO phenomena. As I continue to examine my own experiences and question them, so have I considered the many possibilities of how these things manifest themselves. It is difficult to say whether my sub-conscious could have created "Rohan" in order to express some connection with the subject matter I was interested in at the time. On the other hand, perhaps the entity and the experience are genuine manifestations of a probable future, or of a future that is somehow separate from, and therefore not in competition with, our own present. I've decided to simply approach all my higher consciousness experiences from the standpoint of evaluating the benefits, rather than attempting to prove the validity of the source. When Rohan came to me, I was looking for practical tools to assist me in taking my next spiritual baby step. What I ended up with was more like a spiritual quantum leap.

I happen to think that the Earth is a really beautiful place. I've been fortunate to experience so much contact with other realms and realities outside the Earth, and I appreciate these, but it is here on Earth that we are afforded our only opportunity to *apply* all that we have learned in other realms, whatever those may be. In terms of reincarnation, I happen to be of the mind set that I *want* to come back over and over! I'm not anxious to go anywhere else, no matter what trials may be in store here on the planet, because I think Earth is a pretty great place to hang out, and I don't feel anywhere near done with all the learning I'd like to do here. My feeling is that what I think and do on Earth — however small — *does* have a bearing on the outcome of the future, and I'm going to do whatever I can to add to the collective good, rather than take away from it. I have a long way to go, and I make mistakes, but with my heart in the right place, at least I've taken the important first step.

Rohan's perspective of reality is as someone who lives on Earth sometime after a "probable reality" scenario emerges, in which the Earth's magnetic pole has shifted, creating drastic changes in the terrain and energy fields of the planet. Rohan is a pilot whose distinction as fleet admiral of a specialized air corps also places him as a member of a body known as the "Council of Thirteen." The craft used by Rohan's air corps are capable not only of space travel, but also of time-travel. In the following excerpt from his transmission through me, in a session with Cynthia, Rohan explains something of the Council of Thirteen:

Rohan: *We are one aspect of this Council of Thirteen. We suggest also that you* [referring to Cynthia] *are a part of this council throughout other levels, other times, as well. In some, this is not within the membership, but rather in the capacity of Connector — as in "Facilitator of the Desires of the Collective Consciousness." This is the collective consciousness of the Brotherhood, what some may call the "Christ Energies," although there are many names besides this. These thirteen represent those thirteen star systems that are involved within this quadrant of what would be termed "space." Our Master is here, working to provide the beacon.*

Rohan has described his participation as being one from a future where the technology is of a high order, time-travel is common, and where many interstellar alliances exist. So, I wondered, why are they bothering with our present civilization? His answer was that there is certain information that needs to be made available to the new initiates — the children — whose participation in our present will prepare the way for what Rohan has termed "the coming."

Rohan: *It is our duty, our obligation, our choice, to be part of this coming. Upon the planet — in the now of your present — there dwells already one who is the harbinger — the beacon — of this coming. And indeed, in this other continuum wherein we dwell, that same soul will once again manifest as the one who becomes a beacon of knowledge, or that symbol of the same, returning as the Christ figure. We can tell you that this One is a sequence of personalities which have lived upon the planet at many times, many places. We do not try to say that all must believe that there is only this One, now* *returning after being long away from the Earth. Rather, we imply that very soon — within your own times — the collective consciousness of Earth will recognize this particular reincarnation as that of the Christ figure, and that this realization will signal a major shift in what is understood by all as the best way to approach life on Earth. The realization and the consciousness shift that will follow, we term "the coming."*

Rohan and his colleagues began attempting to project their consciousnesses into our present, he said, in order to accomplish the following goals:

1. To alter events, via communication, so as to change their own reality to a secondary probable reality — one in which the magnetic pole-shift does not occur.

2. To lend assistance or aid to anyone who desires to commune directly with their time-travel corps group at the higher level of consciousness. Those who seek this may then move about the present Earth continuum, affecting others — the pyramid effect, so to speak.

3. To help put in place the necessary mechanism for consciousness transference from the Earth to the borderlands, in case cataclysmic probable realities still do occur. Their concern is that the great influx of souls who would be projected into spirit instantaneously — in the event of a large shift in the Earth's magnetic pole — needs to be ready to make that transition safely.

In the case of such a large number of simultaneous moves away from the Earth plane we now know, the best way to maintain safety is to keep the lower levels from being "crushed" by overflow. This requires spiritual training for massive numbers of people, to assist them in raising their vibratory levels to achieve safe passage. Rohan said that there are schools on the lower planes, to assist normal transfers from death to rebirth. It is how we live each life that determines which level of vibration our "whole consciousness" resides at. Rohan, and those who work with him, are compelled to convey their message to those in our present time. It is their hope that they can avert the catastrophic change that resulted in their own probable future. It is not only a hope, but a necessity that by attempting this the order of the continuum will — at very least — remain intact. It is imperative that the greater consciousness of our whole realm continues to seek its own perfection within the system that was first created, back at the beginning of time.

THE TIME-TRAVELER

In closing this chapter, I want to share one more experience of simultaneous reality. This did not happen to me, but was related to me by a man who came to me for a reading — a teacher at a large city high school.

One afternoon at about 3:30, shortly after school had been dismissed for the day, the vice principal of the school came out of her office and noticed an older man talking urgently to the receptionist in the outer office. The receptionist seemed to be getting visibly agitated, so the vice principal walked over to see if she could help.

"I have been sent here to enroll in your bilingual class," the man declared. "Later, I am to meet my brother in Peru."

The vice principal was surprised, since the school offered no Spanish bilingual classes, and provided no adult education services at all. She took the dialogue over from the flustered receptionist, and explained the situation as diplomatically as possible to the perturbed gentleman.

The strange visitor was adamant, however. "I was told by Mr. Fox, your superintendent of schools, to come to *this* school to register," he said.

Suddenly, the trouble was clear, for Mr. Fox was not the name of the current administrator. There *had* once been a Mr. Fox who was superintendent of schools, the principal thought, but the connection seemed ridiculous, for that name had not applied to the post since the mid-1930's, some fifty years earlier!

At this point, apparently to strengthen his case, the visitor pulled out his card. In addition to his name it showed several stars, and the words "Interplanetary Council." The vice principal couldn't tell if this was a joke, but she wasn't amused by it in the least. Eager to get rid of the man, she suggested that because he had been told the bilingual class would begin in March, and since it was now only February, that he should leave and return next month, closer to the supposed start date of the class. Maybe, she told him politely, they would have some information by then.

The moment the man left, the receptionist told the vice principal what she had seen when the visitor reached into his coat for his card — the lining had seemed to be covered with a complex system of wires and electrical components. The vice principal was alarmed. Concerned that the strange gentleman might have been carrying a bomb, she hurried out to follow him down the hall.

Although she was only a few seconds behind him, and although the hallway was a long one with only one exit at the end, she never saw the mysterious visitor again. The school's security guard, who had signed the man into the building through the only door that was open to the public, told her that he never signed back out. They searched the grounds, but there was no trace of the visitor.

The odd thing about this story is that my client did not tell it to me until my Source made reference to it first, during the course of his reading. In this particular session, my Source had been attempting to explain the concept of time-warps. Without the case that I have just described ever being mentioned, my Source said, *"The visitor to the school was an ambassador from that simultaneous reality of future from which many come. Those who seek to alter the reality of the future time must use the means at their disposal, including travel in time. This visitor was attempting to project further into the past, to make a connection that might later make the correction he sought. He simply missed his destination by some fifty years, the result of a minor miscalculation."*

My client, who was also a friend, then told me the story I've just related. Curious, he later asked the receptionist who had dealt with the visitor if she could remember what he had been wearing. A wide-brim hat and an exceedingly wide tie, she told him. Sort of like the clothes you'd see in a movie about the 1930s. External proof of simultaneous reality? Perhaps. We may never know.

*   *   *   *   *

Out of all my dialogues with simultaneous realities and inner world contacts, Rohan and Ec-Kar are my strongest memories, continuing to bleed through my consciousness, even after all these years. My final simultaneous reality experience was, in fact, a discussion with both Ec-Kar and Rohan at the same time, as if they had melded into one entity. Our communication ended with the statement, *"Soon, who you now are will become a conscious collective of the three energies now known to you as Ec-Kar, Rohan and Gordon-Michael Scallion."*

It has now been some ten years since this last dialogue, and while I can't say I *feel* any different, I have a clear sense that my intuitive awareness continues to grow. Without any "lessons" at all, my understanding of life in Atlantis, life in the present, and life in the future crystalizes more and more each day, becoming somehow one and the same thing. In my mind's eye, I've begun to envision the past, present, and future more as parts of the same Oneness, less as separate things. It is almost as if I see the present moment expanding to include — to embrace — all that exists simultaneously in the past and future.

Despite our fears as we near the turn of the millennium, and despite all of our mistakes as humans here on Earth, I believe with all my heart that this is a joyous time to be alive. Together, we can indeed learn from the mistakes of the past, and proceed into the future full of hope.

Chapter Eleven

Earth Changes

The Earth erupts anytime it is pushed out of balance. It can occur as a result of a cosmic event, such as a comet hitting the Earth, planetary alignments, a shift in the Earth's magnetic field, or as the result of man's violations of the Earth through pollution, misuse of technology, or lack of spiritual communion with the Earth. Regardless, the Earth always survives, as does human consciousness. Both of these are eternal.

— The Dream Teachers

After my last communication with Rohan, I continued to receive visions of Earth changes with greater frequency. Sometimes the messages were similar to what I had experienced in the hospital, and I was shown pictures of what was to come. At other times, my dream teachers would take me on out-of-body journeys over vast stretches of land. This was my own Earth, they told me, but the land looked so foreign, so different from the world I knew that I felt as if they were showing me another planet. Even with all of this input urging me to pay attention to this matter, I continued to ignore it. As the warnings increased, I simply expended more and more effort to put all the disturbing images out of my mind.

*   *   *   *   *

Back in 1982, when I was just beginning to accept my visions as a real experience in my life, I realized that many of them seemed to relate — directly or indirectly — to Earth changes. Further, the term "tribulation" kept coming up to describe a kind of "testing period" from 1991 through 1997, which would be accompanied by the beginning of major Earth changes. My first vision in the hospital had even spoken of this tribulation, although at the time I'd had no idea of what that term meant. When I first began to keep journals of my dreams and visions, one of the things I often did was to draw sketches of some of the strange things that I saw.

It took more than a year of patient record-taking before I had compiled enough information on Earth changes to sketch out a very rough world map which illustrated what I was witnessing in my dreams. I still didn't know exactly *how* these changes were supposed to come about, but I thought that by creating a simple graphic representation, I could at least express what I had seen to others. When I finally completed the map, I made a hundred copies or so, and distributed them to friends, dream analysts, various scientists and geologists, and anyone else I thought might be able to interpret my visions. I decided to leave it up to others who were more qualified than me to determine if any of it made sense.

The reactions I got from professionals when I shared my first crude map-making efforts ranged from laughter, to ridicule, to total disbelief. Embarrassed, and angry at my intuitive guidance system for leading me so far astray, I put all the materials and research I had compiled for the past year in a file cabinet drawer, far to the back, so I wouldn't have to look at these reminders of my wasted effort. Throughout the next few years, I thought more than once of simply throwing everything away, but an inner voice kept me from doing so. Over and over — whenever I remembered the cold reception my message had received and thought to rid myself of the burdensome file of notes once and for all — I heard the word *"wait"* rendered loud and clear in my mind.

THE THREE MONKS

It was in September of 1985 that I had my first "reality check" on the meaning of dream prophecy. Upon going to bed that night, I immediately fell into a deep sleep, and began to experience a lucid dream. In this dream, I found conclusive proof for myself that dreams could be more than merely intuitive — they could be precognitive as well.

I find myself walking towards a thicket in the woods. It is early evening, and the air is crisp, like a spring night in New England. As I near the thicket, I see the light of a fire. I come upon three dark-skinned monks sitting around a campfire. One is an elderly man, who looks to be in his seventies. The other two are much younger, perhaps only in their early twenties. Because of their dark skin and their close-cropped hair, I think they look like the people I've seen in pictures of Tibetan monasteries. Their robes are bright red and made of a billowing, silky fabric. Each man also has a colorfully woven blanket of red, orange and blue stripes. But rather than wrapping themselves in these for warmth, they seem to be wearing them slung over one shoulder, much like a serape. How strange, I think, as I come into the circle by the fire and join them. They nod to me in silent greeting, and I sit down.

"Nothing can be done. It is as it should be, as has been prophesied," says the elder monk. He then turns his face away. He bows his head and closes his eyes.

The two younger monks look dismayed. Both look to me, the light of the flames shining in their dark eyes. One of them asks, "What can we do? There are six million people in that land!"

Before I can respond, the old monk raises his head and speaks again, this time staring directly at me. "Seven thousand shall perish in the city. It is destined."

Tears well up in the eyes of the two young ones. They turn away from their elder. They look to me once again. They ask, "What can we do?"

I respond, "I'll tell you what you can do ... you can get them moving! You can get them moving now!"

Suddenly, the dream ended and I awoke with a jolt. Shaking, I reached for my journal and immediately wrote the dream down. I tried to return to sleep, but I tossed and turned. The feelings and imagery of the dream were still so powerful in my mind that I never did fall back into a sound sleep. I remember spending many hours that night — in a twilight sleep — attempting to puzzle out the meaning of the dream.

The next morning, the twentieth of September, I got up and turned on the radio to catch the early morning news as I usually did. The broadcast that morning changed the direction and purpose of my life forever, in one swift moment. As I tuned in, the newscaster was describing the massive earthquake that had just hit Mexico City during the night. The city's population was six million. Stunned, I listened to the entire report, then changed stations, searching for more information. The death toll was initially reported as two thousand. As terrible as that seemed to me at the time, I was relieved to find that it wasn't the seven thousand deaths indicated by my dream. This feeling was short lived, however. As rescue teams scoured the remains of the city, the number of confirmed deaths increased. The final count: seven thousand dead in Mexico City alone, with an estimated twenty-five thousand deaths in the entire region, all as a result of the quake.

*   *   *   *   *

I felt an incredible responsibility, indeed a burden, weighing upon me. I could no longer view my visions as future possibilities with which I had no involvement. I no longer felt myself to be a passive bystander — aware of what might be, but content to keep my knowledge to myself. I now saw my choices clearly — to speak out or to remain silent. What I did or didn't do could be a matter of life or death! Still, I did not immediately spring into action. Looking back, I think I was so overwhelmed that I may have gone into a state of denial. After all, what could I do? The ridicule I'd experienced when I presented my maps was fresh in my mind, and the sting of it was still powerful. But, as is often the case when I find myself at odds with those realms of logic and self-judgement, the guidance of dream prophecy and intuition came in, once again, to make me face reality — whether I wanted to or not!

I find myself at the edge of a body of water. It seems to be a large lake, rather than the ocean, although the water extends to the horizon, with no visible land in sight. It does not smell like the ocean, I think. Looking down at the sand, I observe that someone has written a phrase in the sand. I back further away, so I can get a better perspective from which to read. The words say:

> *The purpose of prophecy is twofold. On one hand, it allows those who read the signs to prepare for what may come — a warning. On the other hand, it allows some who read the signs to change that which may come to be.*

I woke up feeling recharged, full of energy for the first time in a long while. This was the first dream I could recall in which I could see the hopefulness of the message. In fact, it may have helped me to see the hopefulness in all the messages I had been receiving up to that point.

Spurred by this sudden crystallization of my goals, I began to search for others who must surely have had similar dreams and visions of the future. I sought out other visionaries and psychics all over the country and the world. I met or spoke with over a hundred such people within a couple of months, discovering amazing similarities between our visions. It seemed that as soon as I let myself open to this idea of Earth changes as something to be not only prepared for, but possibly prevented, I felt like I had somewhere to go with the information.

As I mentioned earlier in this book, I had read about various visionaries, such as Edgar Cayce and Nostradamus, but what they had left behind on the subject of Earth changes was very little, and in Nostradamus' case, often shrouded in mystery and therefore subject to wide interpretation. I was, however, encouraged by what I heard from the intuitives who I met as contemporaries. Many told me that they had strong feelings that massive Earth changes would be occurring in the near future, though none had experienced the complete worldwide details that had been shown to me. Regardless, I felt any similarities between my visions and others to be of great value personally. I also thought that — with corroboration — perhaps researchers would be interested in my premonitions, viewed as part of a trend in the collective knowing.

Once again, I took out my map from 1982, dusted it off, and shared it with those people who said they were interested in what I saw. My purpose, I felt, was to ask them to join with me in an attempt to "warn the people," as my message-in-the-sand dream had suggested. Inconceivably, every single person said, "No." Of all the people I spoke with, none wanted to work with me to get a warning out to the rest of the world, before it was too late.

Unfortunately, I was told more than once, no one would pay attention until an accurate prediction came to pass here in the U.S. Somehow I knew they were right. I felt alone now, and once again very unsure of my path. I returned to a state of denial — perhaps the same state my fellow visionaries were in.

*   *   *   *   *   *

During the next several years my visions of Earth changes continued, each time providing me with additional clarity of detail. It was an extremely frustrating time, because I could not understand why I was being shown these things if there was nothing I could do about them. Alternately, I went back to an earlier rationale I'd constructed — that my visions were not prophecies of real Earth changes at all, but merely metaphorical, representing the decline of our society. Maybe the lessons were meant to guide me towards being more of an environmental activist — lecturing about how our planet is being destroyed by nuclear testing, the greenhouse effect, wars, and our general misappropriation of the natural world for our own selfish uses. But this approach — practical though it sounded — just didn't bring all the pieces together to make them fit. I was not really an expert on environmental issues, and besides, how many activists use the destruction of Atlantis to prove the point that our ways here on Earth need changing? I always ended up back at the idea of needing to warn people of the particular Earth changes I saw. The future maps, I felt, were the key. But I still didn't know what to do about them.

For several years after the quake in Mexico, I turned my focus back to teaching intuitive development. The Earth changes dreams had not stopped, but my brief attempt to become a workaholic intuitive-consultant had taught me that this was not the best way to drown out my bothersome dreams. I stopped doing consultations entirely when it became obvious that my health was at risk, and ventured into this new career direction with a full heart. I felt this was a constructive use of my time, and I was able to apply many of the positive lessons I'd gotten from my dream guides throughout the years, regarding the power of mind and our latent intuitive abilities. Cynthia and I conducted weekly seminars, and most of our students — better than ninety percent — were able to significantly increase their own intuitive abilities. These seminars continued to go well, and I felt good doing something that benefited others. When the Earth changes dreams would wake me up at night, or one of my "migraines" would send me to my bed, I simply reminded myself that I had tried to get the word out, but that no one had listened.

Through the late eighties and into the early nineties I continued to dream of events and then watched as they appeared on the news within the next few months — the San Francisco Bay Area earthquake in October 1989, the breakup of the Berlin Wall later that November, the quake that rocked Northwestern Iran in mid-1990, and the eruption of war in the Persian Gulf soon after. All these things came to me first — which I shared with Cynthia, our students, and in a very small newsletter we were publishing at that time — and then came to pass. But this was not what was meant — I was sure — by my dream teachers' calls to "warn the people." I continued to enjoy the most fulfilling aspects of my life — my seminars and workshops, my marriage, friends and family — and resigned myself to silence regarding the catastrophic Earth changes in my dreams.

Gradually, I began to pay a price for my silence. At first, I used increased amounts of work to stave off my visions of destruction, throwing myself into an even heavier schedule of consulting work than I'd attempted before. I figured that I could overcome what I saw as the "negative energy" of my Earth changes visions by increasing the sheer magnitude of my more positive healing work. This tactic failed on several levels. In the first place, it did very little to keep the nightmares at bay. In fact, I actually seemed to dream more and more about this coming period of tribulation, the pole shifts, the alterations in the land, and the struggling migrations of millions of survivors. In the second place, the insane pace I'd set for myself — often seeing up to six clients per day — was leading me rapidly into a state of complete mental and physical exhaustion. Not surprisingly, my health began to falter. I was living in an almost perpetual state of fatigue; the blinding headaches I had gotten in the past when I used my trance state too often had become daily occurrences.

As fear settled in, I made a major decision. I resolved to shut down *all* of my visions completely, and to make whatever effort was necessary to accomplish this. In this way, I attempted to restore my health, and hopefully, my sanity. I stopped receiving clients. I stopped all voluntary communications with my Source. I prayed, meditated, and repeated daily affirmations. I tried to concentrate on improving my health. But the harder I tried, it seemed, the less my life felt like my own. Then the nightmares began.

THE POWER OF NIGHTMARES

One September evening in 1991, I retired early and drifted off to sleep after an especially tiring day. The next thing I recall is waking up with a violent jerk from a particularly vivid dream about Earth changes. I sat up for a few minutes, attempted to center myself, took a couple of deep breaths and did my best to relax before returning to sleep.

When we woke up the next morning, Cynthia and I shared our dreams with each other, something we usually did as a matter of course. The most curious thing about my dream from the previous evening was how closely it mirrored the waking vision I had while in the hospital in 1979. This time nothing but Earth changes events were shown to me, although they were presented in a similar fashion to that first vision — very rapidly, and in crisp, full color. It was as if I were watching a video montage on fast-forward, so I saw the images in such a blur that I could barely understand one before it went on to the next. Cynthia thought it might be an important dream sequence, and that perhaps the reason I hadn't been able to understand was because I was fighting the message. I reluctantly agreed, and before dropping off to sleep that night, I asked my dream teachers to assist me in understanding the previous night's dreams.

As I'd half hoped, half feared, the same dream came again that night. This time, however, the scenes of Earth changes were shown to me at a slower speed, so that I could understand the specifics. The pieces went by so slowly, in fact, that only a small part of the original montage was touched on before the night was through. It was like skimming a book, or reading the back of the book jacket, and then going back to the first chapter and reading it slowly, absorbing each word. The only problem was that this was a horror story to my mind, and I felt sure that every bit of it was real.

Night after exhausting night the dreams would continue, until I was almost frantic, thinking I would never again have a peaceful night's sleep. Each night I would go to bed nervous and anxious, hoping to get some rest. And each night would pick up where I'd left off the night before, as if a dream bookmark was holding my place until the next time; this pattern continued for twenty-nine consecutive evenings. At that point, I'd seen every moment of the original montage a second time, in excruciating detail. In the very first dream in this series of dreams, I remember drifting off to sleep and then feeling a gentle pull on my hands. I heard the usual "pop" sound I hear just prior to going on an out-of-body journey. On either side of me there appeared an angel-like being who was both translucent and luminous, filled with a milky-white light. These were my dream guides, I discovered, but in a new form. As each light-being took hold of one of my hands, I felt myself lifted away from my sleeping body. We traveled higher and higher, until I was in outer space looking back down at Earth.

I don't seem to need any breathing apparatus or ship to propel me about. I look at my arms and hands and see they are blue and golden in color and translucent. I wonder if I have passed over — if I am now a ghost.

An inner voice responds to my thoughts. It is one of my dream guides. "You are not dead. You are out-of-body in your astral form, and have entered the time stream of all that was, is, or is becoming. Watch and remember."

Everywhere I look on Earth I can see lightning bolts. They are flashing and spiraling down into the atmosphere with such ferocity, I can barely keep looking. It reminds me of seeing fireworks on the Fourth of July. I view the moon just coming from around the night side of the planet. Behind it, stars fill the blackness of space, and then one light seems to grow brighter and stand out from the others. At my back is the sun, which seems brighter and more yellow than I remember it. I turn, watching as large spikes of white-yellow energy shoot out from the blazing bright surface — solar flares — and come right past me as they seemed to reach out to touch the Earth's surface. I see dark areas here and there on the sun's surface too. I wonder if these are sun spots.

"Yes, magnetic forces are increasing," my guides answer. "The sun's polarity-reversal cycle prepares now for a new age."

At just that moment, the two light-beings gently guide me back into my bed, and the journey ends. That was the beginning of my twenty-nine night cycle of nightmares. The next night the sequence continued.

Once again I am guided into space by the light-beings. I look away from the sun and focus on a small red planet — Mars. Instantly I find myself catapulted towards it.

"What is the significance of this planet?" I wonder aloud. As I fly through space, I see another light, blue in color and not as big as the red planet from my perspective, but very bright. It appears to be coming from beyond the sun, from behind it. I look for a reference point to mark its location in the heavens, so that I can track its progress. I notice that the blue light seems to be moving in the direction of a certain star in the sky. I ask, "What star is this?"

"Arcturus," my guides answer.

I am being propelled toward the red planet by my constant companions, the two light-beings. As I get closer, I can see that the surface is more orange than red. Craters dot the planet's surface. I see rocks, like rubble, everywhere, and large ditches arranged in a symmetrical pattern, as if they were somehow planned. Some of the pieces of rubble seem highly polished, while most are dull.

"Am I looking at Mars?"

"This is Mars at present," the light-beings respond.

I am very near the surface of the red planet now. I look up to see a small white moon passing over, low on the horizon. I continue to look deeper and deeper into the heavens, almost as if my sight is being drawn to a specific point in the sky. A bright blue-white light appears. I know it is a star.

Time speeds up in the dream, and it is as if I am sitting back and watching it from an outside perspective. There is a quickening, with weeks and months flashing by in minutes. I am back in space now, and I turn back to focus on Mars. I watch as the entire planet begins to wobble on its axis. All of a sudden I find myself being moved half way around Mars, to the opposite side of the planet. I can see the blue star is now brighter and closer. The energy coming from it seems to be building in strength. I wonder if this new sun has something to do with the activity I am observing on the red planet.

Once again I notice the smallest moon in orbit around Mars. It is now moving in a snake-like motion. As I watch, the moon veers crazily away, as if it has suddenly been pushed out of its orbit. In a moment it is over. The moon spirals out into space. I believe that the Martian moon will intercept the Earth's path in the future.

The planet Mars and its moon, Phobos.

As the first week passed, the nightmares continued, usually ending when I awakened abruptly in a cold sweat. Sometimes the events in the dream appeared to be accelerated, weeks seeming to pass by in mere minutes. Other times I see the events in slow motion, as if watching the second hand of a clock. I saw the moon of Mars on several consecutive nights, moving ever-closer to Earth. My dream guides identified the moon as Phobos.

I am afraid that the Mars' moon is going to hit Earth. My dream guides tell me this will not happen. I watch as the tiny satellite nears Earth. As it begins to enter the atmosphere, it turns red from the heat. The angle is shallow, and it looks like it may be deflected off the outer layers.

"I hope it doesn't penetrate the atmosphere!" I think to myself. I watch, my eyes fixed wide open and my heart pounding so loudly I can hear it. I breathe a sigh of relief as the moon ricochets off the atmosphere and continues out into space.

I am now shown Earth at a closer range. The entire planet shudders from the shock wave of the moon's deflected impact. I see large, swirling winds whipping the surface of Earth.

"Winds shall reach two hundred miles per hour, and waves of water shall move across the coastal regions — a mile or more in height," the light-beings say.

I watch storms moving across the planet from the equator to the North Pole. I move closer to Earth until I can clearly see North America. I travel northeast, and recognize the Saint Lawrence Seaway and Great Lakes region below me. To the north, I can see Greenland and the edge of the Arctic Circle. The ice is melting so fast that water levels throughout the world are rising. The channels of the Saint Lawrence swell and the Great Lakes expand. As I watch, the Saint Lawrence becomes a narrow inland sea, feeding into a larger inland sea where the five Great Lakes once were. The water then spills south from what was Lake Michigan, widening the river that flows down to the Mississippi, and on to the Gulf of Mexico. The huge waterway divides the United States in two. Then more water breaks out from the Lakes region, cutting a new river channel through the Midwest to Phoenix.

"This is to become a great river route, upon which the new race shall travel in pilgrimage in the future," my guides explain.

I can see now that the West Coast has become a series of islands. The dream guides continue, "These shall become known as the Isles of California."

The continent has divided into two, separating the central United States from the East Coast. Most of the western territory is submerged, a new West Coast has now formed from Phoenix, Arizona to Denver, Colorado and up to the western edge of Nebraska. The eastern continent is bounded by the new sea created by the widened Mississippi waters, and the Atlantic Ocean, which has pushed back the land of the southern states for many miles. Fully half the land of Georgia, and the Carolinas is inundated. A third of Florida is underwater, as is most of New York, Washington, D.C., and the northeast coastline.

I understood that I was witnessing a future cataclysm. Each night, the details of the Earth changes were shown to me. I watched closely as the scenarios developed, attempting to remember every detail. Having first witnessed North America, I wondered how the rest of Earth would fare. As the second week of dreams unfolded, I saw more than I ever wanted to know. I experienced dream upon dream in which the Earth's surface was erupting with volcanoes and earthquakes, flooding, or sinking under the sea. As I moved from one place to another, I saw that no place appeared unaffected.

In one dream, I watched as Europe sank under the rising ocean waters in a single moment. The light-beings explained, *"The Earth in this region shall be cleansed for nearly two millennia, at which time it shall once again rise from its resting place. Remember that water is the mother — the cleanser. Fire is the purifier."*

My dream teachers would later explain that the inundation of Europe was to occur as a result of the karma of the land, for the many wars which had been waged in this region throughout mankind's history on the planet. The most recent Great

Wars — World Wars I and II — had taken their toll on a spiritual level. The nightmares showed inundations in the Middle East and Japan, as well. I asked whether these were for the same reasons as Europe's demise, and they confirmed that this was indeed the case. The nightmare dreams continued without abate.

I watch as the Atlantic and Pacific Oceans froth white. It reminds me of my sailing days in Florida, encountering a sudden storm with no land in sight. The wind is so severe that the waves are turned to foam, and the blue-gray of the water disappears beneath the chopping whitecaps. Suddenly, large new lands are thrust up from the ocean floor in both oceans, not too far off the coasts of America. Other countries sink below the sea. Japan is gone. Africa is divided into three pieces by seaways forming what looks like a "Y" imprinted on the land.

The land of Canada seems largely untouched, except for the central province of Manitoba, which is largely lost to rising waters. Australia loses almost all of its coastal land. New Zealand rises out of the sea and becomes as large as Australia, a small continent in its own right. South America is separated from the northern continent, and Central America is mostly lost to the sea. As I view the whole Earth, slowly turning below me, I see that every continent had been affected. In their new forms, the lands of Earth are barely recognizable in relation to the familiar map of the world. As I look at my planet — the New World — I feel confused, lost, and sad. I do not know what these changes mean.

*   *   *   *   *

I went to bed on the twenty-ninth evening of this nightmarish dream sequence in a state of complete exhaustion. By now, I had resigned myself to believing that this night would probably be the same as all the others. Yet, as I fell asleep, I realized that it felt different, more like attending a seminar on Earth energies with Ec-Kar than being guided by my dream teachers. In this dream a voice spoke to me while I looked at a slower version of the original montage I'd received on the first night. After all the weeks of out-of-body journeys I'd had in between, I was better able to understand the Earth changes I was seeing.

The voice in the dream said, *"Tonight we will speak to you about the cause and timing of what you have witnessed. The greater changes occur within a cycle lasting between 1998 and 2012. Between 1998 and 2002 are the years when Earth's magnetic field begins to shift its current orientation from the north, moving in steps of six to seven degrees at a time, to the west. This shall occur two or three times. The cause of such changes may be found in the natural rhythms of Earth and the cosmos."*

It seems that Earth does not spin perfectly, but rather wobbles on its rotational axis. This wobbling completes a cycle approximately every twenty-six thousand years. Within this time period, the North Pole axis of Earth points to a different star about every twenty-one hundred years. This is know as "precession of the equinoxes."[4]

Most of us are aware of the zodiac and the twelve astrological signs. As a planet, we are now currently passing out of one sign and into another — from Pisces to Aquarius. During each age, Earth's North Pole is pointed at a different star. Currently the pole star is Polaris — the North Star. Soon, Earth's North Pole will point to a new pole star.

Later Ec-Kar explained more about precession. Approximately every eleven thousand six hundred years the Earth's tilt position, relative to the sun, reaches a critical point. Ec-Kar further stated that if this critical position occurred during a time of solar magnetic reversal — approximately every three thousand seven hundred and fifty years — then a subsequent pole shift occurs instantly on Earth, causing global

---

4 According to *The American Heritage College Dictionary* (3rd ed.), the term precession of the equinoxes is used in astronomy to refer to "a slow westward shift of the equinoxes along the plane of the ecliptic, resulting from precession of Earth's axis of rotation and causing the equinoxes to occur earlier each sidereal year. A complete precession requires 25,800 years." (Boston: Houghton Mifflin Company; 1993), p. 1076.

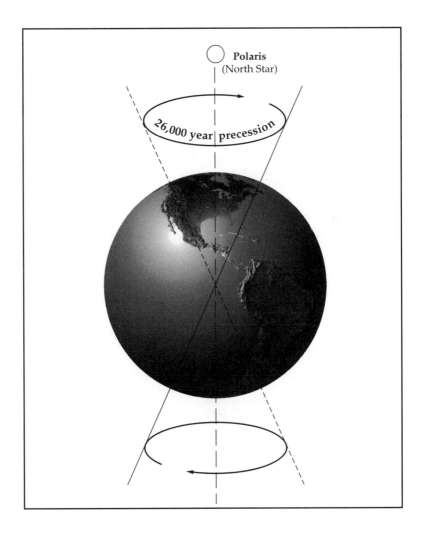

Precession of the equinoxes.

cataclysms of the type that finally destroyed Ec-Kar's home continent of Atlantis. Ec-Kar also stated that Earth is currently at its lowest point in magnetic-field strength — something science has confirmed — and that the sun is now beginning its own magnetic pole reversal cycle. In addition, we are also at the critical point in the precession cycle.

It is interesting to note that in Plato's work, *The Critias*, he describes a war between the city of Athens and Atlantis nine thousand years prior to his time. This war ended, he states, when a cataclysmic earthquake occurred, and the fabled continent of Atlantis was lost beneath the sea. Using Plato's time frame as a point of reference — approximately four hundred years before Christ — we can see that both the precession and solar cycles are due to reach critical points at any time now, and that their simultaneous occurrences will have huge ramifications for our planet.

There is evidence of cataclysmic events in the Earth's ancient past, such as the comet that hit the Yucatan Peninsula about sixty-five million years ago. One theory points to this collision as the event responsible for the extinction of the dinosaurs.

In the mid-twentieth century, Russian scientists discovered numerous woolly mammoths in the frozen tundra. Carbon dated to between ten and twelve thousand years ago, the animals' stomachs and mouths contained undigested grass, an indication that a cataclysmic event froze them instantly as they grazed.

My visions have revealed that this cataclysm was caused by a shift in the Earth's magnetic pole that instantly triggered great changes in weather patterns. These changes resulted in frigid air being sucked out of the polar regions and into temperate and tropical areas, causing winds in excess of two hundred miles per hour.

By examining earth core-samples, scientists have discovered that the Earth's magnetic field reverses itself from time to time. The most recent reversal was at the time of the last Ice Age, a little over ten thousand years ago.

My visions have indicated that the major cause of the com-

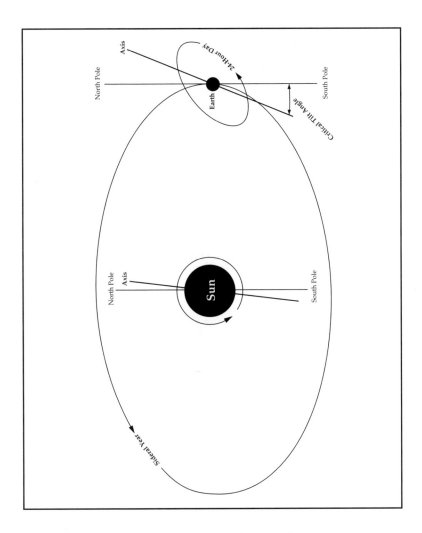

Critical angle between Earth's rotational axis and geocentric axis.

ing cataclysmic Earth changes will be a series of magnetic pole shifts. These shifts are part of the planet's natural cycles and the interaction between Earth, the sun and other planets.

Returning to that last evening of nightmares, I still had many more questions. I wondered if these forces were what caused the Mars' moon — Phobos — to be displaced from its orbit. I also wondered if it was fated that our Earth would enter into this time period of cataclysms in the near future. It was clear to me that *something* was going on already. I had been warned since the beginning — my awakening — that the major Earth changes would be preceded by unusually severe weather — high winds and flooding — followed by increased global volcanic activity, and warming ocean temperatures. At the time of this cycle of nightmares in 1991, these things had certainly begun to happen.

To my questions, my dream teachers responded:

"A magnetic pole shift is already currently underway. It began in the mid 1930's, as a result of a shift in the position of the Earth's core relative to the pole star. Just as earthquakes and volcanoes are caused by electromagnetic forces, so are pole shifts. Plate tectonic movement is only a reaction to these forces. What you have seen in your visions can aid the many. Others shall come forward now to increase awareness of the coming precession and solar cycles, and the beginning of a new age. This is to be a millennium of peace and greater light for all. And yet, as has been indicated to you often, if community is born anew, if there is a spiritual ideal for each entity, if intuition is followed by each, then indeed such a cataclysm as you have witnessed can be lessened."

"Can it be eliminated?" I asked.

"All things are possible. You have witnessed the most probable future Earth. Whether it comes to pass depends upon the people. Warn the people now!"

I woke up yelling, "I'll do something! I'll do something!" Cynthia woke up, startled by my actions, and attempted to calm me down. We immediately got up, went downstairs and talked in some detail about the cycle of nightmares, for I knew, somehow, that it was now over. Cynthia remarked that this last night had been a full moon, and suggested that the number of days and nights — twenty-nine — might be significant. I did find out later that it was no accident. The dream pattern followed a lunar cycle, ending on a full moon, my dream guides told me, and it was now complete.

The next evening my dreams returned to normal — or whatever normal had become for me. But no more dreams of Earth changes. Relieved, I took the next day off. Later that evening, I reviewed what I had written in my journals. The information read like something I could share in a newsletter on Earth changes, and my intuitive senses told me that this was the right direction in which to go. Nevertheless, I could still recall the last time I had put my dreams and visions down on paper — the future map — and the reaction I'd received. I wasn't looking forward to going through a repeat of that experience, but I felt driven to do something, and the newsletter seemed right. The cycle of nightmares had been so clear and real to me, and the desired effect had obviously been achieved — I could no longer remain in denial about what had been happening to me. Cynthia and I talked about it and made a decision — *to warn the people.*

THE EARTH CHANGES REPORT

Between the time we made the decision to warn people about these future Earth changes and the time we actually published the first newsletter, I was scheduled to speak both locally and at an alternative-science convention in Denver, Colorado. After making the decision to publish my insights on Earth changes, I also decided to talk about them at any future speaking engagements. So, I began to tell people about the earthquakes, volcanoes and weather changes I'd seen in my dreams. I also told them about the newsletter we were preparing to publish called the *Earth Changes Report*. The response to my lectures was overwhelming. Rather than people being put off by descriptions of the geophysical changes that I was seeing, many felt that I was correct, and had themselves been sensing great changes on the horizon. Before we had even printed the first issue or made any decisions about how we would distribute our newsletter, we were swamped with requests for subscriptions. It turned out that word-of-mouth was to be the main method of distribution, and in October of 1991, the *Earth Changes Report* (*ECR*) was launched.

In early 1992, I began to sense new changes. I saw distortions in the air and felt them to be encompassing Earth, as if the electromagnetic field of the planet was changing, or being interfered with. My sense was that these changes were mainly the result of a shift in the Earth's core. I published a short-term warning in *ECR*, stating my prediction that three progressively stronger earthquakes would hit the Los Angeles area, a pattern signaling the start of what would be several years of major changes to Earth's topography. The magnitude of the third earthquake would be in excess of eight points.

In March, as we were finishing up the April 1992 edition of *ECR*, I felt very strongly that the first quake of my previous prediction was imminent, and the information I was receiving intuitively grew more detailed. We published an updated warning stating that there was a fifty percent chance that the first of the three earthquakes was about to occur. Its magnitude would be greater than six, and the epicenter would be east of Los Angeles. It would happen between April seventeenth and April twenty-second.

On April twenty-second, 1992, an earthquake of magnitude six-plus hit an area approximately one hundred ten miles southeast of Los Angeles.

In the June 1992 *ECR*, I wrote the following in regards to the second Los Angeles quake: "I believe the epicenter will be approximately one hundred twenty to one hundred fifty miles east-southeast of Los Angeles, with a magnitude in the range of 7.6, plus or minus four tenths of a point."

On June twenty-eighth, 1992, a massive earthquake hit

Landers, California. The magnitude was 7.5. The epicenter was one hundred thirty miles east of Los Angeles.

According to my predictions, the sequence of major Earth changes for the U.S. had begun, and many, many people were now interested in what I had to say. By now our small kitchen workspace — set up to accommodate our two-person mailing and editorial needs — had overflowed to fill our home. Seventeen people were now involved in the newsletter, not only preparing it, but also fielding the massive volume of phone calls and mail we began to receive after the California quakes. We established a company, Matrix Institute, Inc., to orchestrate the newsletter, not to mention the many projects that have been born of the public's response to our work, including my maps — the *Future Map of North America*, and the *Future Map of the World*.

As time went on, this pattern continued. The vast majority of my published warnings were occurring, though certainly, some did not. A major prediction I made that did not occur was in regards to the third Los Angeles earthquake. I predicted this would occur on May ninth, 1993, with a magnitude of 8.3. The month of May came and went with no quakes occurring in that region anywhere near the magnitude I had predicted. I reported it as a "miss" in a subsequent issue of *ECR*. I don't know why this prediction was wrong when the others had been right. Perhaps it was because I misread the visions. Or perhaps the timing was off, and this quake had yet to occur. Being specific about the date of an event is always difficult at best, and often impossible, for any futurist. Maybe the collective consciousness, warned by the first two quakes, was able to shift the reality of the third quake. In some cases, as my guides have stated, we can change events and alter the time stream through our thoughts and actions. It is very possible that prior knowledge of the first two quakes enabled people to create and focus enough positive thoughts and energy on the area to delay or lessen the magnitude of the events. In any case, it was clear to me and millions of others that something was going on with the Earth. And although I had missed on the date, I still felt the third quake would occur.

At the end of 1993, I began to sense that a quake was imminent for the Los Angeles area. In the January 1994 issue of *ECR*, which came out on January first, I stated that I expected significant quake activity on the West Coast to occur "later this month."

On January seventeenth, 1994, a massive quake hit Northridge, California. It was a vertical-thrust quake, and at least a dozen sensors in the region registered higher than 9.0, because of the unusual motion of the quake, although the average magnitude was recorded at 6.6. The quake left fifty-seven dead, eight thousand injured and exceeded $30 billion in damages, making it the most costly natural disaster in U.S. history up to that time.

Earthquakes were not the only events I foresaw in my visions. Extreme climatic disturbances, such as violent winds, tornadoes and hurricanes also figured prominently. In July 1992 one *ECR* article I wrote stated, "I have been issuing warnings from late last year and into this year that Florida will experience two hurricanes. The first will cross the Bahamas at approximately 27 degrees latitude, slamming into Florida's east coast. It will be the largest recorded in Florida's history, with winds exceeding one hundred-fifty miles per hour."

On August 24, 1992, Hurricane Andrew crossed the Bahamas, hitting Florida's southeastern coast with one hundred-fifty mile per hour winds. According to a CNN broadcast that September, Andrew was the worst natural disaster in the history of the United States. (It was surpassed seventeen months later by the Northridge quake).

The response to the information I have been able to communicate through the *Earth Changes Report* has been huge. By creating a monthly forum for my warnings, I have made it possible to get out any new information I receive in a timely manner. I can also remind readers of past predictions that I feel are imminent. Many readers have been able to use this information to act appropriately in the event of emergencies, because they were prepared for them. *ECR* now reaches thousands of subscribers worldwide, and many more people are reached through circulation amongst friends and family. Over the years we have published numerous predictions of Earth changes, as well as forecasts related to many other topics. At the end of this book I have included a listing of significant predictions which have been previously published in *ECR*.

*   *   *   *   *

Natural disasters have become a monthly, if not weekly, occurrence. Destructive weather patterns are increasing; floods are occurring in some regions, and drought in others. The subject of possible Earth changes is no longer a laughing matter, as many felt in 1982, when I first tried to share these visions publicly. A few of my most ardent critics in 1982, have contacted me in the time since, saying, "I never thought you would be right. What's next?" I can understand this disbelief, as well as the eventual changeover in thinking. Even after years of visions on this subject, I myself had trouble accepting the information. Unfortunately, the possibility of these great changes coming to pass, requiring map-makers to rechart the entire world, once seemed remote. Today, in 1997, it seems all too real.

After my successful predictions of the California earthquakes and Hurricane Andrew, we found ourselves overwhelmed with calls coming into our institute. In a single month during 1993, we handled *thirty-four thousand* calls from people inquiring about our work. I should point out that in all the time since *ECR* was launched in 1991, we have never placed a single advertisement of any kind. My guidance simply told me to put this information out, and to let spiritual powers take it from there. Media exposure was a natural outgrowth of the public interest already generated by the newsletter. Although I was hesitant when first approached, I decided — intuitively — that it was correct to accept this exposure. Through the medium of television, awareness of

Earth changes was further increased around the country. Eventually, my work was featured on programs such as NBC's prime time special, *Ancient Prophecies* and Fox television's two regular programs, *Sightings* and *Encounters*.

Of course, everyone who wrote or called us wanted to know what was going to happen in their particular geographical area. Especially in areas which my future maps showed to be unsafe, people wanted to know how long they could remain where they were. I felt their pain and fear. I had also passed through these same stages, and the memory of it was still fresh in my mind.

I explained to those who asked that what I saw was based on my visions of Earth from space. My maps were relative, not topographical. They had been carefully researched, by going through hundreds of taped sessions and compiling the data. The maps were based strictly on what I had seen repeatedly, over a span of several years. By this time, I had instituted a policy that unless I had seen a vision at least three times, no matter what the subject, I would not publish it. I hoped that by doing this, the accuracy of my information would be increased, and the amount of speculation reduced. I also explained that the purpose of the map was *not* to tell everyone to move to safe land. After all, what would really be safe land? Safety from water might be prudent, certainly. But what about wind? What about rising and falling mountains, or lack of food and medicine, or riots? The map serves only to show patterns of what I see to come. It does not show every event or disturbance that will result in the final picture. Most of all, it is not a replacement for listening to your own intuitive guides. Ultimately, only you can decide where you must be in the world, with whom, and when you must go. If these changes are coming, as I believe, we must all look inside ourselves. This is truly the best preparation.

In terms of clues, there are definite, slow changes that we can look to in the present, to see what is already happening. The Mississippi Floods of 1993 and 1995 show — in a small way — how possible it is that the Mississippi is indeed on its way to becoming the inland sea of my visions, dividing the country in half. I knew when I released the future maps that their value would be seen only after the Earth changes truly began. The time during which I released the first future map was the most difficult period of my life. I was out in the public eye, completely, and both attacks and support existed side by side. People were afraid, and I understood their fear. How could we fix this problem in such a short time period, assuming my time windows were correct? The years 1998 to 2012 were just around the corner, and many of my detractors thought I was creating panic with my information. Whenever I began to have doubts, however, my dream teachers would gently guide me back to the path. *"Awareness,"* they told me, *"Awareness is the key."* Like my vision of the three monks had shown, it was time to get people thinking and moving, to *"get them moving now!"*

As people become aware, all things become possible. Even great social change, that perhaps only a few years before might have seemed beyond comprehension, can suddenly shift into being, as people begin to see things and make decisions in a new way. Through the medium of television, over a hundred million people have seen the *Future Map of the World*. Each of those people has now received this idea, giving them the opportunity to tune into their own intuition and to decide if they feel this could be possible. I realized in the beginning that it would take some pretty big events before most people would pay attention. The Northridge, California and Kobe, Japan quakes did it for some, the Mississippi Floods have convinced others. Still, for most, it will take a much larger disaster — the two-by-four effect on a global scale — before they will begin to focus on the state of our Earth.

As with any prophecy, time is the ultimate judge. And the question remains — do we still have time to bring about a change in the probable outcome through spiritual means? The clock is ticking. I continue to be hopeful, but at the same time I have taken what I consider to be appropriate steps in the present. Cynthia and I now live in a rural setting, and we are working towards a self-sufficient lifestyle.

TOWARDS A NEW CONSCIOUSNESS

No event occurs without our prior knowledge. At other levels of consciousness we have full access to the future, as well as the past. We can choose to block this access, as I did for thirty-seven years (my awakening occurred in 1979), or we can allow our conscious self to accept our natural intuitive abilities. Each year it will become easier for all of us to access the "big computer in the sky." This is the ultimate in technology. Imagine, using elements found in the atmosphere as a storage device for memories and thoughts. Imagine further that the "terminal" required to access this super computer is already developed — the human brain.

This super computer has been called by many names. Carl Jung referred to it as the Universal Mind. The late seer Edgar Cayce referred to it as the Collective Consciousness. It has also been called the Akasha. Whatever name we give it, I am convinced that most of the information I receive comes from this wellspring of knowledge. It operates very similarly to the Internet. In fact, I believe we have been developing the Internet as a bridge to our next jump in consciousness.

Our Earth is moving through some exciting and challenging times. I do not see the end of the world. In fact, I see the birth of a new world, and a new consciousness.

I remember a vision I had some time after my Earth change nightmares. In this vision, I was shown a vibrant, living Earth. It was sometime after a pole shift had occurred. Children were laughing, the air was clear, and an Eden-like setting was everywhere. Massive changes or not, Earth did survive, and so did we. Perhaps the age-old prophecy of the millennium of peace — now only a few years away — is indeed possible. Soon, we may find ourselves in the period after the trial, when we have learned our lessons and can finally coexist peacefully with all life forms, and realizing, too, that Earth, like us, is sentient and alive.

Dealing with intuitive knowledge of Earth changes events

each day would be difficult for anyone to live with. It's tempting to leave it up to someone else — like me — to see the visions and to enjoy the benefit of the doubt, that I might be wrong. But in the end, someone else cannot tell you what you need to know. When I'm asked in interviews how I feel about what I see, I like to respond with a question. "What if one day, out of nowhere, *you* began seeing visions, only to find that what you'd seen had come true? What would *you* do? How would *you* feel?"

For me, after I finally accepted what was happening to me, I felt — and continue to feel — a sense of responsibility. In carrying out that responsibility, I rely primarily on my intuition, and I continue to "warn the people." At the same time, I truly believe that if enough people come together in consciousness, at any moment, the events I've seen can be lessened or shifted.

Who can say for certain when a pole shift will occur, or how far it will shift? And who can say when a fault begins to move whether the land will move five feet or five miles? I believe that consciousness in a community can alter such events significantly. I know consciousness can alter weather, and it makes logical sense to me that it can alter our interaction with the Earth's own electromagnetic system. After all, we each have an electromagnetic body, just as Earth does. Sure, it is very small by the Earth's standards, but there are five billion of us on Earth. That's a lot of little magnets running around!

My visions have shown me that in the early 1970s, as little as three percent of the population could have made a significant difference on the outcome of our future Earth, merely by becoming aware of our relationship to Earth. But as when using a lever to lift an object of great weight, the closer we get to the object, the more we must exert ourselves to accomplish our task. Each year, as we move closer to the predicted time of major Earth changes, the percentage of people required to enact a shift in the mass consciousness is increased. Can we achieve such a shift today? Again, as my Source says, *"All things are possible with awareness."*

In our lifetimes, we've seen the Berlin Wall come down, and

the breaking up of the Soviet Union. We've been to the moon and back. We've seen all kinds of miracles in technology and medicine. So all things are indeed possible.

In that light, I believe we have to do several things to get through these changes. We must adjust our lives accordingly, *now*, so that we can become harmonized with Earth. We must recognize the spiritual connection between this Earth we live on and ourselves. We must recognize the spiritual connection between ourselves and each other. We also need to trust our intuition, and prepare for what we feel in our hearts may come to pass. If we choose our preparations by what will truly enrich our present lives, and the changes then fail to occur, we have lost nothing; and, we invariably gain something far more precious than we had in the process.

Earth changes have occupied a major portion of my life now for over seventeen years. As a result, I have learned more than I could ever have imagined about how our planet functions as a sentient being. I have also learned about the numerous levels of reality we experience as a portion of the greater Earth consciousness. The connections between Earth, humankind, and all other life-forms, seen and unseen, never ceases to amaze me. I do not believe for one moment that the end of the world is coming — soon or even in the distant future. I do believe in cycles and change, and that we are about to experience major changes on our world, as well as changes in the perception we know as reality. I am hopeful that the course of the future is determined by the collective, as my dream guides have indicated is so. This means our daily actions and thoughts *are* our future. My Source once had this to say to me about prophecy:

Prophecy only tells you the probabilities. Who truly decides what the future will be? You do!

CHAPTER TWELVE

The Blue Star

> *As changes increase, outward signs occur, such as*
> *spiritual manifestations and signs in the heavens.*
> *One such heavenly sign is the Blue Star.*
> — Gordon-Michael Scallion
> *ECR*, March 1993

After the *Earth Changes Report* was up and running, I decided it was time to reexamine the journal notes I'd kept during my cycle of Earth changes nightmares. I thought I should look for significant elements I might have missed — early warning signs that it might be helpful to get more information about, now that I had a forum in which to share my findings with others. One of the first details that popped out at me was the small, bluish star that I had seen coming around the sun from my vantage point on Mars. What was this "blue star," I wondered? By putting the question out to my Source, I opened myself to receiving a series of dream visions showing the Blue Star's appearance in our sky. Fascinated by what my dream guides had to tell me about this startling new — or rather, very old — member of our solar system, and because it is so relevant to the Earth changes to come, I have included a summarized explanation of the Blue Star on all editions of the *Future Map of the World*. In the March 1993 issue of *ECR*, I published what information I had on the Blue Star, and its significance for the coming years

THE BLUE STAR: ITS ORIGIN

In the mid-1930s, planetary and star energies so acted upon Earth's central core, which was under stress due to twelve thousand years of old ice build-up at the poles, that the core — relative to the mantle — shifted its position. This shift was further amplified by human emotional/mental consciousness, which was at that time, relating to economic conditions then present — the global depression. With the advent of World War II and the birth of the atomic bomb came the underground and aboveground detonations that further increased the shift in the core. A wobble in the axis also began at this time. By the late fifties to early sixties, this ever so slight shift, internal to the Earth, increased — consciousness again acting as the trigger — and Earth changes may be said to have truly begun.

The Host

Prior to major Earth changes and major shifts in consciousness, spiritual forces have sent guidance to prepare us for these changes. This time period of preparation is known as Tribulation — a seven-year cycle ending in 1998. On the physical/mental level these warnings are perceived as urges from within. Later, actual warning signs may be given in the dream state. As changes increase, outward signs occur, such as spiritual manifestations and signs in the heavens. One such heavenly sign is the Blue Star.

Now, imagine a star — a blue star — that moves through the heavens in regular cycles, such as a comet. Except this celestial object is composed of pure spiritual energy; a star made manifest by spiritual forces; a star composed of light-beings. These are angels — souls of the highest level — who by their own spiritual evolution, joined together as a singular Host, to serve.

This star has moved through the heavens at various cycles, passing slowly sometimes, pausing other times, and appearing to remain still at other times. It has visited the Earth many times, most recently two thousand years ago, when it appeared briefly, moving across great expanses of time in just moments. At that time, it came to fulfill the prophecies of old and to announce the birth of the Messenger, whose task was to remind man of his divine nature. This same star also visited the Earth twelve thousand years ago, to warn the world of the coming flood — the sinking of Atlantis. Twenty-six thousand years ago, the Blue Star manifested physical members from its Host to teach the universal laws of Oneness. This brought forth a society known as the Order of Oneness, or the Law of One. Each time, the Star came because it was called, and its assistance was needed during the transitions. Once again, the Blue Star returns.

Time Shift

In the late eighties, the collective consciousness realized that Earth changes would occur unless a majority of those on the Earth could shift their individual consciousnesses. Having realized this, the collective consciousness reached out to the Blue Star for help.

Spiritual forces were asked to intervene, to delay Earth changes, thereby allowing us additional time. The Blue Star responded by blocking the interaction between human consciousness and the Earth's already stressed core, which was acting as a main trigger for Earth changes. The collective consciousness was granted an additional five years to prepare.

During those five years, teachers at many levels have worked in unison to help awaken the many so they could prepare on the mental, physical and spiritual levels for these changes. This time-delay intervention had acted like a rubber band, which when stretched to its limit has a threshold of stability. In the spring of 1992, this threshold was reached — the rubber band broke, and we ran out of time. Consciousness, once again, became the trigger for Earth changes. As a result of the time shift, the many, rather than the few, have had an opportunity to hear the message, to prepare for the coming changes, and with the coming of the Blue Star, will be able to participate in this once-in-a-lifetime spiritual experience fully aware.

His Light Is Seen

During Tribulation, this Blue Star will be seen in the heavens for all who have eyes to see. From a scientific point of view it will seem that a new star crossed the heavens and reached the outer fringes of this system in a moment of time. This star, the domain of angelic beings, shall reach out to all who reside on Earth, both physical and non-physical. The hearts and minds of all who are ready to accept their divinity shall transform as if in a flash. At first many will reject this phenomenon, but as the Light bathes all in this realm of existence, more shall awaken. Before 1998, all will have seen the Light and many will experience higher spiritual vibrations. This shall fulfill the prophecies of old — His Light shall be seen in the clouds.

The Changes

As the Earth comes under the influence of the Blue Star, people will experience many physical changes. The human body will become more sensitive as a result of the new vibrations;

the Earth's frequency doubles to over fifteen cycles per second. With this new sensitivity, many will "feel" the coming changes. These feelings may be used as an early warning system. Pressures and palpitations in the heart may be felt days or weeks prior to the Earth changes. This is a reaction to the shifted electromagnetic fields that are precursors to Earth movements. Electrical sensations in the limbs and spinal column, cramps in the muscular networks, flu-like symptoms, migraine headaches, intense dreams — many of which will be actual warnings rather than symbolic in nature — will be a result of the body's sensitivity to Earth changes. As each becomes more "in-tune" with the Earth, the sensitivity and reaction to the Earth will build. The physical body has already begun to change as a result of the new and changing vibrations, and the subtle bodies are almost completely changed. All life, all kingdoms, shall change as a result. A new light-body is being created.

As the light of the Blue Star permeates the Earth, greater intuitive abilities emerge, as well as healing abilities. An ability best described as "a knowing" shall be experienced by the many rather than the few. With each passing year, these abilities shall increase tenfold, through 1997. Inner urges to become more compassionate, more giving, more loving, shall fill all as the Blue Star shines down upon us. All that is needed to move through these times shall be given.

During the last such major shift, some eleven thousand six hundred years ago, only a handful heeded the warnings. How many will this time? As the collective consciousness shifts, so shall the Earth shift. Old lands shall go beneath the sea to be cleansed, and new lands, clean, fresh and restored, shall rise to support life. New animals, never before seen on the Earth, shall emerge after the changes, as will new plants to be used for healing. Many new elements brought up from the central core of the Earth will allow new non-violating technologies to emerge — all for humankind's use during the millennium of peace. All children born after 1998 shall be telepathic at birth, and many born prior to this shall exhibit such abilities. The physical body shall change to reflect the vibrational changes of Earth under the influence of the Blue Star. The vibrations and colors that govern Earth shall change as a result of Earth changes. Blue, violet and indigo shall rule the next cycle, and the next root race.

When one looks into the sky, two suns shall be present, not one. The new addition will be the small Blue Star, visible in the horizon during the day, and brighter than the brightest evening star or planet. All races of people shall have a bluish tint to the skin as a result. Eyes become cat-like in order to adjust to the new atmosphere and light, with vision becoming both a physical and non-physical sense. Those who choose, shall be able to communicate at will with animals and the other kingdoms, as well as the spirit world. The life span shall be two hundred years — one hundred fifty years of age will be like being fifty today. Rejuvenation techniques using Earth's storehouse shall further extend the life span. All the plagues of the nineties shall be gone, including AIDS. Love shall fill the places where before, hate dwelled. Laughter shall be heard in every corner of the world — children responding to love and joy. This is the true "coming," the Great Awakening, the age of the Blue Star. These are indeed blessed times.

OTHER SEERS PREDICT BLUE STAR

Shortly after publishing my information about the Blue Star, I learned of an ancient Hopi prophecy that is very similar to what I had received. It was told to me as follows:

> *When the Blue Star Kachina makes its appearance in the heavens, the Fifth World will emerge. This will be preceded by the last great war, a spiritual conflict with material matters. Material matters will be destroyed by spiritual beings, who will remain to create one world and one nation, under one power, that of the Creator.*

The Maya have a similar prophecy, as do many other cultures. In the November 1995 issue of *ECR*, we published an article that spoke about different variations on the prophecy of the Blue Star. The following examples of other visionaries' descriptions of the event at hand are excerpted from that article:

> Recent presentations of Mary's messages have said that a new sun will be added to our heavens as part of the evolutionary process.
>
> The Ramala readings of the 1970s predicted that Earth changes would begin with a "Fiery Messenger," a star of great power proceeding towards our solar system.
>
> In the sixteenth century, Nostradamus predicted the coming of a great star that "will burn for seven days at a time, when the sun will appear double."
>
> Four centuries earlier, the German mystic Hildegarde predicted that "a great nation" would endure earthquakes, storms, and huge waves of water when a great comet passed over.
>
> The legends of the Hopi teach that the Creator told one man and his family to travel west. They were led by a dancing Blue Star Kachina, which quit its dancing when they reached the land they were to settle on.
>
> Sun Bear — of the Ojibwa tribe of North America — has reported that the Hopi were also told the Blue Star Kachina would return and dance in their village. Happily, Hildegarde also predicted an age of peace after the great comet.

Does the fact that these prophecies have survived through the ages prove that they have major significance in our lives? Could the Blue Star be so important to our times that its presence may affect our development and perhaps even our existence? Only time will tell.

*   *   *   *   *

What I present next is an inner-world experience on the subject of the Blue Star that occurred in the summer of 1995 and was published in the August 1995 issue of *ECR*.

GMS: Please explain the following repeating vision I've been seeing since 1979. In the vision, I observed our solar system, that is our sun with all its planets, revolving around another sun — orange in color. As I viewed this movement, a small, blue star appeared from behind our sun.

Source: *This is to be. This solar system shall become a binary sun system, when the Blue Star returns.*

GMS: How will this come about?

Source: *All spheres have a cycle. For some — like Earth's cycle around the sun — it is relatively short, in this case 365 days. For others the cycle is long, measured in thousands and millions of years. Now, the sun also has a cycle with other spheres. As it moves across the known and unknown heavens, it comes under the influence of other suns, also on their journeys. What you were shown, relative to the Blue Star, was this star coming into this solar system, making it a binary sun system for a period of time.*

GMS: Is this time period related to the previously prophesied "millennium of peace"?

Source: *It is.*

GMS: Does the Blue Star remain after this period?

Source: *As part of its cycle, it shall disappear behind the sun once more. Though it shall be visible for one thousand eight hundred years, in total, and then a new cycle begins.*

GMS: What will the Blue Star look like during the day and evening?

Source: *During the day it will appear as a silvery light, one hundred times brighter than the morning star, so as to require a new Magnitude scale.* (ed. note: In astronomy, Magnitude refers to brightness.) *During the evening, it will appear as a moon.*

GMS: Please explain the significance of my vision which showed our solar system revolving around the orange-colored sun.

Source: *Just as the moon is held in orbit by the relationship of the Earth and the sun to it, our sun is held in orbit by a companion sun.*

GMS: Please define companion.

Source: *The companion maintains the pulse, establishing those influences which maintain the sun's orbit.*

GMS: Is the Blue Star a companion to our sun?

Source: *No, the Blue Star is a companion to Sirius B.*

GMS: If the companion star is not the Blue Star, then what is the companion star?

Source: *Arcturus.*

GMS: And what is the significance of being shown this companion star?

Source: *These influences shall govern the next root race.*

GMS: How is this possible? Arcturus is so far away compared to the distance of our Earth to the sun.

Source: *Distance is only a portion of the dynamic at work here. Alignment between spheres is the greater portion. See it in this way. Our sun governs all in its system, including the Earth. What occurs with the sun, such as sun spots, magnetic shifts, and its rotation, affects all life, and all spheres in this system. The aurora borealis, or northern lights, is one such visible effect that often disrupts electrical power systems — satellites — as well as animals and humans.*

Now these effects occur on the sun, which is millions of miles away, yet they affect the Earth nonetheless. Just as the Earth is affected by this sun, this sun is affected by other suns. At key times, or cycles, the position of the sun, relative to its companion, is affected in varying ways. Its emanations rise and ebb as a result of inner and outer influences. This in turn causes other spheres, in this system and in others, to adjust accordingly.

GMS: This sounds like astrology.

Source: *Astrology is based upon these principles.*

GMS: How will the Blue Star and Arcturus affect the astrology chart?

Source: *As the Blue Star enters this part of the heavens, the chart-ing of same can give added guidance, for this new sun shall have a great effect on the soul. Remember, astrology only indicates potential patterns, or forces at work. It is the entity alone who determines the outcomes — free will.*

Just as the moon governs the emotional body, and the sun governs the personality, the Blue Star shall govern the soul. Do not misun-derstand here. It is not that the moon, sun and other planets do not affect the soul currently, they do. But the Blue Star shall affect them differently. The soul learns from its experiences through physical incarnations, as well as non-physical. In the very near future, with the addition of another sun in this part of the heavens, a new effect shall be added to the matrix. The vibrations given off by the Blue Star will enable the soul to have an easier time in communication with its host.

GMS: Are you saying in the near future people on the Earth will be able to consciously communicate with their souls?

Source: *They can now. They have always been able to. However, most turned away as the human spirit descended deeper into physi-cal matter and the material world held a greater interest than the spiritual world. This changes shortly, as the new millennium heralds in a time of rebirth. Man shall walk hand-in-hand with God once again.*

GMS: Everyone?

Source: *All that are able to return during the New Age.*

GMS: Some will not be able to return?

Source: *The Blue Star and new vibrations on the Earth and sun shall create a new matrix, or vibration. Where today, for example, all may enter the Earth; shortly only those who have developed the nec-essary spiritual matrix shall find entrance into the Earth.*

GMS: What governs this matrix?

Source: *Those rays coming and going from the Earth. Currently there are seven in number, following the present prismatic spectrum.*

GMS: And in the next millennium?

Source: *There will be three.*

GMS: Are these to be new rays or existing ones?

Source: *Three remain — blue, violet and indigo.*

GMS: How does this influence the cycle of reincarnation?

Source: *It changes, or limits, the opportunities. Whereas currently, with so many rays present, any entity may enter the Earth through birth or other means, in the future only those who have attuned their spirit form to those rays present at that time, shall find entrance into the Earth.*

GMS: What happens to those who have not developed the necessary vibrations?

Source: *They shall find opportunities for lessons in newly created realms. Should they develop the necessary vibration in those places, then it will be possible for them to enter into the new Earth.*

HALE-BOPP

THE COMET OF THE MILLENNIUM

Just after publication of the August 1995 issue of *ECR*, which featured the dialogue on the Blue Star excerpted above, it was announced that two amateur astronomers had sighted what is being referred to as "the comet of the millennium." Since then, many people have asked questions about the comet and are wondering if this could be the Blue Star of my earlier prophecies. To speak to those concerns, we published an informational article about the comet in the September 1995 issue, of which the following is an excerpt:

> At first astronomers thought it was a new comet, "the brightest in twenty years," according to an article in the Washington Post. Named Comet Hale-Bopp, after the two amateur astronomers who — independent of each other — discovered it on the twenty-third of July, 1995, this bright light is located near the Sagittarius constellation. Now, in an article in *The Australian*, Dr. Duncan Steel of the Anglo-Australian Observatory (AAO) in New South Wales says that Hale-Bopp is not

a new comet, but that it has been here before, approximately every few thousand years. "This means humankind must have seen it before, one would imagine," he said. Rob McNaught of the AAO plotted the comet's course back in time and was able to identify it as a faint image on film taken in April 1993. With this information, Dr. Brian Marsden, a Harvard University astronomer, calculates that the comet would make its closest approach to the sun in April 1997. As it comes closer it should be possible to more accurately calculate the date of its last visit to within ten or twenty years. Dr. Marsden said, "It could become the comet of the millennium as it comes towards the sun over the next year or two."

Astronomers have estimated Comet Hale-Bopp to be a thousand times larger than Comet Halley, and large enough to shine in daylight as it comes closer to Earth. Dr. Steel said Hale-Bopp "is, indeed, a bloody huge comet." He says that his "best guess at this stage is that it did come from the Oort cloud, but has passed through the planetary region once, twice, or a few times, with the effect of the planets having been to slow it down slightly, reducing the eccentricity of its orbit."

THE MESSENGER RETURNS

Many people continued to believe Hale-Bopp to be the Blue Star of my prophecies. In the May 1997 issue of *ECR*, I wrote the following editorial, regarding my feelings on the Blue Star:

I believe that every nation and every person is given free access to view the future and be made aware of those signs that indicate cycles for specific events to occur. We are now almost through my predicted time frame for Tribulation, and Comet Hale-Bopp has made its appearance. I believe this comet to be the Blue Star Messenger.

According to NASA astrophysicist Michael Mumma, Comet Hale-Bopp is the largest comet ever, bright as an evening star. It has an elliptical orbit of about four thousand two hundred years, which intersects the plane of our solar system at key times. I believe the last time an intersection occurred was two thousand years ago, about the time of the Wise Men's journey to Bethlehem. If you've recently seen the comet, you might imagine what the Wise Men, students of the stars, thought as they observed a star streaking across the sky seeming to point in a direction to follow.

I believe with all my heart and soul that we are once again experiencing the Messenger Star, whose task it is to signal the beginning of our next spiritual awakening and the millennium of peace. I will make a new prediction here regarding this subject. I believe that between 1998 and 2001, everyone with eyes to see and ears to hear will experience a spiritual event that parallels the event that occurred two thousand years ago. How will this awakening occur? Will a spiritual leader bring the message, or will it be a collective experience? I believe both will occur. I do not believe the Messenger comes to warn us of the end of the world, though we will certainly hear this from others as we approach the end of this millennium, especially with daily Earth changes now occurring.

Now, two thousand years after the last Messenger appeared in our sky, our world is on the brink of cataclysm. Each day forty or more wars rage on in our world, nuclear weapons are still stockpiled, and plagues are on the rise. In early April of 1997, the World Health Organization issued an alarming alert on the rise of both new and old diseases, previously thought to be in check. As a civilization we have turned away from basic spiritual truths in favor of material gratification. A shift in consciousness *must* occur, and perhaps — as my visions have indicated — the Messenger announcing such changes has arrived.

During the last passage of this comet messenger, a Master was born who would later teach how this was possible. His message:

You are all divine. Love one another. Honor all life.

CHAPTER THIRTEEN

The Visitors

STAR BEINGS

Since 1982, I have been receiving information that said "signs" would come to indicate that we are not alone in this vast universe. And in 1987, I started getting specific information on crop circles. During previous sessions with clients, I had been asked repeatedly to respond on the issue of extraterrestrial life. Or more accurately, my Source has been asked repeatedly. The range of the questions is broad: Are we being visited by aliens from other worlds? If so, are they time travelers? Are there good aliens and bad aliens? What is the truth about abductions? What about crop circles and other unexplained phenomena? And the list goes on.

This was not a subject I had any strong personal interest in, especially early on. I was having enough trouble just dealing with what was going on in my own head, let alone what was going on in outer space. Eventually though, the information my teachers shared, as well as my firsthand experiences with certain phenomena, would convince me that there was more to this subject than I'd at first thought. The questions about extraterrestrial life continued to come up with such frequency that in 1993, I finally decided to conduct a session with my Source on this specific topic. The following is taken from the transcript of that dialogue:

CK: You have said before that in the ancient past — just prior to cataclysms — visitors from the stars came to give us warnings. You have also predicted that there will be "landings." Are these two events tied together?

GMS: *Do not think in terms of aliens descending from spacecraft, bringing forth a document forecasting when and where Earth changes will occur. The process used is telepathic. This is not to occur in the future. Rather it is, and has been, occurring for years. Also, do not confuse the increase of abductions and sightings with the messengers we speak of. These messengers are predominately from the Pleiades and Sirius. Their form is not necessarily physical but can be. Form is chosen by thought. They can appear as light, a physical object, a being, or an inner world telepathic messenger. As messengers, they send out telepathic waves to those on Earth who are open to the contact.*

CK: Who or what determines the contact?

GMS: *The soul force.*

CK: The soul of the contactee?

GMS: *Yes, each soul experiences life after life in human form on Earth, as well as life after life in non-physical form. The latter can be on any planet, moon, sun, or other plane of existence in this sphere of understanding. In addition, contained within each solar system is a matrix made up of inner-planes of existence. This sun system contains eight inner-planes, for example. Upon physical death, an entity will pass through, or remain on, these planes prior to a reentrance into the Earth. It is from past experiences on these planes that many connections are made with what is now termed extra terrestrials.*

CK: So contacts are made in the inner worlds first, then telepathically to those open to such a contact.

GMS: *Yes.*

CK: How long have these contacts been going on?

GMS: *Millions of years on Earth: In recorded history, during great wars, during the time of the Moses and the great teachers — Jesus, Buddha, Zoroaster, and others. In recorded myth, just prior to the last great flood and partial pole shift, some seventy-five hundred years ago. And before that, during the final days of the Atlantean world, some eleven thousand six hundred years ago.*

CK: Are there other times when these messengers come to Earth?

GMS: *Between ages, to assist in the transition.*

CK: Such as the shift from the Age of Pisces to the Age of Aquarius?

GMS: *Yes, as is occurring presently. Not all transitions of ages are accompanied by Earth changes. Often they are accompanied by shifts in consciousness.*

CK: You mentioned that there many visitors from different stars. Is there life on any of the other planets in our solar system?

GMS: *Not in the physical.*

CK: In what form then?

GMS: *Spirit. The soul can choose a specific planet for specific lessons. For example, Mars has two levels of consciousness where the soul can attempt to learn how to deal with conflicts.*

CK: Are you saying there once was life on Mars and that the soul sojourns to Mars to recall and experience these lives?

GMS: *There was once physical life on Mars, reptilian-humanoid in form, as part of a group of souls' early experiments in physical form.*

CK: In myth, Mars is known as the red planet, and planet of war. Was it destroyed by planetary disruptions similar to our Earth changes?

GMS: *In part. Great wars occurred on Mars, which subsequently caused volcanic and seismic disruptions. The combination totally destroyed the planet's surface.*

CK: Did any survive the wars and geological changes?

GMS: *Those who were able to leave survived.*

CK: Where did they go?

GMS: *Earth.*

CK: Are there messengers here from other planets?

GMS: *Yes, but at many different developmental levels. Those from the Sirius and Pleiades systems may be thought of as evolved souls. They were known as gods by many cultures. Others are not as evolved, seeing only a portion of the whole. Again, a focused experience.*

CK: What about the inner planes of existence you spoke of? Are there messengers at those levels?

GMS: *Yes. Most sightings come from these realms.*

CK: Please explain that.

GMS: *The Earth has eight realms. Each realm may be seen as another Earth, with each one being less dense. The second realm — the world of spirits — may be seen by clairvoyants. At the fifth realm, or plane, resides the Ethereans. These are souls who, between incarnations on Earth, have so developed in soul experience that they can assist others in passing through the various planes. Guides would be a good word here. Not all guides are from this plane, however.*

Now, the reality in the fifth realm is one of mind over matter. What is thought by a collective body of souls becomes a reality. Technology exists at this level, just as it does on our level of Earth, different vibrations, however. From their perspective, physical reality is no different than ours. When the time-windows are correct, their craft — which we witness as UFOs — can move between levels and materialize on our Earth, so to speak. This is why many of the sightings of objects seem to change color, size and shape, or disappear. They cannot remain in this reality for long, or they become subject to the laws of this dimension and perish.

CK: Why are there visitations from the Ethereans?

GMS: *To increase awareness of life in other dimensions, or realities. With the coming Earth changes, many will find themselves in this realm. All are part of the great Awakening, the coming.*

CK: Are the crop circles seen in England and elsewhere from this dimension?

GMS: *In part. In order for messengers from the Pleiades and Sirius to enter Earth, they too must pass through Earth's realms. Remember, they are not physical beings. In order to do this they work with the Ethereans. It becomes a joint effort.*

CK: How are the circles made?

GMS: *Some are false, created by some to express personal egos. Most are created by highly-charged spheres of light, so compressed as to emit strong gravitational and magnetic fields, and of such strength as to distort time. The spheres move in stylus fashion, creating the messages.*

CK: Messages?

GMS: *They say "You are not alone," and "We have always been here," or "The time portal is now open," and so on. Each symbol is a language of the higher mind. This language is known to all on Earth. So at the higher levels of consciousness, each receives the message. As we move closer to the greater changes in these next few years, the messengers will increase the number of contacts, and we will see a rise in the number of messages left in fields.*

The messages will begin shortly to appear on other structures — in clouds, on rocks, even as birthmarks on newborn children. The messengers will continue to assist in increasing awareness of the changes that are coming, not only geophysically, but spiritually. It is important to remember, there is no death. The physical may fall away, but the soul force is immortal.

* * * * *

In order to seek additional information on visitors from other worlds, I was next led to explore the peculiar phenomenon of crop circles. I had an intuitive sense that extraterrestrial intelligences were indeed responsible for them, but I wanted to get more information than my Source had given me. Often, if I go to the site of a particular event that has occurred, I can receive additional intuitive insights about the history or future of the place. I decided to find out all I could about the crop circle phenomena by going to see them for myself.

CROP CIRCLES: Hoax? Real? Both?

CAMBRIDGE, ENGLAND — One of the most complex crop circle formations yet seen has mysteriously appeared in a wheat field south of Cambridge, in the small community of Barley, near Royston. According to a previously published report, Mrs. Sian Wombwell, an agronomist by trade for some fifteen years, and a graduate biologist, investigated the circles. "I stood in the middle of it. It was quite astonishing," she said. "If this was a hoax it was extraordinarily clever. We know it arrived overnight in a field of wheat thirty inches tall. It would have required floodlights to carry it out. It was incredibly precise. Each circle was perfect, the wheat flattened clockwise, and at the base of the heart it tapered down to a single stalk of wheat. Every stock had been flattened [to exactly] one quarter an inch above the ground."

What may make this Barley circle special is the fact that it resembles the Mandelbrot set — a computer-generated figure created out of the theory of "chaos mathematics."

According to *Today*, in September, two men from England held a news conference in which they announced that they had been perpetrating one of the planet's greatest hoaxes. Using boards attached to their feet, they claimed they would sneak into crop fields around the southwest portion of England and create those incredible circles and designs that have been showing up in England and other parts of the world for several years. It was all a great hoax, they said, a fun thing to do. Pat Delgado — engineer, crop circle investigator, and author of several books on crop circles — was asked to check out their claims and meet with the hoaxers. The hoaxers showed up, but then chose not to be confronted by Mr. Delgado.

Mr. Delgado has investigated numerous circles, and admits some of them are indeed hoaxes. How can he tell? Well, for one thing, some circles are created as a result of a downward compression of the crop, such as would occur by stomping on the plants with boards. But the majority of circles are created by more complex, or mysterious, means. In these, the crop material is bent over in a spiral fashion. The wheat is not broken, and it continues to grow to full maturity in the direction it was spun in. In addition, residues of magnetic forces have been measured at these sites. So what is the story? Who is creating the rest of these circles, if they were not created by the English hoaxers, with their simple board-stomping technique?

— The *Earth Changes Report*, October 1991

CROP CIRCLES & THE ETHEREANS

I can't say for sure that I have ever seen an unidentified flying object, or experienced a close encounter, except within the realms of my own mind. My introduction to crop circles, however, was another matter entirely. I found the idea that these massive signatures upon the Earth might be evidence of intelligent beings attempting to communicate with our race truly profound. So powerful was my feeling about this, in fact, that I was compelled to travel to England with my family, to witness the crop circles myself, and to see what I could gather intuitively on the subject.

* * * * *

My family and I went to England to check out the phenomena firsthand in 1993. Our destination was the site of previous crop circle manifestations — the Avebury and Stonehenge areas. No new circles showed up while we were there. Soon after we left, however, several materialized, some with incredible designs and many occurring on the same evening, although many hundreds of miles apart. Some even appeared in other countries on that same night. I commented to Cynthia, "These hoaxers with boards on their feet sure do get around!"

What we did see at Alton Barnes, which is not too far from Avebury, was an imprint in this year's new crop field. It looked like a shadow in the field, except the shadow had the same intricate design that had appeared there the year before, even though the fields had been plowed this year and reseeded. I found this to be very significant. Somehow last year's crop circle pattern had been imprinted into the soil. This did not lend itself to the theory that human pranksters were simply going out at night and mashing the crops flat with simple tools. Some greater forces, I felt, had to be at work.

Although it's true that I receive communications from many levels of consciousness, most come through visions brought into my awareness through the conduit of my subconscious mind. At times, however, direct communications occur with other intelligences. While I was in England studying the crop circle phenomenon, I experienced this second type of communication. It was the first in a series of contacts I had from a group which identified themselves as "Ethereans." Through them, I received answers to many of my questions about the mysterious crop circles I had seen evidence of with my own eyes, and read about with increasing frequency through the eighties and nineties:

GMS: Which star system are you from?
Ethereans: *We are from the Earth system.*
GMS: Are you speaking of another time, or dimension?
Ethereans: *Vibration would be a more correct definition. You know this realm as the upper mental, or fifth, Earth realm. Just as spirits dwell in a parallel Earth, separated by vibration, so do we. Only vibration separates us from your world. For example, it is like viewing a drop of blood with the naked eye. This same drop can be magnified so that the world of invisible cells may be seen. If you could continue to magnify an object eventually you would reach the point that in order to magnify further you would no longer use an optical system, but rather a system of light, so magnified and condensed in form, as to view another vibration. At this level of viewing, time as you know it becomes bent, having neither past, present or future to the viewer, only a blending of these.*
GMS: How is it possible for me to communicate with you?
Ethereans: *We are a purely mental consciousness, having no specific form. The human brain has the capacity to so establish a matrix — chemically and electrically — to enable the mind, through the brain, to tune to these vibrations. The dream state is such a connection. We communicate directly with your mind.*
GMS: Why are you choosing to contact me?
Ethereans: *You are open and receptive to such contacts.*
GMS: Can you tell me more about your world? Do you consider it a world different from ours?

Ethereans: *All realms are worlds unto themselves — different from your physical world, but comprised of souls who are developing spiritually, just as they are on your physical world. Those of us here are only passing through. One day each of you will pass through our world. Experience, or development, determines the length of stay, though time is measured much differently here. Once a state of development, or attunement, is achieved, we are free to pass on to other worlds. We may return to the physical Earth, another of Earth's seven vibrational levels, or another sphere within this sun system.*

GMS: Do you have physical-looking bodies?

Ethereans: *We do not require sight, thus there is no need for physical appearances. For example, you require an optical system to convey images to the optic nerve, and then to that portion of the brain that processes images. Our process is one whereby experiences occur directly in our minds, where we process all experiences. We are a thought race; we operate in groups, but are capable of individual thoughts as well. It would be like being in a room with seven people, with the ability to listen to each other's thoughts, communicate with each other, and have individual thoughts — to do all of this simultaneously.*

GMS: Are the images you receive by your process similar to images we receive in the physical world?

Ethereans: *Similar in that images that were experienced while on the Earth can be carried over to our world. However, images are not processed in the same way. Symbols are our language. A symbol, for example, would convey perhaps what might take a chapter or even a book, in your world, to convey the same meaning.*

GMS: So can I assume that at your level of consciousness, Earthly desires are not present?

Ethereans: *Yes and no, both.*

We answer affirmative in that our purpose is to perfect the mind in such a way as to free the soul from Earthly desires. All development, at all levels, is for the perfection of the soul. Each level gives the soul a specific opportunity to develop, for it is the desire of most souls to become closer to, or one with, the Universal Mind.

We answer negative in that our sojourn to this plane of existence carries with it those experiences emotionally charged from prior Earthly sojourns. These emotions can often create thought forms of physical cravings that are to be worked on while here. As stated, our world is one of group thoughts, so any thought becomes a portion of the collective group whether it be a thought group of three — the smallest group, or many times that number — multiples of three.

GMS: Do you have contact with other worlds besides the physical Earth?

Ethereans: *All here may communicate with those levels below ours. For some, contact with other intelligences in other star systems is possible.*

GMS: What other worlds are you in contact with?

Ethereans: *Those who were a portion of the earlier root races on Earth — Pleiades and Sirius.*

GMS: Are you in contact with others besides myself here on Earth?

Ethereans: *All that can see our messages.*

GMS: Please explain this.

Ethereans: *We have developed, through our minds, a technology which allows us to travel to other dimensions or levels. Those symbols found in your crop fields that are of such controversy are created by us in conjunction with other intelligences — the Pleiadeans.*

GMS: Are you referring to the crop circles?

Ethereans: *Yes.*

GMS: Why are the Pleiadeans involved in this communication, and not just your world?

Ethereans: *The seeds of this world are from that world. They are your ancestors. and like parents, look over their children with love and concern.*

GMS: I know many people would like to know just how the crop circles are created. Many have been found to be man-made.

Ethereans: *A portion are made by those who struggle to accept their own spiritual identity. The majority are genuine — those that are found to contain magnetic residues from our imaging process.*

To create the symbols, we establish a matrix between our worlds

— a time portal, if you will. Once established, we are able to construct, out of your atmosphere, any object we desire using your known — and unknown — elements. In this case we create a small sphere of red plasma — a stylus, and project it to a favorable magnetic grid region of Earth where we are able to leave our messages.

GMS: Is the cause of the circle formations due to magnetism?

Ethereans: *Correct. The physical cause.*

GMS: Who or what is causing the circles?

Ethereans: *The circles are created by spiritual forces visiting the Earth from the sixth sister of the Pleiades.*

GMS: Are you saying that these are UFOs from the Pleiades?

Ethereans: *Some are craft in your physical sense. Circle craft, as well as other shapes. Most, however, are created by light, magnetically condensed, pulsed and focused in the shape of a sphere. This light is robotically guided by intelligences. In fact, the light is an extension of those intelligences.*

GMS: How does the light sphere create the circles?

Ethereans: *Once the light is created by the intelligences, much as you would create a laser beam, it then selects the area to draw its message. It hovers over an area selected, and descends on the area moving in circular patterns, much as an engraving machine would create an identification bracelet, scribing and then raising up and moving to another area, descending and scribing again.*

GMS: Why are the Pleiadeans creating these symbols?

Ethereans: *They are trying to communicate with their children. They are your ancestors. Slowly, they are opening up the world's consciousness to their existence.*

GMS: What do the circles and symbols mean?

Ethereans: *The circles and shapes are notes, or sounds, containing messages that are not audible within the dynamics of human hearing, but are audible to the subtle bodies of each. Each form contains a specific message. Each message is created by varying the size, shape, width and orientation of the symbol, relative to Polaris. Many are prophecies for this decade of changes. Some are star locations, broadcasting times, or windows. All are a portion of the universal language of the stars. Each knows, at inner levels, their message.*

GMS: Does our government and other governments know of these communications?

Ethereans: *Yes.*

GMS: Why has our government suppressed this information? And for how long have they done so?

Ethereans: *Initially it was for power, an attempt to obtain new means of military superiority. Later, some craft were obtained as a result of accidental crashes, and later some were downed by missiles. Now, it is important to note that the Pleiadeans are not the only visitors to Earth. Many are from other stars and have more physical craft, unlike the Pleiadeans. The U.S. government has known of the existence of these since the twenties. It was not until your American scientists began working on invisibility — using extremely high pulsed electromagnetism — during the second World War, that they had contact. Later, in 1947, they had physical evidence, not only of craft, but of life forms as well.*

CROP CIRCLES DECODED

Upon returning back to the United States from our trip to England, I felt super-charged — my mind raced whenever I thought of the crop circle phenomenon. I had so many questions! I couldn't wait to continue my conversations with the Ethereans, hoping to fill in the blanks from our previous sessions.

GMS: You mentioned that the technology you use to create these circles is a "magnetic lens" system that enables you to create symbols in the crop fields of specific Earth grids. Was this done in ancient times as well?

Ethereans: *Yes. Stonehenge, Avebury, and other sites were built where our symbols appeared.*

GMS: What was the purpose?

Ethereans: *To awaken your race to our existence, our mutual responsibilities, and our mutual source — our divinity.*

GMS: I have received photographs of crop circles created during the 1995 season. Is there a collective meaning to these?

Ethereans: *Yes. Changes are now occurring in your world. These act first as distortions in the time-space fabric that makes up our dimension, as well. In your world, these distortions would be akin to Earth changes. The messages convey the overview of the situation, the scenario, which applies now to your Earth.*

GMS: Why are these changes now occurring in your world?

Ethereans: *Before changes actually happen in your world, they take place in our dimension first. See our world as an outer layer of your world, with each layer being a portion of the other. Your Earth's vibration is the most dense, and the "Akasha" layer, or dimension, is the lightest. A good image here is to see seven separate pictures of the Earth spread out in a row, with each Earth lighter in color and detail than the next.*

GMS: How many dimensions are there?

Ethereans: *Eight, including the Akasha, also termed the collective consciousness.*

GMS: By going through these photographs, could you explain some of these crop circle patterns to me individually, to clarify their meanings?

Ethereans: *Yes, but first let us look to the collective meaning you asked about earlier.*

We have entered a cycle in our combined worlds where actions outside your world are beginning to affect our world. To this end, we

Stonehenge

have presented a series of symbols to your world, that when under-stood from the physical standpoint, will enable your scientists to bet-ter understand the triggers for changes that have begun in your world. Our combined worlds, the very existence and structure of life forms, are governed by activity of the sun. This source, the giver of all life, radiates its energies in cyclical patterns.

Solar-magnetic cycles — pole shifts — occur at the eleven thou-sand six hundred year interval, with lesser cycles occurring at har-monic sub-junctures in the greater cycle. A full magnetic reversal would regularly occur on the sun in the year 2012. However, due to the expansion of thought forms and nuclear activity in your world, this cycle has been modified, and now occurs earlier, before prepara-tions are completed. But knowing these cycles can enable shifts to occur in your world, so that the cycle can be corrected. In doing so, preparation will be facilitated in our combined worlds. The effect of such a solar reversal brings great changes to our combined worlds, making for new seasons, and indeed, new species.

Now, as to the meaning of each individual symbol, present those of interest to you, and we will begin.

GMS: I am overwhelmed. I'm having some difficulty focus-ing on my original intent. So many questions fill my mind!

Ethereans: *Much will follow. Present your first photo.*

GMS: The Litchfield, Hampshire wheat field in England.

Ethereans: *The center of the rings represents the Earth, with each of its vibrations or levels of consciousness. Ours is the fifth ring. The field surrounding the rings represents the Earth force, or night side force. The opening represents a break in the field due to various cycles, such as the solstice and equinox positions, eclipses, and the solar pole shifts. Again, the purpose is to show — symbolically — cycles that affect our combined worlds.*

GMS: The barley crop at Telegraph Hill, near Winchester, Hampshire England.

Ethereans: *The center is once again the physical Earth. The next ring represents the orbit path of the moon — showing the moon's four extreme magnetic-effect points.*

GMS: Does this relate to gravity, tides, et cetera?

Ethereans: *The moon does not control the tides, it only modifies*

Litchfield Crop Circle

Telegraph Hill Crop Circle

them. It is the rotation of Earth and exchange of solar forces at the equator that creates the tides.

GMS: West Overton, Wiltshire England. An oil-seed-rape crop.

Ethereans: *This shows the interaction between lunar phases and the Earth force.*

GMS: What energy system is used for the Earth force or night side force, and are these the same thing?

Ethereans: *The same. As the Earth moves from day to night, the atmosphere correspondingly charges and discharges, much as a battery — or more properly, a capacitor — would. Knowing then the frequency of this force, as well as the cycles and positions of the sun and moon, a system can be — has been — developed to utilize this reservoir of solar force.*

GMS: Has been?

Ethereans: *In Earth's ancient times, some twelve thousand years before your time, and at the turn of the twentieth century in the United States.*

GMS: Is the moon responsible for earthquakes, as has been presented to me in visions?

West Overton Crop Circle

Ethereans: *Often it may be a trigger, but it is not the cause. If a specific portion of the Earth's tectonic system is weak, and if the position of the Earth relative to Mars is in a specific alignment, and if the lunar path is such that it passes near such a stressed area while Mars is in the same sky, then magnetic forces can act to trigger chemical reactions along fault lines, thereby causing a quake.*

GMS: A chemical trigger?

Ethereans: *Yes. Magnetic waves from planets, the moon, the sun, and stars, combine to modulate waves in your atmosphere. Because of their long wavelength, these waves pass easily through the Earth to fault regions, where they can ignite combustible gases, which are present as a result of the chemical reaction from tectonic pressure.*

GMS: Explain Cowdown, a wheat crop circle near Andover, Hampshire England.

Ethereans: *This symbol represents the Earth, with its expanded magnetic field ringing out to other dimensions. The second ring represents our world — in it we are saying, "We Are Here." The final ring indicates the Akasha, or eighth dimension. The pattern of the ringing represents the vibrational shift from the outermost level, the Akasha, to innermost, the physical Earth. Each level becomes lighter*

Cowdown Crop Circle

in vibration, as you move from the physical Earth outward. But from the perspective of distance, all levels are interconnected. The main purpose of this symbol is to show how occurrences on the physical Earth move quickly through all levels of vibrations, like a bell reverberating. What you do on Earth will pass through all worlds.

Once the awareness of other life forms is discovered and accepted by your world, then it may be possible to improve all of our worlds. Each step increases the awareness of the inter-relationship between all life. The statement, "As above, so below" came from our world to remind the people of Earth of their divinity, and their relationship to each other. We are all One.

* * * * *

Since these dialogues with the Ethereans in 1993, I have had no further contact. I can only assume this to be because all that needed to be shared had been given, or at least, all that could be comprehended by us at the present time. Meanwhile, crop circles continue to appear around the world with increasing frequency. Undoubtedly, some of these are fakes, but I feel sure that many are not, and that the messages they contain are real and immeasurably important — not just for our Earth domain, but for the unseen realms in which the Ethereans dwell, as well. Looking at the night sky and speculating on the possibility of extraterrestrial life may be fascinating and mind expanding, but perhaps we need to also look in another direction — one a little bit closer to home — Earth.

CHAPTER FOURTEEN

Life on Mars

Some time back in 1985 I read an article in *Omni*, which showed photographs of the planet Mars that had been sent back by NASA's space probe. The photos, published by the Jet Propulsion Laboratories, showed the surface at close range. One of these images captured a formation which, some speculated, looked to be manmade — a pyramidal structure with its apex blown off. In fact, it appeared that there were two of these pyramid-like formations on Mars. I thought it was more of a sensational, speculative article than a scientific possibility, but my curiosity was strong enough to urge me to ask my dream teachers for information about potential life on other planets. And yes, I thought, why not Mars?

They told me that millions of years ago, before life existed in any form on Earth, Mars had contained life. These were not originated by projections of consciousness, as with the Earth, but had resulted from colonization by other star systems. This race of people were humanoid, although much larger in body size than present-day humans. The Martians were more like the giants — some twenty-one feet tall — who first evolved during the early days of Earth's civilization. The Martian race eventually reached an extremely high order of technology, as well as having evolved spiritually far beyond what we know here on Earth. For tens of thousands of years, the Martians lived peacefully within their cities. They visited the stars, and used time-travel extensively. Then, my dream guides explained, a group of marauders began harassing the Martians' inter-space freight lines.

What? This was beginning to sound like a Buck Rogers or Flash Gordon story! Nevertheless, it is a story that sheds light on our current Earth changes situation, and can help us to understand what may or may not happen to us, and what we need to do here on Earth, together. I relate it here as it was originally shared with us, in a trance session which was conducted in May 1986:

CK: We have had indications of pyramids on Mars. Can you tell us if there was life on Mars?

GMS: *As we find, there was life on Mars and there still is but, in a different vibratory sense, more of what you would term the astral form. This life on another reality level still does exist.*

During the time period of their colonization — their expansion — life did indeed exist there. It existed in numbers that would be counted in the hundreds of millions, and it existed at a time prior to the first projections of souls into the Earth, some eighteen million years ago as we count time from the present.

CK: What were these pyramids on Mars used for?

GMS: *These were used as generators or what may be thought of as cosmic generators. Also they were used for a form of communication — as intergalactic communications — for there is a universal energy flow that connects not only the suns in this galaxy, but also reaches into the other galaxies and indeed into other realities.*

The pyramids that they had constructed were used for these pur-

poses. They were not singular in design, but more of a holographic energy design, where they were used as antennas or receptors for this flow of cosmic force that could then be channeled and used for the generation of energy for various utilities of the day.

The pyramid's secondary force was used for a process of communications. Such structures were not much different from the pyramids on Earth, though the one most closely resembling it would be that of Cheops; there are two in that planet that are larger, some fifteen to twenty percent larger.

CK: Are there other pyramids on other planets that also relate to the ones on Mars?

GMS: *None that remain within this system, but there was a tenth planet that did indeed have life. It was before this colonization, at a time recorded in billions of years rather than in millions of years. Other than that, there is no life, nor are there structures, other than on your moon, that remain. Realize that this does not mean that there are no forms of consciousness or life-force consciousness within the planetary system! But in what you would term physical evidence — or reality — there are no other devices or structures to be found in this system.*

CK: Can you explain the geography and the colors of the planet Mars, and tell us about other life forms that may have existed there in the past?

GMS: *In order to understand this, it would require a reality shift or a consciousness shift. For what was constructed there, and the entities that existed, were much different in their physical reality.*

Earth itself was still in its formation stages. There was animal life that had evolved, but consciousness of man or that of a soul force of man had not yet projected into Earth. At that time, the sentient Mars was already a consciousness that was thriving.

The landscape itself was once similar in nature to that of Earth. Also realize that its orbit was different. It had been moved, or shall we say, pushed from its orbit around the sun and into relationship with that of Venus and that of Mercury. These shifts occurred due to the cataclysmic events that occurred in their land, causing their demise, their final destruction as it were.

In its day — what we would term here its primary day — there was abundance, and there was fruitfulness. This land would have been akin to that of South America. It was a more tropical, torrid type of landscape. The color spectrums of the land were much different than Earth. The hues, the vibratory rays emanating from the sun due to its angular penetration, due to the distance between the sun and its other satellites, were such that the color spectrum would be different than you perceive it today. Realize that it is the optic system of man that determines color. If it was viewed with your vision of today, the natural light that would be seen would be a cast of blue.

As for the activities of the land, the people and the structures themselves were all in a larger format. These people would be termed today as a race of giants. As such, those entities, and the structures of the same, were not only large in nature, but also in spirit — denoting a form of grandeur.

The land itself was occupied by areas that would be termed cities, though unlike the planet Earth, which has continents and also various cities with land between, the two major cities of the Martian's primary time period each filled the whole of a continental land area. These then, were surrounded by large bodies of water. That which is termed today "the canals," were inter-coastal waterways on the land masses. There were large ocean basins, as well, for there was a saline solution, a liquid that was not water; there were crystalline and carbon bases, both present at the same time.

The two cities of the time were populated by hundreds of millions of people, or consciousnesses. This was a spiritually-based culture, attuned to a harmony, or resonance, within the group. Again, this group consciousness must be looked at and viewed differently from your own.

The consciousness of Mars in its day was so different from your own, that its land, its landscapes, its color tones, cannot be described unless viewed with the vision of its people at that time. We have tried to share here for approximation a model which you would understand, the parts that are understandable in your terms. So its environment — mixtures of air, oxygen, and nitrogen — would be thought of as a companion planet to Earth. In fact, in Mars' initial days, they were in identical orbit around the sun. If you could visualize it, you would see Earth on one side of the sun and Mars on the

other side of the sun, never seeing each other, but being approximate-
ly the same distance from the sun. The two planets rotated together,
they moved together. Later, through a shift in the time-space struc-
ture, they came into a different orbiting pattern. This, again, was
due to the destructive forces on Mars in its day.

CK: If Mars and its people were basically a peaceable society,
why do we associate Mars astrologically with warlike activity?

GMS: *To understand, it is important to realize first that much of*
astrology is not truly comprehended at the level of the one reality.
For it is not so much that Mars is located within a certain configura-
tion that affects consciousness, but rather because an entity's soul
has spent time on Mars, and on other planets, that it is so affected
when certain astrological configurations come into being.

The activities associated with Mars are anger, motion, movement
and accidents. All of these are created here in the consciousness of a
time period when Mars destroyed itself. The civilization entered into
a condition where there was a division among the people, even after
millions of years of peaceful activities and spiritual harmony. It was
a negative response to those entities from other star systems that had
chosen to come into this sun system for mineralizing — for forms
of pirating — that drove the Mars people to create a particular
defense system and to become an isolationist colony. And by
attempting to isolate themselves from other star cultures, they creat-
ed a condition for themselves where there could no longer be a move-
ment out to the stars, even those planets which they had colonized,
and to other continuums of time and space.

This defensive stance was successful in one sense, in that it
allowed their culture to continue on. As such, the Martians were
able to operate again for long periods, thousands of years, without
violation. For their screens — the most advanced deflectors their
technology could provide — were impenetrable. Eventually,
though, this created a disturbance among some of the younger people
of the planet, wherein they wished to once again go out to the stars
— to use their minds in this way — which would require a dis-
mantling of the particular defense system. This, of course, created a
situation and disharmony between the generations, and eventually
led to a cataclysmic war.

The war began when the satellites that protected the planet from the marauders were turned around and used against portions of the population itself, as a form of terrorism. Some came to see that if the system was not dismantled, there would be other destructions, but as a people, they could not agree on this as the correct course. This led to a complete technological devastation, since the contingency that was trying to move or manipulate these various satellites did not understand the actual programming. For realize that this had been in operation for hundreds of thousands of years and no one truly understood it any longer. It was simply buried far beneath the ground, operating on a cosmic force requiring no parts, so it would run continuously.

It was thought initially to be a system that would defend itself from anyone. After all, if anyone was to try to penetrate the atmosphere, the system would send out warnings first — clear warnings. It would even send out a ray force that would simply stop the various craft from proceeding on, like a form of anti-tractor beam. If technology was then used to try to penetrate the tractor beam, then the satellites would activate a type of cannon — a pulsating light-activated energy — that would destroy it. No outsider could enter the Mars territory without being clearly warned to turn back or be destroyed. Therefore, they could truly have no blame.

This war activity brought upon the collective consciousness of Mars a total destruction, a devastation. When their weaponry of the day, their defense system, turned upon the people themselves, life on the planet was totally eradicated. The damaging action caused by the inversion of the defense screen continued for a period of more than sixty-five revolutions around the sun, and it completely destroyed all life forms on the planet. There were those that projected out into the stars, and many who came to Earth to colonize. But the planet's consciousness — its aura — became one of war-like activity.

Now, that consciousness still remains, for it is the memory of those souls that projected into Mars at the time this was happening, so that when they are in the Earth realm now, they are still affected by it. It is important to note that all souls in the greater Oneness were created at the same time, regardless of where in the universe they choose to sojourn. All those on Earth were at one time part of the

consciousness of Mars. Or, if they were not part of the original con-
sciousness, so did dwell upon it afterwards in order for the soul to
experience a particular vibratory force. That force is interpreted by
the greater consciousness on Earth as one of war. Also, mechanical
aptitude, industry, and accident or misfortune are interpreted as
parts of the Mars force. And this is true. All of these are a part of
that consciousness.

Venus, by example, is just the opposite. It was a particular system
that did not have physical life, though it had an abundance of life on
a particular vibratory level. On Venus, the soul resides to experience
a vibratory force of love. It has to do with a particular triangulation
in the heavens, and those particular star-seeds that were left to set
up that condition. As such, there are colonies of consciousness still
there in your present time that are based on those principles of what
you would term love. It happens to be a polarization of that of Mars.
But both do exist.

CK: Earlier, we were told how a group of marauders began
harassing the people of Mars, affecting their inter-space
freight lines. Who were these pirates that came into the system, and where did they come from?

GMS: *Some were a portion of that which in these earlier times*
came from the Pleiades. There was another portion that came from
an alternate reality, or what you would call a "dual universe."
Whereas, if you can visualize that in this particular sun system or
the universe as you would know it, that there is also a dual universe,
which may be thought of as the opposite side of the visible polarity. It
is not necessarily that one is good and one is evil, but just an oppos-
ing polarity that pulses in a synchronized frequency with the reality
we know. There are dualities in all consciousness, as there are at all
subatomic levels of matter and energy. Each has a duality, each
searches for a balance or a neutral point. As such, there was many a
consciousness that came from this dual universe to the Mars realm,
through devices of time travel.

As such, there were certain elements of trading — profiteering —
that would move matter from one form to another, bringing in a par-
ticular kind of matter from the dual reality, and then shifting it back
into that reality. Also, the same activity occurred, but in the opposite

direction. It is difficult to explain in terminology that is understand-
able, but it was a kind of cheating through the use of phase shifts,
and the forms brought forth would become forms that had value. In
this way, new technological developments could be brought to the
other universe.

These marauders also came in to work towards bringing back
quantities of what would be termed the richness of Mars — the ele-
ments that it contained. Many of these elements are not yet found on
Earth, not that they do not exist, but there are certain elements that
still remain to be found here on Earth. But they are in abundance on
Mars, even now.

Also, the Martian technology was such that they were able to syn-
thesize other elements from beyond this sun system, by taking the
particular vibratory force, or the light, of sample elements, and then
using technology to recreate the elements. All of these, then, enabled
them to produce again new designs of form. These could best be
thought of as time-travel devices. Mars was indeed, as you would
measure this universe, a pioneer in the field, one who had accelerated
the activities of time travel to a fine art. This was known, and much
of that technology was sought by others in the system. The pirates
made use of the link from their dual universe to profit from what
they could obtain, when others could not penetrate Mars' defenses.

CK: What happened to the people of Mars when their planet
was totally destroyed?

GMS: *As given, the majority passed over to other realities.*
Whereas a portion went to other planets, another portion chose to
move into the newly developing mirror planet — Earth — with
which they had some past history. Realize that the Earth was not in
their optical view, and since the time when they had stopped coloniz-
ing, moving outward, much history had been forgotten. But through
their time-travel activities, a portion of what you would term as the
educators and the scientists — a small contingency — did project
into that of Earth. As such, they began a colonization.

The forms that they took were of a portion of that series of mixed
creatures that were already evolving on Earth, utilizing a form of
melding so to speak. Those originating in the Mars consciousness
would create a shadow such as an astral field, or the etheric field, and

would operate through there. Not that the souls penetrated within these entities, but rather hovered or so did contain themselves about these entities. These were in the area of the Pacific, or the continent of same, at the time, and they began a type of colonization of Earth, along with the earliest projections of souls that came to Earth by choice.

CK: So, if this was in the Pacific, was this then Lemuria at that time?

GMS: *The land mass at that time was without a name as you would know it. It would later be known as Lumania.*

In speaking of this, realize that it is important for most entities to relate a particular name or a sound to an area, such as "Atlantis," "Mu," such as "Poseidia," "Da," and so forth. These names give meaning for us, but realize that in the time period we speak of, there was more of a thought projection that occurred. Language was much different, and a sound would carry much meaning, not only in an activity, but if you can visualize projecting an image, the sound would not only amplify the image, it would add to the emotional context of it. But again, the language was much different than is currently being used. Names as you would know them would be more like pictorial images in the mind, and that these would have meaning.

In later generations — many, many thousands of years later — the area became known as Lumania. The people of this area eventually moved into the land known as Africa, where they became a race of giant stature. Again, keep in mind that this was long before the projection of the five races of man into that of Earth.

CK: Can you tell us some more about the physical appearances of the Martians?

GMS: *Again, they would be as giants, varying from some eighteen feet to some twenty-seven feet in height. This stature was based on their atmosphere, different from the Earth's, heavier in nitrogen and argon content. The head was humanoid in shape, though due to the activities of what would be the optic system, the eyes were significantly larger. Because of the particular climate structure on the planet, there was a deepening of the skin, more of a blue to a blue-green color, thick, almost reptilian, a large portion being reptilian, in fact,* *if they were to be viewed today. Many of those near the aquatic region of the smaller city-continent had scales. Those without scales simply evolved differently, due to the climate, and depending upon whether they initially emerged from the water, or came from the air. On Mars there was always this duality of consciousness — one of air and one of water. (Or rather, one of atmosphere, or gas, and one of liquid, for the elemental composition of Mars was much different than that which is known on Earth.) Whereas on Earth, of course, there are the four — air, water, fire and earth.*

Those that evolved from the Martian ocean had an optic system more closely resembling cat-like creatures than humans. Their sight was used not so much as a vision system, in the way that humanoids would sense, but more as a feline, being attuned to darkness. Also, their vision was designed for more of a distance perception. Those whose evolution began in the air were much different. For on Mars, in its day, there was a greater portion of sunlight during the year than that of darkness. It was similar to Earth, sharing its orbit, but realize that the time difference between then and your present, some eighteen million years, has created different shifts. In that day, there was light on the surface perhaps three quarters of the time — as a yearly average — versus darkness, or night, which was only one quarter of the time.

The activities of the hands were similar, and the arms and legs also similar to humanoid, though there was an additional thumb on each hand. There was also — in the foot region — four toes, instead of five. These are some of the things that would be different, but again, the elements are otherwise similar to humanoid. Do not think of these as alien creatures with green pointed ears, silver eyes and so forth, but rather, see these as giant-like humanoid creatures.

CK: We have heard the story of the souls coming to Earth about eighteen million years ago. Is the story of the Martians coming to Earth this same story?

GMS: *This is a different story. The Earth at the time of the projections — when a large contingency of souls, measuring in the millions, chose to project into Earth — already had one hundred forty-four thousand Martians on it. These souls were on the Earth first, as a colonization. But again, these were "hovering," not here as projec-*

tions. For the first projections of souls that came into Earth were coming directly from being indistinguishable from the Oneness, and they were experimenting. They were simply sampling the waters, so to speak. These were part of a much larger projection of souls, not created at that time but a projection at that time.

Prior to the arrival of the contingency from Mars, other entities had come into Earth to gain experiences, in particular, from that of Sirius. So the Earth has been colonized since its very beginning, or since its molten, or gaseous, days. Different realities, different consciousnesses, apply here. In the physical realm, as you would know it, these first projections of souls some eighteen million years ago would have to be identified as shadow-like creatures. It wasn't until a later time, whence occurred the projection of the five races of humans simultaneously into the world, that a hierarchy of consciousness was set up on Earth.

CK: Is there any way to tell — astrologically — if a person living now may have been one of these projections from Mars in another life? Is there a differentiation in the chart at all?

GMS: *Most of what may be found in charts does not display the activity of the soul, only the tendencies and the desires of the soul in this life. Only an initiate may truly know. An initiate who is an astrologer, an initiate who is simply a channel, or a seeker of answers who accesses the "universal creative force" themselves, thereby initiating their own inner knowing.*

Certain activities, however, or certain tendencies, may indicate the probability of a time spent in that existence. Those that were involved with Mars at that particular time period — the time of the destruction — and did not come to Earth with the original projections that experimented and descended into the race of mixed creatures, would tend even now to move in those vibratory forces that would be closer to bringing about their own attunement. That vibration would be closer to the Blue Ray vibratory forces, since a greater portion of those that colonized from Mars — those that chose to join in the reincarnation process on Earth — came in during the time of Lemuria, and now come in with those new Blue Ray children we see coming in today, and more so in the nineties.[5] So this would be an indication of what you ask, although there is nothing that would be guaranteed in any chart or astrological reading as to this previous life-activity.

CK: What type of culture did they have on Mars? How did they live, and what did they do for work?

GMS: *The activity must be looked at differently, for the life span was not measured in hundreds of years, but measured in thousands of years. It most closely resembled that time period on Earth of the Greek culture.*

For the Martian society, there was much debate that went on, and this became a type of national entertainment, for debates upon a single item would measure in years, not months. They would take very long time periods, what you would measure as a half century or even more, to debate an important item. However, once the consensus on that item was established, it was enacted and remained so for tens of thousands of years without change. So it became a form of vocation of the day to become a debater, like the professional athlete or entertainer is to the amateur in your culture. There were those that were so adept at the art of the debate, that many wanted to witness or experience their great abilities.

Because of the longevity, because of many activities, the population did not shift greatly in numbers. There was no growing population of the planet, no "population explosion," as has been the case on Earth in this and other ages. On Earth, when there was not a growing population, wars would invariably minimize the population further, and it would then rebuild up again. Likewise, Earth changes have collapsed many civilizations, and destroyed great numbers of people. Six times the Earth has gone into a period of darkness — a dark age — only to rise again to great technological heights.

This was not true on Mars, for there was only one great destruction, and in the physical reality, it was complete. As such, those activities of study and intellectual pursuit were greater pastimes, but they were more drawn out, taken slowly, and served more as a pleasure for the individual, not offered as a means of advancing the

---

[5] For context and continuity, it was necessary to include this reference to the Blue Ray at this point in the book. In Chapter 16, the subject of the Blue Ray — and the children born under its influence — is discussed in greater detail.

*culture. Part of the reason the culture on Earth — the most destruc-
tive elements of the most advanced cultures on Earth — is always
trying so hard to progress, to advance technologically, is because
those same souls were often involved in technology-based cultures at
other time periods, and they have a latent memory of what is possible. They are always trying to get back to the more advanced stage
that is remembered. On Mars, there were no such fluctuations in the
technology, but rather it grew slowly over time until it became so
advanced that it brought upon them their own destruction, as has
been related.*

*The work force of Mars was not so much geared towards toil, for
much was done by automated processes. Most of the food was grown
in a format similar to what would be termed hydroponics. They used
a form of generated energy — etheric energy — rather than water, to
grow the various sustenance forms.*

*For the Martian culture, the activities of sports were grand; in
particular, the water sports were enjoyed. Mind and anything that
would expand the mind was a greater portion of the consciousness.
Again, it would be difficult to explain, but to understand the
Martian reality would require a different thought process, for time as
you know it is a confinement on Earth. This was not so in that activity of Mars.*

*A greater enjoyment was that of the activities of travel — time
travel — where consciousness is able to travel through space and
time. There were also those who enjoyed the physical reality of travel,
those who would travel to the stars. This, of course, was closed down
when the marauding began. But again you would have to look at this
as another time period, such as measuring the Roman time period,
the Greek, the Western, and up to today, as being different time periods on Earth.*

*In the activities of Mars there would be similar time patterns. But
their technological advances, their motions and movements, again
were measured much differently. For they came in and projected into
Mars as gods and began at the high level and did not regress, but
maintained a status quo.*

*There was also an activity wherein many of the young of the day
would be involved in various forms of thought or mind construc-*

tions. A school of the day would be where a group would come together to construct physical objects, through the thought process. They would actually build — with their minds — an object that would become physical, and then at the end of the exercise they would disassemble the various atoms and put it back, such as a child on Earth would put away building blocks after playing with them.

Schooling as you would know it was not measured in a period of twenty years or so of education, but was measured in the hundreds of years, for there were more subject matters than can be imagined. The twenty-second century on Earth will begin where they on Mars had begun long, long before. In other words, as you advance into a new reality of thought, this is at a level that the Martians had surpassed many, many times over, and had moved on into other types of activities. Again, without the need for a defense system, for military, for all these activities, it gave more time to what would be termed social activities. And indeed, a large problem for their culture was finding new creative things that would deal with activities to eliminate boredom for the people. This became a great problem after the time-travel lines were closed, for that had been a large portion of how many occupied their minds in that society.

Meditation, a discipline most similar to that as it is thought of on Earth, was also a portion of each day for all people. This is one of the only true junctures from which to understand the Martian culture, in fact, for the act of meditation transcends different realities, transcends understanding. For although there is very little that can be understood by you as to the Martian reality, the act of prayer is universal, no matter what the mode of reality. In that culture, each individual spent perhaps ten or fifteen percent of the daily time period — much longer than your twenty-four hours — in what would be termed prayer. If you could imagine a spiritual group totally attuned to each other, a relationship between all in the society that was one of universal consciousness, this was a greater portion of the experience on Mars.

CK: How did life begin on the planet Mars?

GMS: *As given, all souls were created at once. Each chose different areas of expression. Those, or portions of those, came from other star systems into Mars, though for a greater portion of it, it was a part of* *the first projections of the souls or the first expressions into physical realities. Again, time needs to be taken out of context here, for it was only created to operate within one reality.*

So the answer is, it was from its original projection of thought from the Oneness, and from that original projection, many came from other sun systems and other realities.

CK: And their religion was that of the collective?

GMS: *It can be thought of as a harmonizing. What you today might term as God — the Oneness that always has been and continues always to be — was determined through the defining processes of each individual. Through thought, through prayer, the collective understanding was constantly sculpted and refined, as each had a definition of what that God would be, and daily added an interpretation to the collective spirit-force. For this group, they understood their God to be an embodiment of the collective, the result of their own collective thought coming together. Rather than a Creator that would be in heaven, and a devil that would be in hell, their belief was a form of unity. Knowing all were connected in prayer each day, they were truly one with their God, their own godliness. Their God was the totality of the group.*

CK: Did they have any other structures besides the pyramids that they built?

GMS: *There were tunneling systems that acted as cosmic energy wave-guides. These were circular in form. The control chamber that held the machinery controlling the defense system was part of this matrixing. A series of wave-guides, similar to your atomic accelerators today, were placed around a particular pyramid. The cosmic energy would come in, moving and melding with the electromagnetic energy, which was a form of magnetism emanating from the vibratory force that Mars was constantly creating within its core.*

These wave-guides were finely polished and had specific dimensions which acted as an energy-conversion system in conjunction with the pyramids, which collected the cosmic energy. Each wave-guide was a giant wheel-like subterranean tunnel which lay below the pyramid structure and was connected to it at a hub. These were like machines, but with no moving parts. The Martians used one reality, the cosmic forces outside of time, and combined it with the

*use of electromagnetic forces from the wave-guide tunnels, forces
within time, to create their time machines. So here was a second type
of structure which they built.*

*The dwellings or homes were forms of large dome-type areas, simi-
lar to what would be termed here today as a geodesic structure. But
these were full spheres, suspended by the energy fields generated by
the central pyramid. And these were placed about in an interconnected fashion. Whereas no one lived in a singular structure, but
rather the families lived in the greater extension of a particular
arrangement of dwellings, and these extensions might be called
"pods." Realizing that their lives measured in thousands of years,
these became very large families, each existing within various pods of
the greater complex. These pods would also interconnect. So, if you
can, visualize a series of glass-type pods, suspended all about a central pyramid, and then a series of pyramids, with the tunneling
activities as given, underneath, so that the whole of each continent
— of which there were two — became a vast, interconnected city,
but with each family group residing in its own particular part. Then
you would have a fair understanding of the lifestyle, and also the
mode of power generation.*

CK: Do we have anything similar under our pyramids on
Earth, particularly the Great Pyramid in Egypt?

GMS: *This, as Cheops, remember was a name that was taken, not
one that was given. This is the "Pyramid of Understanding," one
designed by that of Hermes himself, who in a later projection was the
man Jesus. As such, that structure was built as a temple of understanding, a temple of wisdom. Also utilizing the same cosmic forces
as those understood on Mars. A form of time transference, but also
more of an instrument that would communicate with the Infinite or
that of the universal consciousness of the Oneness.*

*It also contains many other secrets yet to be explored and yet to be
understood by man. Underneath is simply granite rock, though portions of various tunnelings still exist and indeed smaller pyramids
between Cheops and the Sphinx still exist which contain the records
and will indeed have reference to that of Mars. This was known by
the Atlanteans, and it was the Atlanteans — or a portion of them
— that so did invade that land of Northern Africa and who con-*

structed the same, with the assistance of the Egyptians.

There are other tunnels similar to the Martian tunnels that exist upon the planet Earth. These are of a time period prior to that of Atlantis. These are of a time period even prior to that of Lemuria. You are referred here to a time period of Lumania and beyond whereas a series of tunnels or tube shoots were created. These were to move or convey people. Realize that it wasn't that these were all tunnels, but realize that the shape of the Earth has changed so much as to bury these further down. Whereas, in its time, these were not so deep into the ground, but were more conduits of transportation. These still do exist and many have been found, though not understood.

CK: How does the story of the Martian wars, and the destruction of their planet, relate to us today?

GMS: *The lesson for today is simply that there is no technology that can simply defend a system; that you cannot be isolated; that what is required is a harmony and a unison. The lesson is that when peoples come together to communicate, to pray, to work together for the good of the whole — the greater whole — then harmony and peace does exist.*

There will always be challenges from those who would wrongly use their power under the names of great causes, under the names of the Creator himself to bring about change. And when these conditions do occur, there is separation, and there are eventually destructive forces which come into play.

The lessons for today should be that it is more important for all to attune together. It is important for all to put peace and the greater whole above themselves, and look for harmony. In doing so, there can be an elimination of a potential reality of Earth's peoples entering such a totally destructive phase themselves, as the Martians once did.

* * * * *

So part of our ancestry here on Earth began with a small colonization from the nearby planet Mars. I wonder how many other visitors have come to Earth? Are we a composite of many life forms from many universes? My teachers say that the connection between Mars and Earth life forms will be known and understood before the close of this century. At the very least, this means that it will become widely known that there was once life on Mars.

We are aware of but a brief time period in what we call civilization — some six thousand years, the Bible would have us believe. But each year, it seems, this date needs to be pushed back, as religious dogma (which is quite different than true spirituality or faith), gives way to scientific truth. I am convinced, and evidence is slowly being uncovered which agrees, that humans have existed far longer on this planet, and probably on other planets, than we currently know.

Time does not necessarily mean that we grow spiritually, that we learn more. We are confronted constantly, as I am sure we have been since the first great thought, with choices for expression. There may never come a time when all is perfect, when life on Earth is a nirvana or Eden. Since each soul is independent and also part of the Oneness, there are always those possibilities of movement from one level to another. We can only do the best that we can at whatever point of focus we are currently in. This is true for us as individuals, and as a society, too.

My teachers say that energy — when built to a high level of harmony and resonance — attracts to it similar energies from the greater universe. People, and groups of people, that choose not to be drawn to a positive source will search out energies more familiar, more similar, to themselves. And they will do this indefinitely, until they decide to be different, thereby attracting different types of energy to them. Whether it be on Earth, or at any of the levels of reality, energy is constantly, eternally, searching for other like energies.

As an individual, your choice is always one of deciding what type of energy you want to generate, to emanate. What comes from that choice — what comes to you — follows naturally. Concentrating on refining the energy we put out, rather than searching outside ourselves for that which we feel lacking, is perhaps the most important lesson we can take from the story of the Martians' demise. Our own story could certainly end up like theirs, depending upon what energy we decide to put out into the universe, as a collective. But it might just as easily go in an entirely different direction, as well. Ultimately, I am hopeful that we can create, here on Earth, the kind of energy that might have saved the culture of Mars from destruction — the kind of energy that can move our planet toward harmony, balance and peaceful coexistence.

CHAPTER FIFTEEN

The Pyramids of Egypt

In late 1994, I began to receive a series of dreams which I thought at first were reruns of my Mars visions, or perhaps even an update to them. It turned out, however, that I was receiving entirely new images. These were of the long-forgotten land of Dar, in what we now know as Egypt.

In these dreams, I saw the great pyramidal structures — massive as they are now, but faced in stone polished to a glassy smoothness — and the familiar form of the Sphinx, also in its original state, low in the foreground. These were hyper-vivid scenarios, full of sensory experiences. I could smell the fresh, damp air of the lush landscape, and exotic scents from a culture long vanished. I could hear the running water of public fountains, and I saw people in strange clothing going about their business. In some of the visions, I watched the bustling activity on the Nile in its original form, not as the river we now know, but when it was clearly a manmade channel, perfectly straight, with sides constructed of massive, cut stones. Over the course of a few nights, the images and impressions in these visions began to reach an almost intolerable intensity, coming at me in rapid-fire montages and overflowing with exciting curiosities, none of which I seemed to be able to slow down enough to examine in detail. I decided to ask my guides for a dream that might ease this sensory overload.

That night I had a dream in which a character calling himself Darune came to me and spoke. *"Come to the Temple of Light,"* he said, *"and you will understand."* When I awoke the next morning, I somehow knew that I must go to Egypt, sensing intuitively that there was something important to be discovered out in that vast desert — clues that I was now being asked to unravel. By then, I had learned the importance of trusting my instincts, so there was little debate on the subject of whether or not to go. The very next day, Cynthia and I began to plan the trip, and we booked passage for early January.

Since my first intuitive experience in 1979, I have seen many visions of ancient civilizations and buried temples. If I visit a specific site, then the visions become technicolor, and I am able to project my mind below and inside these structures. This is what I did during my stay in Egypt. The place where I spent the most time was the large complex known as the Giza Plateau, a few miles west of Cairo, Egypt. Notable structures located there are the Sphinx, The Great Pyramid of Cheops, eight other pyramids, and various temples. Most of these are in question as to who, when, and for what purpose they were built. Current Egyptologists have speculated on the age of this complex, and many believe that it was built around 3,000 B.C., or five thousand years before the present. My information dates the construction and rebuilding of this complex at closer to 10,500 B.C.

A great difference exists in time periods between current scientific fact and my intuitive belief. Another seer has likewise dated these structures to over ten thousand years old. Edgar Cayce, who died in 1945, often spoke in a trance state about an ancient cataclysm which occurred over ten thousand years ago, destroying much of Earth's civilization.

THE GREAT PYRAMID

Considered one of the seven wonders of the world, the Great Pyramid, located at Giza (also known as the Pyramid of Khufu, the Egyptian king for which it was built, or Cheops, to use his Greek name), has stood as an enigma for thousands of years. And it continues to do so, even in our technologically advanced twentieth century.

We have built space ships that have transported men safely to the moon and back, and still, with all of this marvelous technology, we do not know how the Great Pyramid was built, who built it, and most importantly, why it was built.

Egyptologists currently date the construction of the Great Pyramid at around 2,600 B.C., as a tomb built for the pharaoh, Khufu. They theorize that a primitive people working with copper and brass tools constructed this monument, using a hundred thousand or more slaves over a period of twenty years.

Let's look at some of the scientifically known facts about the Great Pyramid, beginning with its location, or position, on the Earth. If we were to look at a flat map of the continents and oceans, we would find that Cheops is located precisely at the geographical center of the total land surface of the world — at approximately thirty degrees north latitude, by thirty degrees east longitude. Further, we would find that the pyramid's position, relative to true north, is only six seconds of one degree off of today's exact polar north direction.

The Great Pyramid is constructed of almost two and a half million blocks of stone, each weighing at least two tons, with some stones estimated at over fifty tons. (For comparison, the average weight of an American automobile is approximately two tons.) These massive blocks were cut, moved, and then fitted together with such exactness that a thin blade cannot be inserted between them. The pyramid has a vertical elevation the equivalent of a forty-story skyscraper — over four hundred feet. Currently, no capstone exists on the structure, and much debate exists as to whether one ever did exist. The base of this massive monument measures over seven hundred fifty feet on each of its four sides, and covers an area of thirteen acres. (Again, as a comparison, an average city block in New York City covers just under two acres.) The four sides of the pyramid are perfectly oriented towards the cardinal points — north, south, east, and west. The base is level with a divergence of less than one inch in its total circumference.

Whatever culture built the Great Pyramid must have had an advanced knowledge of mathematics and Earth's measurements, as well as their exact position — within seconds of a degree — relative to the North Pole. One has only to visit this structure to realize it must surely have been built by an advanced race of people. Its perfection is like nothing found in the world today.

Conventional Egyptology theorizes that the Great Pyramid is four thousand six hundred years old, which is in itself an enigma. We know from archaeological discoveries that copper and bronze were used at that time, but not iron. Yet even today, to cut these stones to such an accuracy — especially the granite used in the inner chambers — would require tools of the precision used to cut diamonds, but on a massive scale. The engineering, mathematics and technology needed to construct such a monument is, even now, far beyond our comprehension. In fact, some years ago, an attempt to construct a small-scale model of Cheops was attempted. With funding from Japan, researchers, mathematicians, computer experts, engineers of all types, machinery, and anything else the twentieth century could offer were brought to the Giza Plateau. After months of hard labor and millions of dollars, they gave up. Even with all of the global technology of the twentieth century at their disposal, all they could say was, "How did they do it?"

After visiting the Great Pyramid, I wondered if those who believe a primitive culture built the Great Pyramid have ever been inside the structure. If the sheer size and perfection of the outside doesn't astound you, the inside surely will. My visit inside the Great Pyramid and into the Grand Gallery induced visions of an order and magnitude that I have never experienced before. Here was a passageway — one hundred fifty-six feet long and twenty-eight feet high, at an incline of twenty-six degrees — perfectly aligned. The stones here are granite, many weighing over fifty tons! I live in New Hampshire — the Granite State — and my house is set on a granite foundation, so I am well-acquainted with the difficulties inherent in trying to manipulate and work with this particular mineral. Have you ever tried to break, let alone cut, granite? Even with diamond saws and grinders, a feat of engineering such as is evidenced by Cheops' Grand Gallery staggers the imagination. The granite stones in the Gallery are finely polished, too, as they are in the two chambers that lead into the Gallery — the Queen's Chamber, and the King's Chamber. And remember the currently accepted theory of construction: one hundred thousand slaves, twenty years, copper and bronze tools, primitive people, and no technological advancements. It seems impossible, doesn't it? The pieces just don't fit neatly together.

Unequivocally, our visit to Giza and the Great Pyramid changed my life. I do not make this statement lightly, especially in view of all the incredible changes I've experienced since my health crisis in 1979, and my subsequent thrust into the world as a visionary. However, reviewing all the changes I've been through, my experience at the Great Pyramid has had the most profound effect on my life and direction of service of anything else I've experienced. Perhaps, as Edgar Cayce said, "The Great Pyramid was built as a temple of initiation." I certainly experienced my own visit as an initiation.

Actually, many seers have pointed to the Great Pyramid as a place for initiation. Some have even suggested its purpose was to stabilize the world so as to prevent an axis shift.

Scientists continue to contend that it was a tomb for Khufu, though no mummy, or records referring to the structure being a tomb for Khufu have been found. Unlike other structures in Egypt, the Great Pyramid contains no hieroglyphs that might shed some light on its purpose. It appears that if the pyramid's builders wanted to record any message, they did so through the only process that would surely survive — the massive size and ingenious mathematics of the structure itself.

The visions I received at Giza were quite different from the visions I'd otherwise been receiving since 1979. Typically, when I see a vision it is like viewing a split screen, like watching two or three aspects of the same scene. Not so at Giza. My first vision occurred before I ever entered the pyramid. I was sitting on our balcony at the Mena House, which faced the Great Pyramid, maybe a thousand feet away, when I found myself seeing a vision of workers clearing the plateau in preparation for construction of the Great Pyramid.

I found myself being drawn into the vision, so that instead of it being an optical experience where I was viewing an event, I had become part of the scene I was watching. I had actually traveled back to the time of construction.

I see large birds in the air which remind me of prehistoric birds. The terrain is much different than in my present — semi-tropical, with lush vegetation, a mild temperature in the seventies, and water surrounding the entire plateau. The area surrounding the hotel where I had been when the vision began is now underwater.

Also in the air, I see large cigar-shaped flying machines which resemble hot-air balloons. Cables hang down from the craft to anchor points below. Workers dressed in white kilts and cloth hats that have long flaps extending down to their shoulders, are removing stones from cradles that are housed below the craft. The activity reminds me of helicopters that transport heavy materials on platforms, supported by cables. I can see other air ships coming into the area, being guided by anchor cables from point to point. Each ship carries a cradle, one stone in each, with markings on each stone in glyph form. Here, I realize, is an unconsidered possibility in the pyramid puzzle. These

air machines were used to transport the stones from quarries to the
site — not barges, rollers, ramps and slaves!

If this experience stops at this point, I tell myself, I will still con-
sider it the most amazing vision I've ever witnessed in my life. I con-
tinue to watch the building of what will become — thousands of
years from now — one of the seven wonders of the world.
Astounded, I listen to the voices of the workers, and the screeches of
the mammoth birds in the sky. I bask in the humid heat of the day.
My thoughts are running so fast that I am barely aware of the throb-
bing in my head — a familiar sensation which indicates I am push-
ing too hard to receive information. I back off a little bit, and the
scenery changes.

Pictures began to flow by, like a river of consciousness. I
wondered, "When is this occurring?" Immediately, my inner
voice responded with an answer.

"The time frame is 12,553 years before present."

My thoughts dashed to a list of questions I had written for
myself back in New Hampshire, prior to our trip. During our
travels, I had hoped to find clues to the secrets of the Sphinx
and the Great Pyramid itself — what their significance was,
and answers to why I had been drawn here. Now, here I was,
tapped into a super-consciousness database — a library of
sorts — where I might do a tad better than clues. Concerned
time would run out and I would lose the connection, my
thoughts raced, but I was committed to staying in this time-
stream, and allowing whatever I was presented with to occur.

"What was the original significance of the Giza complex at
the time it was first built?"

"This would depend on which civilization, as the purpose varied
depending on the root race then present, for there have been many
evolutions there, and many groups have come and gone. In the
beginning, this country was one of the first of the in-dwellings of
man."

"What time frame?"

"Here we would need to turn back time to more than ten million
years from the present. The people were similar to a collective

thought form, physical in some respects, but light in density. If they were viewed in the present they would appear shadow-like. The society was one that was constructed or built upon a conscious relationship with the One — in constant communication. It was taken for granted in the same way a breath of air is taken for granted today.

"With the greater changes and the shifts of the Earth's axis — numerous times — this site has been occupied longer than any other land on the globe. In the time frame before the last geophysical pole shift, some fifty-four thousand years ago, this site — Giza — was occupied by the peoples from the Gobi who had moved into this area and joined with the people already present. The giant Olmec heads that may be found in many lands today would be a close kin to these people.

"After the shifting of the poles, this land became a wasteland of sorts and eventually became overgrown, tropical in nature, and a different geological formation. Even the oceans were much different during this time period. Slowly the area shifted once more and became more habitable, and then there were the migrations of those peoples from Mu, Alta, and other lands that came into that region, developing a high level of society some thirty-eight thousand years before present. This would be termed here the beginning of the current Giza site — not the first, mind you — for even during this time period there was research going on to determine who the original inhabitants of this land were.

"During this time frame there began the construction of the first of those monuments still present at Giza — the great head of the king of that time which has since been modified into what is now called the Sphinx. This was done by those who came into the land some sixteen thousand years later. Civilization continued until there was the greater destructive forces from the Atlantean land, thirty thousand years before present, when there was the warring activity between them and the land now known as China. This caused global cataclysm, bringing the world into another dark age.

"This site lay dormant and did not reemerge again until approximately eighteen thousand years ago. At this time we would find the beginning of what was to become a solar cult, and the beginning of the current Egyptian civilization. Growth was slow until twelve

thousand five hundred years ago, when other races of people from Zu, Ur, Dar, and Alta, entered into this land. It was during this time period that great technological, spiritual and scientific advancements were achieved on Earth. Here began the initial thoughts and plans for what was to become a series of complexes, above and below ground: a great avenue containing buildings dedicated to science, medicine, history, astronomy; an observatory; buildings dedicated to astrology and numerology;, and more. Today it would be similar to the Library of Congress, the Smithsonian, the Cairo Museum, the Mount Palomar Observatory, and various universities.

"Now, during this time frame, the Nile was much closer to the complex and there were canals that had been dug allowing the Nile to reach the site. So, from the Sphinx, for example, we would find the Nile to be five hundred to a thousand yards, depending upon the turn or the curve of the waterway. This channeled water into the site and the plateau could be seen as an island unto itself. Whereas, if you looked at the plateau now, you would find that the area that is now the ancient cemetery, as well as the new cemetery, situated to the east and facing the Sphinx, would have been a waterway. So imagine an island, rectangular in shape, with a docking port many feet below and on the east and west sides of the Sphinx. This would give you a fair approximation of the site during this time period."

"Was the Great Pyramid like a church or temple, where people came to pray for enlightenment or experience initiation?" I asked.

"You seek a name to call this structure, a name to describe its purpose, do you not?"

Still somewhat fearful that I would loose the contact, I thought, trying not to be too excited, "Yes, that's exactly it."

An immediate response came back. *"The Great Pyramid is a time machine."*

This response was not one of the possibilities I had considered! How could it be possible? Television and movies in the present are just beginning to explore the possibilities of time travel. For comparison, look at what we have achieved in the past century — electricity, the automobile, atomic power, lasers, space travel — all within the short span of a hundred years. Now, imagine where our civilization might be in the next hundred years. And that is exactly where these people were over twelve thousand five hundred years ago! Civilization does not necessarily develop technologically, with time. Rather, it rises and falls, depending on the lessons that civilization — that particular group consciousness — desires.

"Who built the Great Pyramid?" I asked.

"Atlanteans, in conjunction with Egyptians and Dareans."

"How does this machine work?"

"The machine's purpose, as constructed, was multiple in design. Bending time was its focus, so as to provide a process for initiation. However, the manner in which this was accomplished provided other benefits for its people. These varied from increased crop yield, weather control, a form of electrical power, and a learning institute for the study of the heavens — astronomy, astrology and cosmic forces, mathematics, chemistry, inner world dimensions, and the seven levels of initiation. All were part of its design."

"Like astronomy and astrology," I thought.

"Yes, it was used as an observatory. The builders knew the cycles of the stars, their individual and collective emanations relative to the Earth and sun, their effect on consciousness, and the fact that life was not limited to the Earth. To this end, windows were known and so recorded in those chambers, known and unknown, to indicate times when communication was possible with people from other worlds — both inner worlds and physical worlds. Knowing these things then, it became possible to construct such an instrument that could attune to those forces emanating from stars and other dimensions, amplify and modify them so as to bend time. This then allowed those in resonance with the instrument to enter the time-stream where all inner-world communication occurs relative to this sphere."

"What did these people hope to attain through time traveling?"

"A way to communicate with the Lord and His angels."

Stunned by this answer, I felt the familiar electrical sensations course through my body, and suddenly found myself back on the hotel patio. I was intensely disappointed that my lack of control had caused me to break the contact. My head throbbing from the experience, I decided I would try again the next day, and fell asleep for the afternoon.

Realizing the importance of timing and consistency regarding intuitive applications, I attempted to induce a vision the next day at the same time and location. Colorful visions emerged, showing me the topography of the region, the position of the Nile at that time, and more views of the construction process. These were the more conventional visions that I usually receive — more of visions blending into other visions — each lasting only seconds. After fifteen minutes or so, these stopped.

Later that day we visited the Sphinx, where we spent an hour or so. Upon leaving the Sphinx area I walked to the top of the plateau where the Great Pyramid and two smaller pyramids — those for Kings Mycerinus (or Menkaure) and Chephren (or Khafre) — are located. I stopped at a turn in the road, about a thousand feet away, and gazed at the three pyramids, enjoying their magnificence. Suddenly, I heard a popping sound, and found myself once again witnessing the construction of the Great Pyramid. The experience of the previous day had prepared me, or rather focused my thoughts towards what I felt was important to observe. I never expected to repeat the interactive experience, but hoped I would be able to go back to the point I'd left at the day before.

There are no pyramids present on the plateau, only the beginning construction of what will be the Great Pyramid. I recognize the Sphinx, although the styling is much different than in my present; there are a few other buildings, as well, rectangular in shape, and a few mound-like structures that seem to be very old. The monstrous birds I'd seen in my previous visions continue to fill the sky. I notice several men making strange motions. In one hand, each holds a sling of some sort, which carries a weight at one end. They begin spinning these in a circular fashion. A high-pitched screech is emitted, causing the prehistoric birds to scatter, and me to cover my ears. A few moments later, a large air ship enters the plateau.

Illustrator, Ken Southwick's depiction of GMS's
dream voyage to ancient Egypt.

I prayed I could keep centered and stay as an "observer." I took a deep breath, and felt an electrical sensation run from my shoulders to my neck. Carefully, I asked my first question.

"What is the relationship between the Great Pyramid being both a time machine and a place of initiation?"

"Life is initiation. Each thought, each action, is a portion of initiation. Man once walked the Earth with full knowledge of the Oneness. All thoughts were one. All actions one. Then, with a single thought, an infinite number of thoughts — separate and collective — were formed. It was the creation of souls. A portion of these souls came to this sun system to experience individuality, though they

remained connected to the Host. With time, magnetic forces and will, communication with the Host and other spiritual realms became so blocked as to cause a separation. To aid in the reconnection, a process of initiation, or training, was established. It utilized the Great Pyramid as a communications instrument. In this way, contact would be possible for those who, through their dedication, could communicate with their soul mates and the greater collective consciousness."

So many questions were part of my consciousness, but I grabbed onto the first one I could, so as not to loose the connection again. "Why so large a structure?"

"The size and mass chosen was required in order for the instrument to contain the gasses within the structure, as the machine operated. The shape chosen, acted as an antenna — collecting those particles that precede light from the heavens, that are forever being drawn to this sphere."

"Could you explain the term 'antenna'?"

"This specific pyramid shape, in conjunction with its position of latitude, acted as a lens, not optical, but in focus, drawing to the machine those rays necessary for communication."

"Explain what is meant by 'gasses within the structure'?"

"Stones in specific portions of the instrument were set in place with a sealer-adhesive, which allowed for airtight chambers and passageways to exist. The gasses were a mixture brought up from deep within the Earth, and combined with gasses created by the alteration of elements, as created through the instrument. The principles used here are similar to the laser used today, but developed differently because of conditions then present."

"Was this gas invisible?"

"Green in color when active, invisible otherwise."

"Is this gas present in the world today?"

"Only at times in nature when those magnetic vortexes that may be found in the world become active."

"What is meant by 'active'?"

"Transition points — polarity shifts in the solar cycle — June and December currently."

"And what is the purpose of the passageways?"

"*Multiple in purpose. These were used as service tunnels, sighting tubes, and to channel large quantities of gas to the appropriate chamber.*"

"And what about the main entrance to the ascending and descending passageways?"

"*The main entrance has not been found. It will be discovered deep below the base — nearer the center of the pyramid — with a passageway leading up to the apex, as well as to the Sphinx and other structures. What is now thought to be the main entrance, was at that time used as part of the machine. At that time, a hinged door was set in the opening which, in one mode of operation, acted as a safety valve for the release of gas. In another mode, the door was held open by a lever, allowing the sighting and tracking of specific stars. This was so the Earth's exact position, or axis relative to specific spheres — currently Polaris — could be determined. When used for such alignment, light from the star entered the doorway and fell upon the instruments, located at a position along the descending passageway.*"

"If the entrance was below the base, how did one get to the Queen's and King's Chambers?"

"*Access to these chambers were not required as they were a portion of the instrument — harmonically-tuned rooms. By way of a stone staircase, travel to the top — or capstone — was possible, as was travel to the lower control rooms many hundreds of feet below.*"

"So there was a capstone?"

"*Yes, made out of the metals of the day — hollow.*"

"Are there other chambers above the base besides those we know as the King's and Queen's Chambers, and the Pit?"

"*Yes. Seven in number, above the base as chambers.*"

"What is the purpose of those shafts found in the Queen's Chamber?"

"*These are for monitoring and controlling the gasses, internal to the structure at that location.*"

"What is the purpose of the Grand Gallery?"

"*This is the tuning circuit of the instrument. Along its length, tracks were fitted — above, below and on each side — in which a tuning device was housed, in a carriage. The carriage, then, con-*

tained the likeness of a creature — part bird, part beast — holding
a large crystal in its talons. The tips of the creature's wings reached
to the height of the Gallery, and contacted the upper tracks. This was
then powered, through induction, by magnetic forces. These propelled the carriage up or down the Gallery. When tuned properly —
for depending on the chamber selected, different desired results could
occur — the time-space fabric would shift within the instrument,
allowing a portal to open."*

My head continued to throb as vision after vision filled my
mental screen. The realization of what I was experiencing
began to overwhelm me. My first thought was to give control
of what was occurring over to some external force. But my
inner voice responded, correcting me in a gentle, yet assertive
manner.

*"You are aware most times of the real you and your connection
with the inner worlds. You must now push your consciousness out
further, and acknowledge the experience as being within. Do not
misunderstand. This is not to indicate that other spiritual forms are
not assisting, or are at times present, but these occur as guides to
assist in initiation, not to fulfill initiation. The more the inner self is
accepted, the greater the development. And yes ... risk is the price
that must be paid. But what is being risked here? We would suggest
it is the ego. Without risk, there can be no gain. Safety is but an illusion."*

I took a few deep breaths. I thought, I know this, so why do
I continue to question, to resist? I felt a glimmer of understanding. It is part of the initiation, I thought. My mind
relaxed, and I continued with my questioning about the Great
Pyramid.

"Who, or what, determined the selection of a chamber?"

"The initiate chose, with the assistance of the priest."

"Please explain this."

*"Better here to explain initiation. As given previously, all of life is
initiation. Each experience, each act, each deed — especially
thoughts — are a portion of initiation. Initiation then is a process
whereby the entity — the soul force — is given the opportunity to
develop spiritually. This means, that when the soul chooses to*

improve itself — to move towards a greater light, the soul-body so changes its vibration as to remove from its spiritual fabric those attachments detrimental to its path upward.

"An analogy here would be to imagine blindness that has been a part of the physical body from birth. Then, through surgery and the removal of blockages, vision is very slowly restored. At first, light may be detected, void of detail or meaning, but nevertheless, a new experience. Slowly, shadows appear in the vision. Another new experience. Shadows then give way to form and detail. With each new visual experience, small shifts in awareness occur. Lastly, color fills the form and a new interaction with the other senses occurs. At this point, a whole new world opens up — the applications of sight. Initiation operates much in the same manner.

"Now as to the process of initiation. Each soul is at some level of initiation at birth, as a result of previous, as well as future, incarnations. Even those souls who have fallen are still at a level of initiation. Initiation can be either an upward movement towards a greater light or downward towards the darkness."

"Are the two known passageways — ascending and descending — related to initiation?"

"Descending — to decline or regress. Ascending — upwards towards the Great Hall and final initiation in the King's Chamber."

"It has been speculated in some books that these passageways contain evidence of Biblical prophecies. Is this correct?"

"In part. The passageways contain a time line. This marks significant dates of all major religious movements since man first entered the Earth. The time line ends in 1953, with the entrance to the King's Chamber."

"Why 1953?"

"This marks the time period of 'the choosing.' The choices of humankind, from 1953 to 1998, will determine how the development of the next civilization, or root race, will unfold."

"Does the time line pick up somewhere else?"

"Rather, it points the way."

"To where?"

"The tomb."

"Does this refer to the empty sarcophagus?"

"*Yes, though this was part symbolic, in form, and part of the machine.*"

"What does it symbolize?"

"*The final test — passage from the physical world to the spiritual and back. The continuum of life.*"

"And how is this part of the machine?"

"*It is a resonant device tuned to the frequencies required for the seventh level of initiation. This then worked in conjunction with the room's additional workings. What appears to be the ceiling of the King's Chamber is but one of several tuned circuits. Forces collected by the pyramid were captured, focused and directed downward through the stones, into the open sarcophagus. These frequencies, in conjunction with other forces created by the crystal in the Great Hall, and the initiate himself, made possible the test for the seventh level of initiation — travel to other worlds.*"

"So the sarcophagus by itself has no power?"

"*In the hands of an initiate of the seventh level it has great power, even today.*"

"Are there other devices like this in the world?"

"*The one most remembered and still preserved is known as the 'Ark of the Covenant'.*"

I decided, despite my curiosity to know more about this, that I would make better use of this opportunity by staying with the subject of initiation. I hoped that some day I would be able to learn about the Ark, and some of the other areas touched upon. I continued with the original line of questioning.

"Since the initiates were not physically present in the chambers, how was travel to other worlds possible?"

"*Through spiritual forces. Let us more fully describe the process of initiation and the workings of the machine. While the process of initiation is a spiritual process it occurs with and through physical laws; however, it is the brain, and ultimately the mind, that has the experience.*

"*There are seven chambers above the pyramid's base — one for each level of initiation. Additionally, there are seven chambers below the base, cut deep into the plateau. More than twenty years were spent constructing the base and lower workings. A portion of the pyramid's outer stonework was fashioned from the lower cuttings. The chambers below may be seen as a mirror of what is above, plus the addition of control rooms and other passageways. Each chamber below is an exact harmonic of the chamber above. They are connected through vibrational waves. 'Out-of-time' would be the correct definition here. Seven waves, fourteen chambers — seven above and seven below — make up the workings, each tuned through the mechanism in the Grand Gallery.*

"As the process began, an initiate who had so prepared himself for testing would enter the appropriate chamber below. The priest, having already perfected all levels of initiation, would join — psychically — with the initiate. As they journeyed to the inner world, the priest would act as guide and guardian."

"What determined a successful initiation?"

"The journey itself. For if the entity was not attuned to the level he was to experience, he would be unable to journey with the priest. Again, the machine only provides the framework, or mechanism, for initiation, not the experience. It is vibration that determines the experience as all is vibration regardless of level, worlds, or universes."

"Please describe the destination of the initiates in their journeys."

"In this world there are eight realms, or what may be imagined as seven Earths, each lighter in vibration. The eighth may be seen as the totality of the seven — the Universal Mind. Within each realm there are seven sub-levels of initiation. In the second realm may be found ghosts and departed family members, also known as the astral realm."

"So initiation is directly related to preparation for death?"

"Yes and no. Initiation prepares one for the process of perfection of the soul. Currently, all may easily enter the physical Earth, leave through death of the physical, and enter again."

"Currently?"

"After the greater changes occur between the years 1998 and 2001, the vibration on the physical Earth, as well as the inner Earth, will change so as to alter the process of initiation. This has already begun

in the astral world. While now all entities may enter the Earth, shortly, only those whose spiritual vibration matches the new Earth will find entrance, should they choose, during the next thousand years. Thus bringing the millennium of peace, as so prophesied."

"What happens to those entities who have not reached these levels?"

"They will find themselves in worlds that mirror their soul's vibration. However, the numbers of entities occupying these levels shall increase significantly. Additionally, some levels will be no more, and others will merge into one another. A new process of initiation shall be born, and the levels for development shall correspondingly change to accommodate the need."

"Will there be a reduction in the total levels of initiation then?"

"There will be an increase to fourteen."

At this point, the throbbing feeling in my head returned, and I found myself losing the vision portion of my experience. Realizing I was losing contact, I thought of one last question.

"How can I experience this type of communication, fully conscious, again?"

A period of silence followed which seemed to go on forever. Then came the response — only four words:

It is all Vibration.

THE GREAT HALL

Before we left Egypt, I was able to enter into one last dialogue concerning the hall of records — the Great Hall.

"Is there a place in the Giza Plateau where there are records indicating the purposes of these buildings?" I asked.

"These are placed in many temples, not a singular one; whereas, in the lower chambers of the Sphinx may be found the plans and purposes. Below, and in front of the Sphinx, or guardian, lies the Great Hall, which details all knowledge contained in the world up to that time. While most seek a singular building or a temple of records,

what should be understood is that there are many, both above and below ground."

"How does one find these temples?"

"These temples may be found — after the inner dimensional shift takes place, this year — along a line drawn from the center of the south wall of the Great Pyramid, to the center of the hind paws of the Sphinx. We would find temples to the east and west of this line."

"And the Great Hall?"

"We find entry to the Great Hall service begins through entrance to the west of the temple of Isis, or below what is now visible of the Sphinx's right front paw. This will require the removal of the outer casing layers, applied many years after its construction, when the site was sealed. This leads downward many feet passing through, note here — through — the great Sphinx, and those channels leading to the other temples. Turning east leads to one of three guardian protectors who were left to guard the underground complex and Great Hall which is itself a pyramid. Records found, and those to be found shortly, at the rear left paw of the Sphinx, indicate much but only lead the way."

"What was the purpose of the Great Hall?"

"To preserve for future history, much as a time capsule, a history of our world up to that time."

"And are prophecies for our times contained in the Great Hall?"

"Both in the Great Hall and the Great Pyramid."

"In what form?"

"In the Great Hall, records are cut into a tablet made of an emerald stone, and inlaid with the metal of the day — these are in hieroglyphic form. In the Great Pyramid, the prophecies are contained in the very construction, geophysical position, and alignment to key stars of the structure itself. Each gives prophecies covering both ancient times, or the first root race, to when a new race begins, between 1998 and 2001."

THE EMERALD TABLETS

Just prior to the sealing of the Great Hall, some twelve thousand years before the present, specific prophecies concerning the twentieth century were added, to give direction to those who would next discover the hall and its contents. At the time of the sealing, two people existed whose intuitive abilities were developed to such an art, that not only did they know all about the past and future, but all about the alternative realities, as well. Their names were Ra-Ta, the priest of the land of Dar, and Hermes, the Avatar of the Atlantean lands. With the aid of the Great Pyramid — which they called Gizeh — these two masters were able to go beyond even their own formidable abilities, and see clearly into our time period — the final days of this current root race. We, who began some two hundred twenty-thousand years before the present, and will last through the year 2001, are the parents of the next race — the children of the Blue Ray.

The following is my understanding of the meaning of the emerald tablet records, which pertain to the years 1932 through 2001 A.D.

Tablet I
Our work is now complete in this age, and soon the forces of nature shall let loose their fury, as floods purify Ta (Earth).

Tablet II
Before the next millennium comes, this Great Hall shall be covered with the waters from the sea. Protected from all elements, it shall survive this and the next flood — four and one half millennia from now.

Tablet III

Twelve millennia from now, the Great Hall shall be opened, as a new race emerges. What has been placed here is for the children of the millennium of light.

Tablet IV

So that all may know when these changes are to come about for Ta (Earth) — heralding mankind's rebirth in a new age — the days leading to it shall be filled with turmoil. Ta (Earth) shall erupt, and the stars shall shift their positions.

Tablet V

The beginning of the new cycle may be known. Find what we have left for you — an instrument of detection to aid in your preparations. This is a method of determining — within a few solar cycles — the beginning of the pole shift in relation to your pole star (Polaris).

Tablet VI

When the light from your pole star shines through the observation door of Gizeh (the Great Pyramid), down the passage of descent, unto the collector of liquid metal (mercury), then you may know the days are short before the pole star comes anew.

Tablet VII

Osirus (Sirius) will shine brighter than any other in the heavens, and Ma (Mars) shall turn bright red and leave its orbit. Then the alignment between the center of Ta (Earth) and the pole star shall change.

Tablet VIII

Study then the star charts we leave for you. Ta (Earth) is governed by the stars. Knowing the orbits, cycles and rays will aid in the preparation.

Tablet IX

We shall return, along with those who through their dedication to the uplifting of the spirit of mankind, shall aid in bringing hope to a world who has for so long cried out. The time shall be known when our light is seen in the clouds, and yet the sun is at rest.

Tablet X

A single sun now becomes two, for the new race. One to govern the mind of mankind, the other to govern his soul group. Yellow for one. Blue for the other.

* * * * *

So ended my dream voyage in Egypt. Since that time I have thought of a hundred questions I wish I had asked. But in the end, I know I probably did the best I could under the circumstances. Since returning from Egypt, I have worked diligently on my own initiation. Fortunately, I have been able to call upon my Source and successfully journeyed several more times, always exploring new subjects. Interestingly, I do not consciously choose the subjects, nor the times for these journeys. They continue to occur in a random fashion, as do my visions. It appears that contact occurs in order to fill a specific need — to bring forth new information that can be shared with others.

What I have learned from my dream voyages is that each of us are limited only by our own levels of trust and belief. If we are willing to risk, the gains we find are so staggering that we may wonder — as we enter the process of initiation — why

did it take so long to begin? When I asked this question during one of my inner world contacts, this was the response:

> *It does not matter when you begin the process of conscious
> initiation. It is only important that you begin. Each day,
> from sunrise to sunset, is a new initiation. Each day, new
> opportunities arise. For all on the Earth, there has never been
> a time, since Man's entrance, when there has been such an
> opportunity for these great gains in consciousness now pos-
> sible. From 1953 onward, the Earth has been vibrating at
> rates never before experienced. From 1995 to 2001, the
> Earth's vibratory force will double. Movement through levels
> of initiation that may have taken a hundred or more incarna-
> tions, may now occur in one. These are blessed times.*

Gordon-Michael and Cynthia at the Giza Plateau, Egypt, in January 1995.

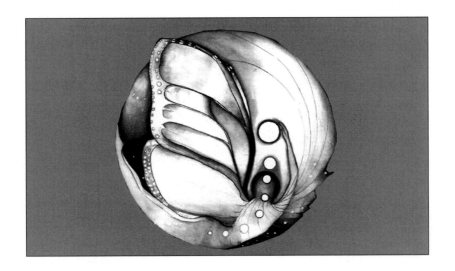

CHAPTER SIXTEEN

Children of the Blue Ray

From nearly the beginning of my intuitive awakening, I would occasionally experience dream voyages in which I viewed children wearing strange clothing. Their physical appearance was familiar — much like children of the twentieth century — although certain characteristics were strikingly different from the children I knew. I felt intuitively that these were children from a future Earth reality. But since these visions occurred only rarely, and the information did not seem to relate to the rest of my transformation, I kept notes, but otherwise paid little attention to them. That is, until 1985, when the phrase "children of the Blue Ray" started coming through during the personal readings I was giving for clients at that time. My curiosity was piqued; nevertheless, I wasn't sure what to do with the very sparse communication I'd received on the subject.

Then, in 1988, Cynthia and I were conducting a session to follow up a client's request for some specific information. Intuitively, Cynthia was guided to ask a question that would lead into a full dialogue about the Blue Ray children. Since that time, this subject has become our most requested topic by far, exceeding even my Earth changes predictions as an area of interest. This overwhelming response to my information on "the Blue Ones" baffled me in the beginning, but as I notice the new children coming into the world throughout this past decade, I wonder why I didn't see the significance earlier, for it is now obvious to me that these children are everywhere. The following is a transcript of our original session dialogue, regarding the remarkable young people now entering our Earth realm.

CK: I would like to ask you some questions about the new "Blue children" that you have referred to in the past. Just who are these children, and what is different about them?

GMS: *These are the forerunners. They are those who come to prepare the way for the next race — what may be termed as the next root race.*

Their origin in the inner world has come from those planes of existence that you would call the mental levels. It is here that, through their particular sojourning, they have congregated, banned together under the ray that would be blue. Not so much as their skin color would be blue, though this indeed will be a portion of the next root race, but rather their vibratory soul group is of the blue vibration.

This overlays a time period, and a land, known to you as Mu, which later became known as Lemuria. Whereas those projections, those early soul projections, did so dwell in that continent in what is now the area of the Pacific. Their evolutionary process, their karmic process, was one of spiritual attunement, being close with the Creator, not having separated or lost from same. A secondary division or a portion thereof manifested in a portion of the Atlantean land. Greater separation occurred with this group. These may be thought of as the yellow race. Not as in color, but as in soul force vibration, that ray governing same.

CK: When did these Blue Ray souls begin coming into Earth?

GMS: *The projection into the Earth School system began for this group predominantly when Uranus began to affect portions of the United States, and indeed the globe.*

As to their projection into that of the United States, a few thousand have incarnated throughout the time period of the seventeenth to twentieth centuries, predominantly in the area of the Southwest. A smaller group — a few hundred — were born into that of the northeastern section: Virginia, Kentucky, and the Ohio Valley. These were also of the same group, but may be thought of as forerunners of the group now coming in large numbers — many hundreds of thousands — throughout the continent. In the 1950s, in particular, they began as the peacekeepers.

CK: Why did these Blue Ray souls choose these time periods to enter the Earth?

GMS: *So that you may have an understanding of the incarnational cycle of groups and the preparations of cycles, we would bring your focus to that time period of the turn of the last century, in particular, just prior to World War I. Whereas a major influx of souls of the yellow vibratory force — or the Atlanteans — did so come to dwell in the Earth School. This has brought to Earth technological advances, as well as warring activities. These were similar energies to the Atlantean time periods of twenty-eight thousand, eighteen thousand and fourteen thousand years before the present. During this time period, a small portion of the Blue Ray force also incarnated, to add balance in the world.*

In the fifties, another window opened up that provided an opportunity for a different vibratory force. Those souls who were attuned to the blue vibratory forces while in between worlds — in the borderlands — found compatibility in the Earth system. This group became the peacekeepers of the sixties.

In the sixties another main group incarnated, and became the political activists. Many of these were the earlier Native Americans — previously Lemurians — reincarnating once more, to complete and work the cycle of preparation. All of this moves towards a grander cycle that will have lasted approximately twelve hundred years in its major focus, through the time period of the turn of the century. It will then move for approximately eighteen hundred years in a sub-harmonic of this, which may be termed a lesser cycle or a preparation for the completion of a grand cycle.

CK: How are cycles chosen, and who chooses them?

GMS: *Entrances or projections into Earth may be thought of as windows or portals of opportunity — lessons for souls to once more choose between applying spiritual forces to the positive or the negative. These cycles are governed by the spheres themselves. Who chooses? The souls themselves.*

CK: If these Blue Ray souls haven't been on Earth for hundreds of thousands of years, why do they come now?

GMS: *These Lemurians, or the Blue Race, have chosen this particular window of opportunity because the vibration of Earth is becoming more closely attuned to their original projection onto Earth. Their goal and purpose was originally to achieve a greater attunement with Earth. Through a co-partnership with the Creator rather than a separation from same, they gained much. As such, they may be thought of as the guardians of the planet and its inhabitants. The children incarnating in this time period are driven towards peace and unity, a caring not only for Earth, but for the universe in its totality.*

Those things that would deal with nurturing qualities — this includes the five elements of Earth — will become part of their total consciousness. They will begin to incarnate in even greater numbers as the vibratory force begins to build. So while an earlier portal of opportunity — such as the 1940s — was a narrow band of color tones of the blue, a greater portion opened up in the fifties, sixties and seventies. In the eighties, nineties and in the next century, millions will enter.

Their function, their purpose — what may be viewed as their karmic desire — is to express themselves in a peaceful manner, utilizing Earth in its original form. They seek to be allowed their existence as co-habitants with the various elements and the sentient Earth form. Understanding would be best if you would view the Blue Ray children as predominantly teachers.

CK: How can these Blue Ray children be identified?

GMS: *The Blue Ray children may be easily distinguished from* *those of other vibratory forces by the structure of their auras. Those who are clairvoyant may recognize them. They have about their skin a cast that would be blue in nature. Realize that this is not true for all soul groups and their vibrational color tones, but for this group it is predominant. Also, within the eye structure, if you will focus on the iris of the eye, you will notice a peculiar wavy action, a shifting or movement, within the color. This is an energy, a force, that emanates from the structure of the eye. Clairvoyant vision may detect these waves as a milky white substance, a form of ectoplasm. This is, in actuality, a life force that is projected out. During the Lemurian time period, it was this same ability which gave these individuals the power to move and molecularly reorganize objects, using the optic system as an appendage, as you would use your hands to do the same. This ability is still there, latent in force, and may be applied as telekinesis.*

CK: You mentioned they are teachers. What will they teach?

GMS: *They will move towards those teaching professions that would deal more with the activities of environment, and will head up and move into positions of authority. Another portion of the group will be the peacekeepers, the negotiators, or those that will bring about a unification of peace. These, however, are more of hybrids, more of those portions of Lemurians who also had Atlantean experiences. They have already gone through the various shifts and changes, what would be termed warring activities or misuse of powers. It is not difficult in today's world to simply look upon these groups and see that they have already begun to manifest. Though, as we perceive, they are only in their very early stages. Again this is cursory, for they are the forerunners of the initiation — such as the purification energy of the baptism. They prepare the way for the coming of the beacon, the Master, and the coming of a grander awakening upon the planet.*

CK: How do colors govern their lives while they are on Earth?

GMS: *You will find that their abilities are expressed directly through activities of color. They are drawn to color in a grand way. They will work with color in such a fashion as many today might use the pencil and ruler for sketching. Likened to the difference between* *those who choose to draw in black-and-white versus those who paint in color, one is not better than the other. Rather, it is simply a different perspective, different dimension, different activity. Within the various colors that these Blue Ones will gravitate towards, you will find them drawn most to pastels, and in particular, to the color mauve, or hues of mauve. This is another way for them to become aware of their group presence, and their projections outward.*

Longevity is another portion of their totality. For with this vibratory force, the age of their life extends some fifteen to eighteen percent. So as you move through the turn of the millennium, you will notice a longevity — a continuing youthfulness — in the earlier members of the group.

You will also find within this group that they become teachers to the parents, having abilities at birth to excel in music, art, writing and psychic communication between all kingdoms of consciousness, plant, animal, human and Earth. All of these gifts are latent in their consciousness, and awaken early. They come into Earth consciously aware of most of their abilities, and of their own presence. If nurtured early, these abilities become manifest at a very early age and begins to project out — where they are teaching others by the age of four to five. By the time they reach their twelfth year, the Blue Ones would be equivalent to an average adult who has spent perhaps twenty-five years as a teacher. These are correlations in general, not taken to be specific. But it is a good overview of their ability, if nurtured early.

CK: How would a parent recognize an infant as being of the Blue Ray?

GMS: *Much of this has to do with the ability to sleep and to move. They will walk early and seem to need little sleep. They will also have the ability to penetrate with their eyes — a certain look, initially — from soon after birth to the age of eighteen months. It is a piercing almost, as if looking into deep wells. The eyes would be the strongest indicator during this earliest segment of life. It is here that their telepathic abilities are the strongest, too.*

Also watch for the ability to understand, move and talk with the invisible world. This sounds more like babble, initially. But if listened to with care, you will find the babble has a rhythm to it, a cadence that obviously conveys meaning, even if you yourself cannot understand it. It is not much different from the language that was first conveyed during their time period some eighteen million years ago, as we count time from the present. Whereas the inflection of the sound wave was more of the language, rather than the spoken word itself.

CK: How can a parent or teacher best nurture these children?

GMS: *By bringing color into their environment. Large areas of color, whether it be walls or panels, are best. In particular, use the hues as given, in the mauve ranges, moving perhaps two or three tones above and below. These set up a rapport between their natural vibratory forces and the available environment, enabling a communion to occur, an awakening, an acceleration of consciousness.*

For aural environment, music that mimics the sounds of the elements — like the sound of running water — would emphasize the correct vibration. Also the music of the flute, or music that would be in the form of chanting, or drumming. What we are describing here is a rhythmic cycling — a humming or beating pulse, soothing, not agitating. It may be thought of as the flute operating in the higher octaves, and the drums in the lower vibrations. Both give an attunement with the infinite, and also with the Mother herself, Earth.

CK: What about diet? Is there any special diet for these children?

GMS: *This is preprogrammed, initially. These souls have always been vegetarian, and as such will turn away from any sustenance in the form of meat, including that of fish and fowl, preferring vegetables and grains instead. That is not to say that they will not have a sweet tooth for the cane! But meats are not in rapport or harmony with the Blue Ones, for the density of the vibratory force which would come through eating meat separates them from their basic life force — Earth. The Blue Ones draw most of their power from the Earth force, rather than the greater cosmic force; the planet energy runs strongest in them, so their diet conforms naturally to that which most benefits the planetary balance.*

CK: So the parents shouldn't be concerned then if they don't eat meat, and they should try to balance their diet as best they can with vegetables and grains?

GMS: *It is only necessary to provide a variety upon the table. They will be automatically drawn to those vibratory forces of necessity for them. In particular, the difficulty here will be more of the vitality of the particular vegetable, rather than the type of vegetable. They will sense automatically, not favoring specifics of flavor or familiar tastes, but gravitating towards that which is freshest, or most alive, on a vibratory level. Their sensory abilities — particularly in those meridians on the thumb, index and middle finger — are receptors which are attuned to the vibratory force of foods. This is an interesting point to note at this time, for all of humankind have this ability, though the Blue Ones have the latent knowledge, or understanding, of its use. They can feel vibratory forces through the electromagnetic structure of foods — not its etheric web, but its electromagnetic, or bonding, force.*

CK: So it's a good idea to let them touch their food?

GMS: *It will be a natural process for them, thus encouragement in the environment facilitates their growth. This follows that used as a secondary sense, which would be the olfactory activity, or sense of smell. The Blue Ones use such as a confirmation of the primary sensory attunement. In your present, little is known about aromatics, though much understanding will be emerging shortly, especially as those of the Blue Ray grow into their teaching facilities, communicating what they already comprehend — that life force may be taken directly from the fragrances of flowers and foods. This group will use both the primary and secondary senses to detect the correct vibratory levels before consuming food. If there is not a harmony or resonance with the food — if they know it will not provide the necessary sustenance, which is based on energy, not the rules of nutrition as they are currently understood — they will simply dismiss it. They will not eat it.*

CK: Are these children coming in to any particular type of parents?

GMS: *As given, much of this will have to do with lessons. But the familial structures, while they may be diverse, will be based on a kind of "need" activity. This is to say that the parents will tend to be needy, rather than having a greater nurturing quality. It is not that they will be unable to nurture the children, but more that they will*

*lack a greater awareness of consciousness, or an evolved sense of the
Oneness of the whole. So the parents themselves will often have a
form of need. This is a stronger need, perhaps, than soul groups even
in the sixties, seventies, and so forth, because although they will possess the latent abilities of the Blue Ones — their offspring — they
will be more open to the learning process than those souls of earlier
decades. So the children must become teachers unto them, which, of
course, was prearranged through the choices of all souls involved.
The parents of children of the Blue Ray are not likely to be from
Lemuria; more commonly, they will represent a wide variety or
diversity, entering from many other vibrational levels. Part of the
lesson and part of the purpose of the Blue Ones is to teach all groups.
Some will teach in a broad sense, such as in the classroom; others
will teach through forms of writing, art, music, productions or other
such activities; others still will manifest as the peacekeepers; and
finally, there are some who will simply teach the parents, as part of
the karmic cycle.*

*Many of the Atlanteans who are on Earth today — which are the
majority of souls at present — will have a need for new lessons, to
learn the new vibratory forces that are soon to govern the planet in
the coming age. For in the time period from the turn of the last century through to the year A.D. 2250, only those souls who have particular vibratory forces will be able to incarnate in this Earth reality.
It is not that some are being restricted as a judgment of purity or
goodness. Rather, this is a natural process, wherein the vibratory
force of the soul must match the vibratory force of the time period, in
order for passage to occur. Earth itself will soon be beating, pulsing,
at a different frequency than it has in previous times. It will have a
different vibratory force, and its pilot frequency will change, moving
to another harmonic. Earth's harmonic will increase to more than
two times the current rate of cycle. As such, those souls not properly
attuned through other incarnations, will not be able to resonate or
find harmony within the Earth School. The Blue Ones come to aid
and assist in the present, so as many as possible may take part in the
coming of the next age.*

CK: Can you tell me the difference between the Indigo Ray
and the Blue Ray, and describe the people of each?

GMS: *It is important to note here that the color spectrum — moving from what you might call the denser or the red, up towards that of the totality or that of the white — is an ascension. It is an ascension, as in moving towards a greater unity with the Oneness. Do not be confused, however, by thinking that someone who is working at a particular vibratory force in the present, say as a yellow or a green, is not as evolved as someone who is currently in that of the indigo, the blue, or the violet. For the present entity is only a small piece of the higher self — the whole consciousness — which chooses particular lessons that it wishes to develop, so that its entirety may be more perfected. The vibratory level is simply an indication of the particular range of lessons, activities, or opportunities being explored. As such, depending upon the focus, which you might term as time, or time period, the entity chooses and selects a particular group to work from. These soul groups have similar vibratory needs, and manifest naturally in the correct period for the lessons they require.*

Soul groups, such as those of the Blue Ray, have sub-groups within them. These can be thought of as hues or tones in the color range. Each of these sub-groups band together, as a form of collectiveness. For example, there is what is termed individual karma, and also group karma — group as in nation, or group as in continent, or group as in planet. These band together in space and time, for it brings to them many of the other souls who are working on a similar collective energy. It might be to shift consciousness in a particular country, for example, or to bring balance to an area of Earth. So they move together for this collective experience.

The Indigo Ray may be thought of as those who are teachers of teachers. This, again, only comes as an example, and should not be taken literally, for there can be teachers of teachers in any of the color groups. The Indigo Ray group, Cynthia, of which you are a part, is the vibratory force of what may be termed here as a greater expansion of consciousness. You are working together as a group, on the psychic level, rather than individually, or within a specific time-space. So those of the Indigo Ray group become entities who are teachers that reach out and touch many. Presently, this group is comprised of those Masters who are now working upon Earth —

some quietly, some in an expansive way — to bring about shifts of consciousness for the entire collective.

CK: Are there any distinguishing characteristics about the children of the Indigo Ray?

GMS: *The majority of these had their incarnations in the Atlantean framework, or portal, having come in during the times given earlier. All of the current time is part of an awakening within them, for they have been the forerunners of the Blue Ones. They have set up the modules of opportunity, those frameworks and conditions which will allow the newest projection of souls. They can be thought of as the grandparents of the Blue Ray children, the new root race.*

CK: Did the Indigo Ray also have incarnations in Mu, as well as Atlantis?

GMS: *There were portions thereof, but the spectrum qualities at that time were much different. The spectrum as you now know it was not the same. The vibratory forces, the atmospheric conditions, the alignment and positions of Earth within the sun system was different. The vibratory forces during Mu were shadow-like. Such colors, as you now know them, would not relate to that time period. The blue vibratory force was dominant. It would be like today looking through glasses that allowed only the narrow band of color pertaining to the blue spectrum to enter your vision. This narrow band drew those souls seeking communion with the spiritual forces of the Earth. The Indigo Ray forces passed into another spectrum — creating the Atlantean land.*

* * * * *

After that session in 1988, I received almost no new information on children of the Blue Ray. Until the spring of 1997, that is, when Cynthia's daughter, Shari, brought her family out for a visit.

Now, in our family we have several very young grandchildren who are already clearly demonstrating Blue Ray characteristics. During Shari's visit, though, I had the opportunity to witness firsthand a true child of the Blue Ray, demonstrating those uncanny intuitive abilities which to the Blue Ones seem only natural, a part of their very essence.

Cassie is Shari's young daughter, and she just turned five years old this past January. Spending the weekend together at our rural New Hampshire home was a treat for all of us. It's a great place for kids, and adults too. We have a fish pond with a little paddle-wheel boat, all types of wildlife, many acres of woodlands, and of course, our cats Ichabod and Pepin, and our three llamas, Damiana, Hermes and Bright Stars. In other words, there is a lot of fun things to do, and Cassie, like our other grandchildren, enjoys them all. On the second day of Cassie's stay, she woke early — as she normally does at our house — and announced that she had had a special dream. Of course, everyone asked her to talk about her dream. She complied, but only barely, mentioning those details that stood out to her — a rainbow, a waterfall, and her new baby sister, Nicola.

A little later in the morning I was over in our studio, which is about a hundred yards from our house (working on this book, as a matter of fact). I heard a knock on the door, and Cassie let herself in. She had told her mother and Cynthia that she *had* to go to the studio to see me. The studio is another one of those fun places on our property. We have large dry-erase boards to write on, and lots of colored markers. We also have a recording studio, with both audio and video capability, including lots of lights, props and buttons to push — a veritable playground for all kinds of pretend-games. But Cassie did not want to play with any of these things, or with me, but wanted instead to talk. I asked her what was on her mind, and like many five-year-olds, she simply shrugged her shoulders. I waited. And waited.

Finally, she said, "Gordon, I had a dream last night."

Taken aback by her seriousness, and having missed out on her earlier explanations back at the house, I said, "That's great! What was it about?"

"I lived under a waterfall, and I was swimming underwater. But I had to hold Nicola, because she couldn't swim." She paused. "There was a rainbow, too," she added.

"Is there anything else you can recall?" I asked.

"No."

I knew, intuitively, that she wanted to explore the dream further, but that she didn't know how to go about it. Suddenly, my intuition snapped into action, and I went to our recycled-paper bin and got out about a dozen pieces of paper which were blank on one side — great for kids to do coloring. I quickly folded the sheets into a book, and stapled the centers together. I handed it to Cassie, and asked if she wanted to make a dream book.

Her eyes lit up. "Oh, yes!" she said.

I said that to begin, we would need some crayons, and a title for this dream book. I quickly supplied the crayons. Cassie decided the title should be "Cassie and Nicola Under the Waterfall," and set to work on her book.

Delicately, page after page, Cassie drew detailed pictures of her dream. The first one showed her underwater. She explained to me that she could breathe underwater. The next showed her under the waterfall holding her baby sister, Nicola. Nicola, however, had not yet learned how to breathe underwater. The color blue dominated the pictures (as you might imagine), with water and rainbows as the main motifs. She was also using other colors — greens and browns — with almost equal intensity.

Looking over at her project from time to time, I was taken aback when I saw the next page, showing a picture of Nicola's face. It was blue! But a very light blue, more of a tint. I asked her why her face was blue, thinking perhaps it was to show the color of the water. She said that was the way Nicola was supposed to be. And she — Cassie — was supposed to be blue too! Cassie completed many pages, explaining to me in great detail the meaning of each. Now, I've had some experience with dreams myself, and have a working understanding of dream symbolism. What Cassie described was clearly not a creation of her imagination. She was recalling, in detail, a very special dream that described not only her feelings of love for her sister, but how she knew — intuitively — that both she and Nicola were somehow "blue."

To me, this was a dream of spiritual expression and love. The symbolism of the rainbow may be different for a child than for an adult, but they share many things in common. For both, it can represent a feeling of joy, good fortune, luck, or a way of pointing to another dream symbol, such as Cassie's waterfall. The combination denotes an intense feeling of overflowing joy. To breathe underwater can also represent strong emotions, and a feeling of strength or power — as if to be a part of the water is as natural as breathing, becoming one with the life force. Water often represents the collective consciousness, the all-knowing Oneness. In Cassie's dream, her baby sister could not yet breathe underwater. But, Cassie explained, she would be able to very soon.

"Why?" I asked.

"Because she is blue, silly," she replied.

* * * * *

This experience was to be a catalyst for me, because shortly after Shari and her family left, I began to receive new insights on Blue Ray children. These new characteristics are presented below:

1. Blue Ray children have dreams that are highly evolved, and they begin dreaming and remembering dreams at a very early age.

2. They have an affinity for languages of all types. Many speak more than one language, if exposed, by the age of three.

3. They are determined, and at times can be quite stubborn.

4. They invent pretending games in which they take on the role of healer, using the laying on of hands.

5. They are drawn to water, more than any other setting. They

often stare into space at length, especially when near rivers, lakes, oceans or even the blue sky.

6. They have an understanding of how animals feel and think. They explain this to others in a matter-of-fact — "Don't you know?" — manner.

7. By the time they reach their teens, many have the desire to go to other countries — often attempting to urge their parents to take them, or going so far as to plan their own trips. South America and New Zealand will be favorite destinations for Blue Rays.

8. Their personalities seem to fluctuate between two extremes — from being serious, single-minded and focused, to being dreamy-eyed and distant.

Since first publishing the Blue Ray material in 1988, I have received significant amounts of mail from parents describing their children, who they believe to be Blue Rays. There are far too many similarities in all the material I have received for these traits to be merely coincidental. As such, I feel it is important — perhaps for our very future — that I do everything in my power to support a continuing awareness of these gifted children. One way I can do so is by publishing new Blue Ray material in our newsletter, the *Earth Changes Report*. I will also continue to publish letters, and to make comments on correspondence I receive from Blue Ray parents, relatives, friends, or even Blue Rays themselves, if given permission to do so. Please keep me posted if your child is a Blue Ray, or if you know of one.

CHAPTER SEVENTEEN

The Third Millennium

In earlier chapters, I have given a fairly concise description of predictions I have seen occurring between 1998 and 2012, as well as specific details about the forerunners of the next root race — the children of the Blue Ray. In this chapter I wanted to share other visions I've received for the time period 1998 to 2012 as well as a special dream voyage into the third millennium which shows a quite different Earth, one that is spiritual, peaceful and vibrant.

A few days before this book was to be sent to the printer, however, something quite surprising, almost mystical, occurred. While working at my word processor, new material of a cryptic nature was presented to me. This material was identified as "The Milios," and apparently relates to events in the millennium to come — after the year A.D. 2000. While I have not been shown their meaning by my dream teachers, my intuition told me to include them at the end of this chapter in the hope that others might assist in determining their meaning.

PREDICTIONS: 1998 — 2012

Geophysical

As Earth changes increase in earnest on the west coast of America, I see cars from California snaking across the desert at night, their headlights strung out like Christmas tree lights in the darkness. There is only one direction to go — east — and their destination is the high desert, where camp-cities are being set up. I see flocks of Chinook helicopters with National Guard insignias emblazoned on the undersides coming in to land, the desert sands blowing in every direction around the massive machines as they touch the ground. Troops are unloading food and medical supplies from the helicopters as fast as they can land. This, and other tent cities like it, are spreading up and down the California landscape, just west of the Arizona and Nevada borders. There are hundreds of thousands of refugees, many of them children and elderly people.

Other survival camps in the western region are located in Nevada, Colorado, and New Mexico. There are survival centers throughout the United States. In the Great Lakes region — Iowa, Illinois, Ohio and Kentucky. In the northeast — southern Vermont, western Massachusetts, east-central New York state, and western New Hampshire. In the south — central Virginia, central North Carolina, and north-central Florida.

In the coastal areas of western Canada, the land is "pushed back," or inundated for two hundred miles or more. Survivors migrating from the west coast of Canada move into Alberta. On the eastern end of the country, coastal land is pushed back one hundred miles or more. Survival camps are located in the centers of Nova Scotia and Quebec, Ontario and the Great Lakes region.

From Japan, many people escape to China and Russia, as the Japanese islands go beneath the sea. In the United Kingdom, the mountains in the upper northeast portions of the coast become a survival area. In Australia, early warnings allow people to flee the coastal areas, and many move hundreds of miles inland, creating a significant migration to central portions of the country. In New Zealand, populations are forced away from the coasts at first, which are inundated by tsunamis — caused by the sinking of other lands — and subjected to severe quaking due to rising land masses that will soon expand this territory to more than double its current size. On the European continent, there is a great loss of land. Those that can leave their homes before it's too late find refuge in the mountains of Spain and Switzerland. In South America — the region of longest lasting Earth changes — hundreds of camps are set up in the high mountains along both coasts of the continent.

Weather

Currently, it is estimated that eighty percent of the world's volcanoes are located in the oceans. At the end of this century — and into the beginning of the next — the number and intensity of eruptions from these underwater volcanoes will increase exponentially. The result of this action will be significant thermal heating of the oceans, which upon reaching the surface will be translated into an atmospheric change, drastically affecting Earth's current weather pattern systems. So as the oceans are heated by these volcanic eruptions, high-velocity winds shall be created and driven over the land. Areas between the Tropic of Cancer and Tropic of Capricorn shall experience the greatest exposure to these winds.

Over time, the winds change the natural patterns of vegetation on the planet, and create dramatic shifts in the climate and temperatures of various regions. The system of worldwide agriculture is thrown into turmoil, as seasonal weather patterns go into flux, or are altered permanently. In order to preserve many species of plants — and in some instances entire ecosystems — invention and intervention are required. Hydroponic growing techniques and improvements on artificially created growing spaces, like the biosphere, aid in the production of food and medicinal herbs, and will save some smaller forms of wildlife from extinction. During the climatic changeover, cooperation and sensitivity to current conditions, rather than a dependence upon past rules and trends, are crucial to survival.

The power of these winds and storms should not be underestimated — in many ways they present the greatest threat to life on Earth during the period of changes. For although the land shifts and floods appear to be the most catastrophic events, these are localized occurrences, and relatively brief in duration. The winds, on the other hand, dictate new patterns of life throughout the land. Cycles of pollination, migration patterns and regional precipitation are affected. Many wild species of plants and animals cannot survive the dramatic shifts in temperature; this is not because the increase or decrease is so huge, but because the *cycles* change so drastically. Hibernation patterns no longer apply. Growth cycles for many plant species are disrupted, and this will be felt throughout the food chain, devastating many species at the high end of the chain. Mankind is in many ways the most susceptible to these changes, but is also in the best position to anticipate and prepare for them. An understanding of science and technology, in conjunction with a greater attunement to the Earth as it goes through this transformation, does much to ease the devastating effects of weather on our life support systems.

Conflicts

Before the turn of the century, war breaks out in Turkey and spreads throughout the Middle East. Soon, other nations are drawn in — creating a third world war scenario — as alliances are established.

Economics

Due to Earth changes and war, country after country falls into a state of economic depression. Initially, gold and silver become highly valued. Gold trades at over $2,500 per troy ounce, silver increases even more in value, trading at over $75 per troy ounce. Paper currencies become devalued in every country. Commodities rise sharply. Stock markets close globally. There are runs on the banks in almost every country, Switzerland included.

Politics

The United States becomes a series of colonies, thirteen in number, as a result of land separations. Each is independently governed, with no connection to a central government, at least in the initial stages. Eventually a new government is established to tie the colonies together. Some Canadian provinces join with the northern colonies of the Unites States. Other provinces choose to stand alone.

Russia becomes an agrarian society under a single leadership once more. An uprising then occurs, which places a spiritual teacher at the helm. The same occurs in New Zealand and two of the U.S. colonies.

The United Kingdom is reduced to a small series of islands, and joins with what remains of the current European countries to form a new government similar to the colonies in the U.S. The seat of this government is located upon new land which rises from the depths of the Atlantic, off the coast of Portugal.

Australia remains fairly stable politically, and like portions of the U.S., Canada and Africa, becomes a center of food production for the rest of the world.

As people attempt to restore order and govern themselves after the first large wave of Earth changes, attention is somewhat shifted away from politics and trends towards nationalism, isolation or colonization. People the world over are more concerned with the local issues of providing food and medical attention for those nearest to them, reconstructing habitable environments, and maintaining orderly conduct amongst themselves. Although many areas are decimated by an inability to cope with these new problems — violence and looting leading to a state of anarchy in many places — many communities of healing and cooperation are borne of the need for reorganization.

Science

After the turn of the century, science begins to make great strides in medicine, especially in a new area of study showing how the human body is affected by the subtle vibrations of Earth. A method of limb rejuvenation is perfected, useful for up to twenty-one days after severance of a limb. Vision is correctable to 20/20 for both near- and far-sighted people, through a chemical process. Eye color can also be changed — as a cosmetic procedure — by a similar process.

Education

In the U.S., education becomes private to a significant degree in the coming century. Urban areas cannot handle the economic hardships of reorganization after the first wave of Earth changes. As schools close, instruction is sub-contracted out in some areas. Eventually, a voucher system emerges and becomes the norm in several of the colonies, wherein there is still some attempt to track a standardized level of education. In other colonies, at-home education is openly supported, and a new form of communication network links them together, providing a cohesive program, and allowing for a more interactive learning process. Many individual home-study programs merge into community-based programs, especially in rural regions.

Technology

Because of shifts in planetary and solar magnetic forces, our current system of electricity is not seen in the future. New technology is developed, based on natural forces found in the Earth — standing wave forces. This technology, first developed by Nikola Tesla at the turn of the twentieth century (and applied throughout the twentieth century by military factions), emerges effortlessly. To access this energy system, each structure requires only one small unit — about the size of a toaster — for all power and communications use. Satellite technology all but ceases as the funds and equipment to maintain it are lost. Vehicles will utilize a power-cell propulsion system, though very few individuals will have access to one.

Cities

What cities remain by the early part of the twenty-first century — those not destroyed by Earth changes — find themselves in turmoil. With no funds to maintain services, the quality of life in most urban settings crumbles beyond repair. People leave for rural areas, or try to migrate to other countries. By A.D. 2012, population in the U.S. has shifted and regrouped into smaller, rural communities.

Health and Healing

Due to magnetic shifts in the sun and Earth, many plagues such as AIDS and tuberculosis disappear overnight, because the destructive cells cannot support their own matrix in the new magnetic environment. During the early years of the new millennium, most cancers are eradicated by the discovery of a naturally occurring blood additive. The global birth rate swiftly declines, further decreasing the population. Healers emerge in all corners of the globe. Most seem to wake up one day with a sudden "gift" for the laying on of hands. Many point to God's assistance and blessing during these times.

Spirituality

After difficult times at the end of this century and the beginning of the next, society begins to emerge as a spiritually conscious community. Wars are replaced by a spirit of cooperation. Food is shared globally through a system of food banks. Life in the next millennium is based on unity and a respect for all life. If you were to ask various national leaders in the next millennium, "What do you consider to be your country's most valuable treasure?" most would respond emphatically, "Our children!"

Telepathic abilities become common for children born in the next millennium. Earth consciousness is taught in all schooling programs. Children are born with what would be considered "gifts" during our current time period. Telepathic communication with family members over long distances becomes a common practice, as children of the Blue Ray teach their parents how to access these inner resources. These same talents are used to communicate with loved ones who have passed over into the next realm. Fear of death declines rapidly as a result, as people are able to adjust slowly to the separation.

DREAM VOYAGE INTO THE THIRD MILLENNIUM

As I attempted to project myself farther into the future while writing this, hoping to discover more information on what our world will be like after the Earth changes, I saw a bright, white light with rays of gold pouring forth from its center.

I gaze upon the globe of light, and I can clearly see the likeness of a child. I cannot see whether this child-being is male or female. It has no hair on its head, which is strange, and although it is not at all unpleasant in appearance, it has other features that seem quite different from a human child as well. Its skin is the color of a pink honey-

suckle blossom — rosy, but with a blue tint. Attached at the center of its back, near its shoulders, are enormous wings that rise several feet above the being's head, and reach down almost to its delicate ankles. The wings are of a soft, downy membrane, skin-like, but almost as if the skin grows in fine layers, so that it has a feathery quality. The being itself is thin, and perhaps four feet in height.

Looking harder into the light, I see that the first child-being is surrounded by others of a similar type, although these appear to be older, more like young adults in their twenties or thirties. These others have wings as well, but their skin is a different color, more white than pink, but still with a tint of blue. The child-being beckons me forth, and I move forward. As I reach the child, it holds its hand out to me and says in an adult voice, low and melodious, "Come, and we will show you the miracles of the third millennium." I take its hand, and within a moment I find myself moving along with the child and the other winged beings.

We are flying through the air, effortlessly. There is no sensation of movement, no feeling of air on my face or velocity, but I can see clouds, and then the Earth, moving past us, around and below us. It is as if we are in a protective bubble, devoid of all external sensations, but with a clear vantage point of what exists outside the bubble. We seem to be traveling over the Earth, at a distance of perhaps a one to two hundred feet above the ground. I can see that we are approaching a futuristic city of some type.

The Dome City

As we approach the city, I can see vast fields — crops that seem to be growing higher and greener than any I have ever seen before. All the buildings are domes, perfectly round and clear, as if formed by a large, translucent ball that was cut in half and placed face down on the ground. As we enter the city, I see that some of these domes are quite large. Their surfaces glisten like water or ice when the sunlight strikes them just so, and I think that they are beautiful to look at.

"These are the homes and factories of the future," the child angel-being says. "These structures are grown from an organic substance, much in the same way as you might grow a vegetable. The shapes are *determined by a master mold, and the genetic encoding is established by designers to meet specific need requirements. The shell provides heat and cooling for the interior, and also acts as a collector for solar rays, utilizing a process similar to photosynthesis in plants."*

I am in awe of the sparkling structures. All around me I sense a thriving life force. The crops, the people on the ground, why even the buildings, seem vibrant, vital, and totally alive.

The being continues to explain what we are seeing. "Electrical forces generated by the dome shells themselves provide all the energy necessary for the appliances used in this age. Nothing operates through the use of fossil fuels. No pollution is created by any means of energy production. It is against the 'Charter of the Chrysalis' to do otherwise. The homes and buildings you see are developed and produced at regional factories, and delivered to communities such as this one."

I can see clusters of homes sprinkled over the landscape for miles. They seem to be blended with the surroundings so perfectly, they appear almost to have grown naturally. I cannot see any roads or power lines at all. Each housing cluster seems to be comprised of three separate but interconnected domes, which are in turn joined at the center by a much larger dome. There are perhaps fifty of these clusters in a one mile radius. At the center of this community of clusters is a huge single dome, perhaps ten times larger than the domes residing at the center of each cluster.

The angel-child says, "The central building acts as a terminal of sorts, a conveyance system."

Coming out of the far end of this terminal I can see a tube, perhaps fifty feet in diameter, which extends beyond the clusters and disappears over the horizon. I imagine it connects to another terminal dome and more interconnected clusters. It reminds me of something made out of Tinkertoys. The tube is perfectly round and seems to float above the ground, with no apparent means of structural support. Its walls are made of the same translucent substance as the domes. I watch as a vehicle of some type comes through the tube and arrives at the central dome. Its shape is cigar-like, perhaps fifty feet long.

Our protective bubble floats motionlessly above the city, and the beings who are my guides seemed to be patiently waiting for me to observe all that I might. I can see children playing outside in a park-like setting. Sculptures of all types adorn the playground. Many of these are in the likeness of familiar animals, common to the twentieth century. Strangely, though, I notice that I have seen no real animals anywhere here — no cattle, no horses, no sheep. Birds, however, are everywhere in abundance, and colored as strikingly as the exotic species of any rain forest. In the park, there are many birds that resemble parrots, but they are at least three times larger than any parrot I've ever seen. Flowers are plentiful, too, although also in varieties that I've never seen before. Clearly, new species of birds and plants are part of the third millennium.

I focus on a group of perhaps twenty children, who are gathered in a circle around an adult woman, their teacher. They are all sitting on the ground in the park, and the woman is showing a photograph of what looks like New York City. Slowly, she shows the children various pictures of different cities, talking as she holds them up for viewing. I recognize Paris, Los Angles and Detroit. One little girl reaches out and touches the image of the Eiffel Tower, and I think how foreign that structure must look to the children in this city of domes. The teacher shows other pictures of familiar landscapes — one of Three Mile Island, another of a factory with black smoke bellowing out of its multiple stacks, and still another showing a congested interstate highway, with cars sitting bumper to bumper for miles, mired in a gray haze of exhaust fumes.

At the other end of the park another group catches my eye, and I focus on them. Here there appears to be a diverse mix of youngsters — perhaps ten to twelve years old — and elderly people. The ratio of children to older folks is three to one, and they are clustered in small groups around what look like branches of trees or plants. Each group has a different kind of plant, and it is clear to me, even from within our protected bubble, that several heated discussions are going on. The expressions on everyone's faces are quite dynamic, and the elderly people, especially, seem peculiarly vibrant compared to what I am used to seeing. I see one older man make a silly face as he gestures with the branch, and the members of his group, children and adults alike, join in robust laughter.

I turn to the angel-being and say, "They seem so happy!"

"Yes," came the reply. "And they will be so for most of their life-times, which during this age shall be three hundred years. Disease as you know it no longer exists. The conflicts and wars of previous ages are absent from the third millennium. Do these blessings not also contribute to their laughter?"

Nodding in agreement, I look up and notice the sky. It is not the usual blue color, but a strange blending of teal and fuchsia. The clouds, while white in general appearance, have a bluish, rosy tint to them.

I turn back to the child-being and ask, "Is it summer?"

It responds, "There are now only two seasons for much of the plan-et — spring and summer."

I look into the sky as if searching for some indication of why this is so, and find myself instead thinking about airplanes. Airplanes are nowhere to be seen, nor are there any of the other more common methods of transportation such as cars, trucks or buses on the ground. I have seen no roads at all since arriving, not even ruins of old ones left over from my own time period. I wonder how people travel, and how goods are transported from place to place.

The angel-child reads my thoughts. "Within the city, people walk, for it is not far from any one place to another. Rarely, to move larger objects, there are hover-transports available which do not require paths or roads. To traverse longer distances, this city and others like it are linked by the tube system connected to the main terminal."

I turn my attention back to the domes. I wonder about the inside of these structures and find our bubble instantly moving closer to the nearest cluster. Up close, the domes seem to have varying levels of transparency. Some parts are reflective, almost mirror-like from the outside. Others are totally transparent, like glass, and the people and furnishings inside can be seen easily. We approach one dome and our bubble stops about ten feet from the shell.

Inside, a group of more than one family is dining together. There are some adults, but mostly children. The kitchen and dining area is quite large compared to the other spaces in the dome. I see two adults and several children preparing food in the kitchen. Bowls, clear as glass, are sitting on a stone-like surface, and I can see that the con-

tents of one is boiling and a vapor is rising from it, although no con-
trols of any kind are visible, nor is there any indication on the surface of where cooking elements might be. Positioned in a recess of the
counter top to the right of the stone cooking area is a rectangular
box, perhaps four feet square. It has a door, and I suspect that it is a
cooler of some kind, but when one of the children opens it, I cannot
see anything resembling the design of a familiar refrigerator.
Everything inside is translucent, except the sides of the device which
are white, and these give off a soft, white light, although I can see no
bulbs or other light sources other than the material itself. Inside,
there are many shelves on either side of a central series of bins. Each
bin contains food — vegetables and nuts or grains of some type.
The food is contained in the device itself, and none of the familiar
bottles of condiments or plates and containers of food are present. If
this is a cooler of some type, I wonder, then, why there are no liquids
stored inside.

I next turn my attention to another counter area and a series of
tubes, again translucent, about an inch in diameter. These tubes pro-
trude out of the side of another device which is about the size of a
breadbox. I watch as one of the adults approaches this device and
positions his glass on the counter top below one of the protrusions.
Liquid flows from one of the tubes into the glass and stops its flow
automatically when it is three-quarters filled.

In another room, I can see several adults sitting around a small
cube which is positioned on a low hexagonal table made of the same
stone-like material as the cooking area and counter tops. On the surface of the cube I can see light emitting from it in waves of color,
reminding me very much of what I witnessed during my first vision
in 1979. I watch as a mist forms, and the lights turn into holographic images. I concentrate on this scene for several minutes and then
turn to my angelic guides. With all that I have witnessed, I feel as if
I understand something. They nod and smile at me in unison.

The child-being says, "When one age ends and a new one begins,
all is not lost. There are no ends, only cycles that blend into other
cycles. In the third millennium much will be different, and yet, that
which you now hold dear shall be carried forth. You have witnessed
the most probable reality of what is to be. There are now in your

world — your time — millions of thoughts that are joyful, giving, compassionate, creative, healing, and loving. These thoughts are now in the process of creating what you have just witnessed. As your society today thinks, so shall tomorrow become. This is what the Avatar meant when he said, 'You must be as a child to enter the gates of heaven.' The third millennium can be such a heaven. How choose you all?"

With that, I suddenly found myself back in my studio at my computer. I could see the aura of my hands glowing, radiating an electric blue. I could see the light from my aura reaching far out from my body — farther than I could ever remember having experienced before. This had not been a typical dream voyage. In the time since, I have read my notes of this journey many times. Each time, I revisit the experience and smile with joy. I feel so blessed to be on Earth at this time.

THE MILIOS

As I was finishing up this book in June of 1997, I decided to scan our database of previously published material, to see if there was anything else readers might be interested in. As I waited for my computer to complete its search, somehow the scan was canceled, and a word processing document opened up instead. Startled, I pulled my hand back and stood up, for this action had occurred without any conscious intent on my part. My heart pounding, I recalled the dream voyage to the third millennium and wondered if I was about to repeat the experience. I went outside for a walk. Fifteen minutes later I returned and decided to give it another try. Perhaps I was stressed from all the deadline pressure I was under to complete the book. When I returned to my desk, I once again opened my database file and began a search. Once again I canceled it — without intention — and opened a new blank word processing document. It was now clear that some part of my consciousness was trying to tell me something. It is not unusual, as I mentioned in a previous chapter, that the computer becomes for me a high-tech method of accessing higher states of consciousness. In the old days of spiritualism at the turn of the century, mediums used a process called automatic writing to bring forth messages from the dearly departed. Perhaps, I thought, this is the modern way of doing it. I took a deep breath and tried again.

What followed was unlike any of the material I have ever brought through in the past. Two separate messages — each presented to me a day apart — came to challenge the thought process of the members of my staff, Cynthia, and indeed myself. Puzzled, we are still not sure just what these strange verses mean. But one thought we all had in common was that since I was doing a chapter on the third millennium, perhaps these messages were prophecies. We also thought that possibly this new material had a entirely new purpose. Again, we remain open-minded about what it all might mean.

I thought of not including this new material in the book, waiting to publish it after we had taken some time to decode the messages. However, just as I was reflecting on what to do with this material, guidance came through, which is often the case when I am about to take a wrong turn, so to speak.

"The Milios," my inner voice said, "is for the people who prepare for the third millennium. All initiates may learn their meaning. Allow them to assist."

After this experience, my staff and I agreed that it felt intuitively correct to add this material to this, the final chapter of *Notes from the Cosmos*. My sense is that more of these "Milios" will be presented to me as time goes on. Should that be the case, I will share these in our newsletter, as well as any helpful comments we receive from those who choose to work on interpreting them.

The First Milios

The ten, standing with pomp and glitter, race
*   to their vaults.*
Crowds, angry and wild, storm the shops in
*   reaction.*
Who amongst them knew in advance?
The eagle? The bear? The crown? The sun?
Nay, the skies seemed clear, the road straight,
Destiny was not a consideration for this race.

The Second Milios

Fireworks heralded their day,
Returned have eight to prepare the way.
Blue light from beyond sets the course,
As death retreats before Michael's presence.
He'll walk and talk with all those that wish,
Oh what joy, this age shall be!

What do the above "Milios" mean? It is too early for me to know, and I may never understand them definitively. Perhaps they are being presented to me at this time in order to share them with you, so we can begin our next level of intuitive development — working together as a group to access the collective consciousness of the third millennium. I am only too aware of the power of collective thought. Perhaps the Milios will serve as a bridge to a new consciousness, one that in the next millennium, now only three years away, everyone will be able to access.

For now, it may be the task of those initiates who choose to work with the interpretation of these stanzas to establish a thought colony — a realm of collective thought — where the unified energy of thoughts will make it possible for each of us to more easily access that great reservoir of spiritual thought — the Oneness — of which we are all a part.

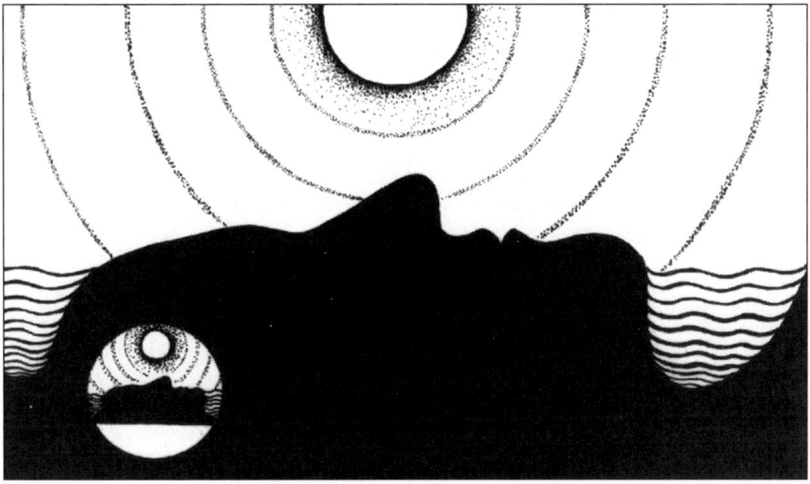

CHAPTER EIGHTEEN

How to Become a DreamVoyager

For the first half of my life, I barely knew what intuition was, let alone that I might actually possess it. In my case, it took the health crisis I experienced in 1979 — and what could truly be termed a "rude" awakening of my psychic senses — before I was willing to turn my attention fully to the choices available to me. Basically, I could either open my mind to the possibilities presented to me, or I could attempt to deny all that I had been shown and return to my previous life, continuing to cultivate a blindness to my intuitive self. I am glad I had the strength to choose an honest exploration of the intuitive world, for it has enriched my life more than I could ever express in words.

Intuition is just like any other life-skill one might develop. Once you have grown proficient in the techniques and come to appreciate the finer aspects of the discipline, you naturally want to share what you have learned with others. Having moved through the frustration of being a new initiate, sticking with the learning process until the successes outnumber the failures, you eventually come to love the practice which at first seemed so impossible to master. It is this love that manifests as teaching, when one has discovered the joy of practicing any challenging skill. And such has certainly been the case with me, in terms of my spiritual awakening.

As I have continued to grow in my own intuitive development, I have also continued to teach these same skills to others. The vast majority of these skills can be learned by anyone within an amazingly short period of time, typically within a twenty-eight-day period. The benefits at that point are generally so obvious and satisfying that it becomes easy to continue on your own.

The only requirements for developing intuitive skills are:

1. Belief — that you **can** develop your intuition.
2. Trust — that with **practice** you will develop your intuition.
3. Purpose — resulting from a clear **desire** to develop your intuition.

As part of this book, I wanted to share with you one of the simple techniques we teach in our DreamVoyager intuitive-development seminars. If you are willing to spend a few minutes per day doing a simple exercise, then twenty-eight days from now you will have undoubtedly made a significant start towards honing your intuitive skills — *regardless of the status of your current intuitive belief system, or any abilities you may already be aware you possess.*

My intuition training work is based upon a single tenet — you are already intuitive! This means we are born, each and every one of us, with this natural sense — intuition — already present in us. Think about it for a moment. Do you ever need to say to yourself, "I must breathe now," or "Heart, please beat now"? What about seeing, hearing, tasting, smelling or feeling? All of these are natural senses we take for granted, because we are taught to use them as a matter of course. Our intuitive senses, on the other hand, have not even been accepted as valid in our society, so virtually no time is spent on developing them. In fact, most of us were programmed — beginning in childhood — to deny our intuitive senses, ignoring and discounting them until they dwindle — as adults — from lack of use.

As an example of this, think of all the television commercials you've watched. Every seven minutes or less, a program is interrupted by a commercial touting all the things you need to buy in order to live happily and comfortably. Every seven minutes, we are being told what we need, who we are, what we should do, and of course, what we should purchase. None of these products seem to address our spiritual needs, and indeed, the very process of advertising assumes that we are incapable of discovering what we need for ourselves. It is no wonder that we — as a society — are not following a spiritual path! Most of us have shut down or blocked our most important spiritual tool — our natural intuitive sensitivity.

DISCOVERING YOUR PERSONAL INTUITIVE CYCLE

The first step on your path of intuitive exploration is to discover your own personal intuitive cycle. Everything in the cosmos has a cycle: the revolutions of the Earth, moon, and planets; the seasons; birth; life and death. All things, especially living beings, exist in this way. In our own bodies, we have literally thousands of cycles going on simultaneously. Each moment, new cells are being born, while others complete their life cycle. Our brain functions require hundreds of individual cycles. One of these is creativity. Another is intuition. Through extensive experimentation, Cynthia and I have discovered that creativity and intuition, while always present at some level, rise and decline in intensity, following an obvious rhythmic pattern which repeats every twenty-eight days. I believe this cycle is established at birth for each of us. It varies for each individual, depending on where and when we were born, and the polarity of the sun's magnetic field in relationship to the Earth's at the moment of birth.

I have also discovered a way to validate and track this cycle. In fact, it is the discovery of this simple exercise that first enabled me to become a DreamVoyager. The tracking mechanism I am referring to is, of course, your own dreams.

Dreams, like eyes, have been called the windows to the soul, and my own personal experiences have borne this out. I've experienced literally tens of thousands of dream voyages, both during the sleep-state and while awake. During these journeys, I have encountered many intelligences; some have become good friends, while others have merely stopped by to offer encouragement and advice. But even with all I have learned from my communications with these intelligences, I still find that there is no replacement for regular contact and communion with our own personal dream teacher — the higher self.

The Higher Self

The higher self may be thought of as the greater whole-consciousness of our being — all that we are now, have been, or are building towards becoming. Each higher self is then tied to all others that are within a specific color Ray group, of which there are seven, following the prismatic spectrum — red, orange, yellow, green, blue, violet, indigo. Each Ray group is then connected to the collective consciousness — the total super-consciousness of mind that many refer to as God.

Each of us experiences communication from our own higher self during our nightly dream states, as well as during our waking states. Because most of us have shut our intuitive processes off, though, we seldom "get" what our higher self is saying to us. Meditation, prayer, attunement exercises, and activating altered states of consciousness are some of the practices through which we can relearn how to listen to our higher self. Any of these, over time, will bring about a clearer under-standing of — and attunement with — our higher self. Some of these may work better than others, depending on the individual, but over an extended time any of these will lead to more vividly remembered dream-states, and a clearer "intu-itive" understanding of the messages our higher self is attempting to communicate to our waking self. And the pri-mary message — the single most important reason for culti-vating our intuition — is to guide us on the path that leads us towards a better understanding of our life's purpose.

INITIATION

Each person comes into this world with a life's purpose. Dreams are designed to assist you in achieving this purpose. This process of discovering and fulfilling those learning expe-riences desired by your higher self is called *initiation*. Think of it as a cosmic continuing education course, wherein your soul moves from lifetime to lifetime, attempting to refine and per-fect itself. Other souls will be of assistance along the way, just like students forming a study group, and your higher self is always there, too — gently reminding you what the assign-ment is. And the teacher? Well, this is an independent study course, so your own higher self *is* the teacher. This life — your life — is the lesson of the day.

Dreams offer the initiate — you — advice, support, heal-ings, encouragement, solutions, gratification, and of course, warnings. Why is it then that we seem unable to recall all of our dreams? And if dreams are supposed to assist us in our initiation, why are they often so cryptic? The answer is simple. Dreams are the language of the soul, and of the higher self. In the dream world, all of us are able to communicate with one another, regardless of race, language, or location — even those of us from another star system, or currently residing on a non-physical plane!

The physical world we live in is only a single aspect of our overall existence. Our awareness at this level does not necessarily convey the "Big Picture," so what may seem cryptic to our waking mind is not necessarily lost on us; communications from the dream-state are seeping into our sub-conscious mind at many levels simultaneously. During dreams, we leave our physical world focus and enter a world of timeless reality. From this perspective the past, present, and probable future all exist simultaneously. These two spheres of reality — the physical world and the dream world — interact with one another constantly, regardless of our perception. However — and this is a *big* 'however' — the initiation of our higher self moves forward by absolutely fantastic leaps when we choose to integrate perception of *both* worlds into our lives. And when you do — wham! — you have become a DreamVoyager.

TRACKING YOUR DREAM CYCLE

It is beyond the scope of this book to teach you *everything* you need to know to work with and interpret your dreams; however, I can start you down that path by assisting you in the discovery of your own intuitive dream cycle. As I said earlier, the experiences I've had since the beginning of my transformation have enriched my life more than I could ever express. Each day I feel like a child at a candy store, with a whole dollar to spend. (Well, when I was a kid, a dollar would buy a lot of candy.) And while my journey has had its challenges and detours, I would not trade away one moment of it.

As I stated earlier, our research has shown that each person's dreams, intuition and creativity follow a natural rhythmic cycle which lasts approximately twenty-eight days. The location and time of our birth establishes our initial cycle. Relocation only modifies this cycle, as does the lunar cycle. Each cycle rises and falls in a perfectly repeating wave. At the low end of the cycle, our brain and those glands associated with higher levels of psycho-spiritual energy are operating at lower levels than during the middle and high ends of the cycle. Our research has shown us that for about two-thirds of the cycle, we are accessing higher levels of psycho-spiritual energy.

Once you know your cycle parameters, you can learn to work *with* — instead of against — your own cycle. On low-cycle days you might read a book, go fishing, go for a walk, do things that are more physical than mental, or just relax. Take advantage of high-cycle days to solve problems, write, paint, be creative, or attempt to program your dreams for something specific.

To get you started, I have included a chart on the next page for the purpose of charting your own psycho-spiritual cycle. The chart includes space for twenty-eight days of charting along the horizontal axis. Along the vertical axis, you will rate the intensity of any dreams you may recall for that day. There are six levels of intensity for dream recall, as delineated below.

> **Zero** — no dream recall.
> **One** — recall few fragments of one dream.
> **Two** — recall substantial fragments of one dream.
> **Three** — total recall of one dream.
> **Four** — recall fragments of two or more dreams.
> **Five** — total recall of two or more dreams.

Those days when you are unable to recall a dream — a zero day — you will place a mark on the zero line of the vertical axis. On days when you are able to recall dream fragments or complete dreams, note the level on the vertical axis, according to the above scale. As the month proceeds, you will see a pattern emerging. This pattern will be your creative-intuitive cycle.

Any new skill requires patience, and this is no different. Once you begin to see results, even tiny ones, let it fill you with confidence, and your intuition will begin to expand.

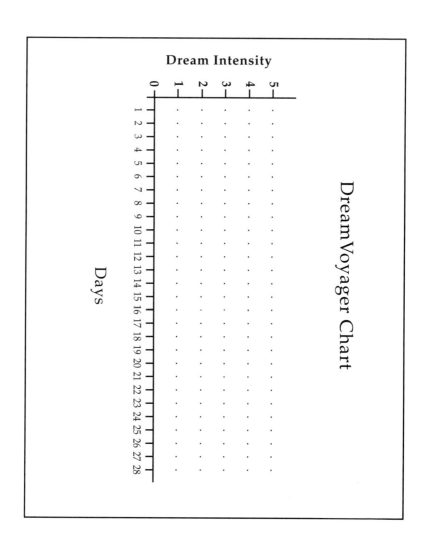

Remember, *belief, trust,* and *purpose* are the keys here. Don't give up!

This simple exercise of charting your dreams is designed to show you that your dreams, intuition, and creativity do indeed follow a pattern. Once you establish this truth, your conscious mind will begin to focus on the intuitive and creative messages coming from your sub-conscious mind. The reason some people feel they don't dream, rarely dream, or aren't creative or intuitive, is that they have not taken the time to become familiar with their own intuitive-creative cycle. Your cycles are real. Believe in them.

*   *   *   *   *

In closing, let me just say that most of us want nothing more than for our families, friends and ourselves to live happy, healthy lives. Working with and trusting our own intuition is by far the best way to assist not only ourselves, but everyone around us, in this universal — perhaps even cosmic? — pursuit. Maybe as we all become more intuitive, we will also use our intuition to assist our home planet as we would our friends, family, and loved ones. This book is dedicated to all of you who feel this way. God bless you all.

Supplementary Section

The following is an alphabetical listing, by subject, of Gordon-Michael Scallion's most significant predictions that have already occurred between 1991 and June 1997. All of these were originally published in past issues of the *Earth Changes Report*.

Archeological Discoveries

Prediction: *Major archeological discoveries prove the existence of intelligent humans and advanced technological civilizations dating back over twelve thousand years.* (ECR 1/95)

In the summer of 1995, ancient carved tools were discovered in Zaire. Researchers dated the tools at more than eighty-thousand years old. In September 1996, archeologists announced the discovery of artwork carved in huge sandstones at Jinmium in the northwestern part of Australia. Archeologists believe the artwork to be fifteen thousand years older than any other rock art in Australia.

Prediction: *Discoveries will come from China, the Yucatan, and Egypt. The greater [archeological] discoveries will come from the Giza Plateau.* (ECR 1/95)

In May 1995, several major archeological discoveries were made in Egypt. Sixty-seven chambers were found that go back to the time of Ramses II, who ruled from 1290 B.C.

through 1212 B.C. Later in the year an ancient Egyptian canal was discovered near the pyramids of Giza, built about four thousand five hundred years ago.

CONFLICTS

Prediction: *War shall spread throughout the former Soviet Union, Africa and the Middle East. Time frame: 1994 to 1997.* (ECR 1/94)

The *New York Times* reported in January 1995 that conflicts in Africa had escalated to unthinkable proportions during 1994. Later, in Rwanda, several hundred thousand Rwandans were massacred as part of a conflict between the Hutus and Tutsis.

In December 1994, war broke out in Chechnya, a former member of the Soviet Union, when the country attempted to secede from the Russian federation. Russian troops, tanks, and bombs began a steady decimation of Grozny, the capital of Chechnya.

Prediction: *Not during the coming year [1994], but before the end of the century, terrorist acts involving chemical and explosive devices shall occur.* (ECR 1/94)

On April 19, 1995, a huge car bomb destroyed the Federal building in Oklahoma City.

On March 20, a Japanese cult was accused of spreading deadly nerve gas throughout the tunnels of the Tokyo subway system. A dozen people were killed, and more than five thousand five hundred were injured. In April 1995, fumes spread through a train in Yokohama, causing more than five hundred passengers to be hospitalized.

During the 1996 Summer Olympics in Atlanta, Georgia, a bomb went off, killing at least one person and injuring several more.

Prediction: *Ireland politically goes through very positive changes in 1995, even greater changes in 1996. (ECR 1/95)*

In June 1995, the first British army base was dismantled in Northern Ireland. An agreement reached in November 1995 created an international body to oversee the removal of arms from the IRA and Protestant guerrillas.

EARTHQUAKES

Los Angeles Three-Quake Scenario

Prediction: *The Los Angeles area — up to one hundred fifty miles east southeast [of the city] — is to have three earthquakes, the third of which will be in the magnitude 8 range, and will cause severe damage. (from ECR 11/91 and 1/92)*

Prediction: *The first Los Angeles quake ... range 6.5 to 7 ... has a fifty percent chance of happening this month, April 1992 — most likely between April 17 and 22. (from ECR 11/91, 1/92 and 4/92)*

On April 22, 1992 an area one hundred ten miles east southeast of Los Angeles was hit by a 6.1 earthquake.

Prediction: *Multiple earthquakes to hit California — many reaching magnitudes in the 6 to 8 range ... Los Angeles area ... between May 8 and July 13, 1992. (ECR 5/92)*

Prediction: *The second of the three-quake scenarios for L.A. now has a sixty-five percent probability of occurring. I believe the epicenter will be approximately one hundred twenty to one hundred fifty miles east southeast of Los Angeles, with a magnitude in the range of 7.6 plus or minus .4. There are to be additional quakes in the 6 to 7 range. (ECR 6/92)*

On June 28, 1992 Landers, California was hit with a 7.5 quake. The epicenter was located one hundred thirty miles east of Los Angeles. A 6.5 quake hit Big Bear Lake on the same day.

Prediction: *Sri Lanka ... should be watched as an additional early warning sign for inundations and the beginning of the super megaquakes in the Hawaiians, Japan, and the West Coast U.S.* (*ECR* 1/93, written the last week of December 1992)

On December 7, 1993, Earth tremors shook Colombo, the capital of Sri Lanka. They were recorded at 5.5.

Prediction: *If we are going to have significant quake activity this year — magnitude 7.0 or greater — it will most likely occur later this month ... on the West Coast.* (*ECR* 1/94, published the last week of December 1993)

On January 17, 1994, Los Angeles was hit with a 6.8 quake centered in Northridge, a suburb of Los Angeles, fulfilling the Los Angeles three-quake scenario (although it fell short of the predicted magnitude).

The California Fracture

Prediction: *[Between] May 8, 1992 and May 8, 1993, the first of a series of California fractures occur. Sections of land along the "fracture" line from Eureka to Bakersfield to the Baja separate. Gaps occur along this line from several feet to hundreds of feet.* (*ECR* 5/92)

On June 28, 1992, the 7.5 quake that hit Landers, California caused a forty-four mile long "fracture," or tear in the Earth along the given fracture line (south of Bakersfield and west of Los Angeles.)

Hokkaido, Japan Earthquake

Prediction: Japan will have a 7.5 earthquake soon. (*ECR* 12/92)

On the fifteenth of January, 1993, a 7.5 quake hit Hokkaido, Japan.

Bolivian Earthquake

Prediction: *Globally, if we are going to have quake activity this year above 7.0, it will most likely occur this month. If not, the next active window is late spring.* (ECR 1/94)

On June 9, 1994, an 8.5 quake, three hundred seventy miles deep, struck Bolivia.

Earthquakes Throughout the U.S.

Prediction: *In the U.S., the areas to watch for quake activity greater than 5.0 ... Los Angeles, California, Oregon, Washington, Alaska, Arizona, Utah and Colorado.* (ECR 1/94)

Northridge, California, was hit by a 6.8 quake on January 17, 1994. Also during January, 1994: three quakes greater than 5.0 hit Southern California; two quakes greater than 5.0 hit Oregon; many quakes greater than 5.0 hit Alaska; one quake in Colorado registering over 5.0; and one in Utah, greater than 5.0.

Worldwide Earthquakes

Prediction: *Major quake activity, greater than 7.0, this summer and fall in Japan, Taiwan, South America, New Zealand, and the U.S. (ECR 7/94)*

The following earthquakes were reported in the months following the prediction:

Sea of Japan, 7.8, July, 21, 1994

Hokkaido, Japan, 8.3, October 4,1994

Taiwan, 7.3, September 17, 1994

Northeast of New Zealand, 7.1, July 4, 1994

Off the coast of Northern California, 7.2, September 1, 1994

Ring of Fire Four-Quake Scenarios

Prediction: *Quakes greater than 6.5 will follow a sequential pattern:*

1 — Beginning in Japan

2 — Followed by quakes in the Indian Ocean and/or the South Pacific

3 — Followed by South America

4 — Finally the West Coast of North America.

The sequence will occur in weeks rather than months. (ECR 2/95)

The 7.2 Kobe, Japan earthquake of January 17, 1995 was the first in the series, followed by these earthquakes: South Pacific, New Zealand, 7.1, February 5, 1995; South America, Colombia, 6.4, February 8, 1995; North America, off the coast of California, 6.7, February 19, 1995.

Prediction: *A similar scenario will repeat itself in the same areas, beginning in May, with quakes in 7.0 range. (ECR 3/95)*

The following quakes occurred as predicted: North of Japan, 7.6 , May 27, 1995; South Pacific, Kermadic Islands, 7.1, July 3, 1995; South America, Chile, 8.1, July 30, 1995; North America, Mexico, 7.5, September 14, 1995.

Prediction: *A third four-quake scenario will begin sometime [between] December 1995. through January 1996, with the magnitude increasing to the 8.0 range. (ECR 3/95)*

The following earthquakes occurred as predicted: Kuril Islands, north of Japan, 8.0, December 3, 1995; Indonesia, east of Borneo, 7.8, January 1, 1996; off the coast of Peru, 6.7, February. 21, 1997; near the coast of Oaxaca, Mexico, 7.1, February 25, 1997. (The last two quakes of the third scenario were slightly under the predicted magnitude.)

ECONOMY

Prediction: *The cost of grains will rise because of Earth changes. (ECR 1/94)*

The last months of 1994 brought devastation to much of the world's harvest due to extreme global weather conditions. Cambodia's drought caused the loss of an estimated seventy percent of the year's rice crop. Heavy storms and floods destroyed many of China's grain-producing areas during the 1994 growing season. Crops in South Africa produced only fifteen percent of expected returns. And Australia, suffering from the worst drought in its recorded history, estimated the winter grain harvest to be less than a tenth of the yield for the previous year.

Vietnam experienced 14.4 percent inflation in 1994, with rising food prices among the principal causes. Official figures showed that exceptionally high food prices were due mainly to floods.

EDUCATION

Prediction: Last year I suggested that the voucher system of education will emerge ... watch for this in the coming year. (*ECR* 12/92)

In the fall of 1993, two thousand low-income students in Cleveland, Ohio got tickets to start school at private instead of public institutions thanks to the voucher system. Cleveland battled in court to win the right to offer low-income parents the option of choosing private religious schools for their kids. According to *USA Today,* the controversial $5.25 million program gives each participant $2,250 in tax-funded tuition vouchers, so that they may enroll in one of almost fifty parochial schools in the region. The parents are also required to cover a small part of the tuition each month, based on their income.

Prediction: *Education shifts, due to economic strains.* (*ECR* 1/93)

USA Today reported in June 1997 that twenty-two states were considering takeovers or some other drastic intervention in their district-run schools. Several others are considering "school bankruptcy laws." One of the most serious concerns is underfinancing.

Prediction: *The educational system in the U.S. begins a major transformation [this year].* (*ECR* 1/95)

According to an article in *USA Today* in late January, two new trends in education appear to be on the rise: home schooling and privatization of some or all of the operations. Contracting private firms for just administrative or for both administrative and instructional areas is being considered by more than half the nation's school boards.

FIRES

Prediction: *Fires sweep across the Pacific Northwest and California ...* (*ECR* 1/96)

Hundreds of fires have raged across the Western States and Alaska during June and July 1996, burning hundreds of acres.

GEOPHYSICAL

Prediction: *I see magma pushing a large land mass upwards. [It] extends from hundreds of miles off the West Coast all the way to the Rockies. This upward movement is caused by the inner core of the Earth shifting its position. It is a prelude to a magnetic pole shift which I believe is already happening. [Changes in the magnetic pole] occur when magma at the Earth's core moves. I have predicted that a six to seven degree magnetic pole shift is to occur between 1993 and 1995.* (from *ECR* 5/92, 9/92 and 9/93)

Seismologists from Harvard University have discovered an unexpected tilt in the Earth's core according to a report in the April 16, 1994 issue of *Science News*. Iron crystals in the core that once pointed toward the poles may now indicate changes in the Earth's magnetic fields.

HEALTH

Prediction: *A new strain of AIDS is discovered.* (*ECR* 12/91)

A new AIDS virus without HIV has been found, according to a *New York Times* article dated July 23, 1992.

Prediction: *The third of the seven plagues ... attacks the respiratory system.* *(ECR 12/91)*

An article in the *San Francisco Chronicle* in January 1992 stated that a new strain of tuberculosis is now out of control throughout the world.

Prediction: *... new diseases are to come that have not been on the planet before.* *(ECR 4/92)*

A mysterious disease struck and killed several people in the Southwest according to June 1992 reports in *The Arizona Republic* and *USA Today* . The Hanta virus, thought to be the cause, has never before been associated with the symptoms manifested by the victims.

Prediction: *Alternative healers emerge as more turn to natural healing methods.* *(ECR 1/93)*

A recent *Newsweek* report stated that one third of all Americans now use alternative health modalities, and spend $14 billion each year doing so.

Prediction: *New Plagues emerge, affecting the optic nerve and causing blindness.* *(ECR 1/93)*

A May 1993 *New York Times* article reported that thirty-four thousand Cubans have been afflicted with a mysterious epidemic of partial or total blindness.

Prediction: *The barks of many trees can be beneficial to healing during Tribulation, as they adjust to the changing Earth forces through their root structure.* *(ECR 2/93)*

Researchers at the University of Illinois reported in the October 1996 journal *Nature*, the development of a new anti-cancer agent, betulinic acid, extracted from the common white birch. The new drug specifically affects the cells of melanoma, or skin cancer.

Prediction: *There will be an increase in those diseases that attack the respiratory systems, as well as blood disorders, skin cancers, and heart failure.* (ECR 1/94)

USA Today reported in October 1994 that new strains of tuberculosis, resistant to antibiotics, have surfaced in the U.S. and in third world countries. In one major U.S. city alone, 352 cases of whooping cough were reported in one year, compared with 542 cases over the previous thirteen years. A penicillin-resistant meningococcal bacteria has emerged in the U.S., infecting the blood and then spinal fluid, often causing life-threatening septic shock. Heart failure is now reported as the "most common cause of hospitalization in people over sixty-five," and is the "only cardiovascular disease increasing in frequency." Incidents of heart failure have more than doubled in frequency in recent years.

Prediction: *Between 1992 and 1997 ... plagues and new diseases will occur.* (from the *Future Map of the United States, 1998-2001,* published in 1991)

In July 1994, the U.S. Center for Disease Control and Prevention warned about diseases that have developed uncommon resistances to antibiotics and traditional medicines. Among those diseases listed is the streptococcus-A bacteria — also know as the "flesh-eating" disease. The World Health Organization announced in April 1997 that the world is on the brink of a medical disaster because of new and mutating strains of bacteria and viruses, as well as the reemergence of frightening communicable diseases such as the plague and tuberculosis.

Prediction: *New and unknown diseases will emerge.* *(ECR 7/94)*

The April 1995 issue of *Science* reported that a "mystery illness" which killed fourteen horses and their human trainer in Australia, has turned out to be a new strain of virus.

Hemorrhagic fever viruses are among the most threatening examples of emerging pathogens, one of which is a previously unknown strain of Ebola virus, which was first isolated in 1995. According to a report in the October 1995 issue of *Scientific American,* an Ebola epidemic killed more than one hundred ninety people in Zaire this past spring.

Prediction: *Herb sales will soar as more people seek alternative methods of health care.* *(ECR 1/95)*

The USDA Economic Research Service reported that an increase interest in health and alternative medicines has expanded the market for herbal remedies and opened opportunities for growers in recent years.

INSURANCE

Prediction: *The insurance industry begins to collapse, in part because of hurricanes and other disasters.* *(from ECR 12/91, 7/92 and 8/92)*

Insurance claims for 1992 were a record $23 billion for catastrophes, including Hurricanes Andrew and Iniki. Catastrophe losses usually run between $3 and $6 billion. As a result, insurance companies stopped writing or refused to renew policies in high risk areas, according to a May 1993 article in *USA Today*. Others have had to put a limit on coverage in coastal areas, and they are reexamining their policies for areas prone to earthquakes.

Prediction: *The insurance industry further collapses because of high claims due to Earth changes.* (ECR 1/93)

Prediction: *Insurance claims will once again be in the billions — I see it more than double last year's claims!* (ECR 4/94)

According to Gannett News Services, catastrophic losses to the U.S. in insurance claims were estimated at $5.7 billion in 1993. A report issued in December of 1994 stated that catastrophes nationwide cost the insurance industry $12.7 billion in the first nine months of 1994 alone. Losses for Hurricane Gordon and the Texas floods had not been added to the total yet.

JUPITER-EFFECT

Jupiter Effect — Earthquakes

Prediction: *Jupiter-Effect Prediction Window — [from] twenty-four hours after the comet hits Jupiter through [the end of] 1995 ... Expect deep quakes (a hundred miles or more) throughout the Ring of Fire in the Pacific.* (ECR 7/94, published June 27, 1994)

Comet Shoemaker-Levy 9 broke into twenty-one fragments and bombarded the surface of the planet Jupiter from July 16 through July 22, 1994, an event categorized as the most violent in the recorded history of our solar system. The following earthquakes were reported in the following months:

On July 21, 1994, a 7.8 quake struck 348-miles deep in the Sea of Japan.

On November 15,1994 a quake estimated at 335-miles deep hit Indonesia.

In December 1994 there was a quake 114-miles deep on the Peru/Bolivia border in South America.

Also in December 1994, there were two quakes over 145-

miles deep, one in the South Pacific, and one north of Japan.

In January 1995, in Fiji, there were two quakes over 300-miles deep.

In March 1995, in Sea of Japan, there was an earthquake 261-miles deep.

In April 1995, in the South Pacific, there was a 470-miles deep quake.

Jupiter Effect — Weather

Prediction: *Jupiter Effect Predictions (within a window of twenty-four hours after impact through the end of 1995) — Weather will become erratic at the sea and coastal regions. High winds will occur between the Equator and the Tropic of Cancer.* (ECR 7/94)

Hurricane Emelia hit north of the Hawaiian Islands on July 21, 1994, with sustained winds of one hundred sixty miles per hour, and with gusting winds of one hundred ninety miles per hour, making it the most powerful central Pacific hurricane ever recorded.

MEDIA

Prediction: *Media programming on metaphysics, the world of spirit, and phenomena expands.* (ECR 1/95)

In the January 1996 TV Guide, weekly series included *Mysteries, Magic & Miracles* on the Sci-Fi Channel (hosted by Patric Macnee, it covers unusual phenomena), *Miracles & Wonders* on The Learning Channel, and the hit show, *Touched By An Angel*, on CBS. Fox Channel's *The X-Files* is also one of television's most highly rated series.

PHENOMENA

Prediction: *As changes increase, outward signs occur, such as spiritual manifestations and signs in the heavens. One such heavenly sign is the Blue Star ...* (ECR 3/93)

Comet Hale-Bopp was discovered on July 23, 1995. Dr. Duncan Steel of Anglo-Australian Observatory, says that Hale-Bopp is not a new comet, but has passed by before, approximately 3,250 years ago.

Prediction: *Most crop circles are created by highly charged spheres of light ... the spheres move in stylus fashion, creating the messages.* (ECR 6/94)

According to the publication *Beyond Boundaries*, crop circle researcher Colin Andrews said that a man camping on a hilltop near Wiltshire, England in August 1996 captured footage of the formation of a crop circle. The film shows two white spheres moving across a field in an arc-like movement. As the spheres spiraled across the field, a circular pattern flattened to the ground in a matter of seconds.

Prediction: *Phenomena increase in the world.* (ECR 1/95)

According to a report in the *Guardian* newspaper in October 1995, at least thirty-nine new crop circles appeared throughout England during the summer of that year.

Sightings of Mary and angelic sightings have occurred recently in over one hundred countries. The *Fortean Times* in July 1995 reported that in Italy figures of the Blessed Virgin Mary have been weeping blood all across the country, with more than fifteen cases reported. On the island of Cyprus, villagers claimed to have seen icons weep in St. Catherine's Greek Orthodox chapel.

Medjugorje, a pilgrimage site in the former Yugoslavia,

has mysteriously escaped any damage throughout the civil war that has raged nearby since 1991. Six local children continue to see the image of the Virgin Mary, who first appeared to them in 1981. Marian apparitions were also reported in Canada, according to an August 1995 report in the *Toronto Star*.

On March 13, 1997, thousands of people in Arizona reported an enormous object in the night sky. According to a story in the June 18, 1997 issue of *USA Today*, the V-shaped object was more than a mile long, with extraordinary gas-like lights — seven of them — six on each prong and one light trailing away from the others. The object was videotaped by numerous witnesses.

SPACE

Prediction: *1996 will be the year of space discoveries.* (ECR 1/96)

In October 1996, scientists found a huge planet in an egg-shaped orbit around one of twin stars in the constellation Cygnus. It is the first planet to be discovered outside of our own solar system.

Prediction: *... the origin of the moon will be known.* (ECR 1/96)

In December 1996, officials announced that the spacecraft Clementine, while orbiting the moon, had picked up unmistakable evidence of a vast pond of frozen water deep inside one of the moon's craters. The discovery offers new clues about the possible origins of the moon.

Prediction: *By 1997 sunspot and solar flare activity begins to exceed the normal range, and will continue to accelerate in the nineties.* (ECR 3/92)

In April 1997, a solar storm erupted from the sun and

headed in our direction for the second time this year. Solar flares are expected to increase and peak over the next few years, when eruptions ten times bigger than average will occur several times every day, and storms a hundred times larger than normal will occur once every two or three days.

TECHNOLOGY

Prediction: *[I see] a photovoltaic breakthrough using living crystals. The system works as follows: suspended in a liquid matrix are living crystals that, when exposed to sunlight, begin to grow. By controlling the growth rate and life cycle, the matrix is able to give off energy in the form of heat which, through its chemical matrix, develops direct electricity.* (ECR 1/94)

According to an article in the July 7, 1994 issue of the journal *Nature*, scientists have discovered the structure of a "light-harvesting pigment protein" that could herald the development of artificial photosynthesis. Information revealed by electron crystallography could be the basis for new energy-producing technologies.

Prediction: *A system of reusing spent fuel will emerge in the world. This system will have the ability to neutralize nuclear waste so as to return it to a safe state.* (ECR 8/94)

In the November 1995 issue of *Science*, scientists at Armed Services University of Health Sciences in Bethesda, Maryland, reported that the radiation-resistant bug, *deinococcus radiodurans*, can withstand fifteen million to three million rads, a very high level of radiation. The Department of Energy is funding research to program the bacterium to consume radioactive material.

Prediction: *A new fuel-cell power system emerges — fossil-fuel and pollution-free.* (ECR 1/95)

On October 4, 1995, the *Los Angeles Times* reported that researchers have developed fuel cells that produce electricity without recharging, using a non-fossil fuel source.

VULCANISM

Prediction: *Volcanic activity will hit Mexico between ten and twenty degrees latitude this year.* (ECR 1/94)

On December 21, 1994, Popocatépetl erupted. Over 75,000 nearby residents were evacuated from the area.

Prediction: *New Volcanoes are born; Iceland grows and eventually merges with Greenland.* (ECR 12/94)

Prediction: *I see major volcanic eruptions occurring shortly in the Arctic, Italy, Caribbean and U.S.* (ECR 10/96, published September 15, 1996)

In October 1996, Iceland's Loki volcano, about one hundred twenty miles east of Reykjavik, erupted. It broke through the Vatnajökull glacier and causing major flooding.

On September 18, 1996, the Soufriere Hills volcano erupted in the Montserrat region of the Caribbean, causing the surrounding area to be evacuated. It erupted again in January 1997, and continued off and on throughout the early part of 1997.

Throughout the month of November 1996, the Pavlov volcano in Alaska erupted, with lava flows and huge bursts of ash and steam.

WATER

Polar Icecaps

Prediction: *The ozone hole ... increases [global] temperature, thus melting the caps and [creating] movement of glaciers. This is to signal the greater inundations of coastal areas.* (ECR 12/91)

As of September 9, 1995 a U.N. panel, the Intergovernmental Panel on Climate Change, announced it was convinced that global temperatures have warmed during the past century because of human activity.

According to a Reuters' news service report in January 1996, the Earth's temperature in 1995 was the warmest on record since global record-keeping first began in 1860. The report stated that the rise in global temperatures is due to emissions of carbon dioxide and other greenhouse gases.

Prediction: *... water will rise because of a melting of the poles. This occurs over years, beginning slowly in 1993, accelerating from 1995 to 1997 and completing [the cycle] between 1998 and 2001.* (ECR 10/93)

For the first time in recorded history, according to a March 1995 report by the British Antarctica Survey, it has become possible to circumnavigate James Ross Island. The ice shelf which formerly occupied Prince Gustav Channel and connected James Ross Island to the Antarctic Peninsula has completely disintegrated.

WATER POLLUTION

Prediction: *As Tribulation builds, water is to be of prime importance. (ECR 10/92)*

During the Great Flood of 1993, potable water was often difficult to come by in the Midwest and Northeastern U.S., because of flooded water treatment plants and contaminated wells. At least two major cities, Milwaukee and New York, had contaminated water systems in 1993. According to a September 1993 Natural Resources Defense Council report, there were over two hundred fifty-thousand public water violations in 1991 and 1992.

Prediction: *As Tribulation occurs, water will be of prime concern. (ECR 2/95)*

According to a report by the U.S. Environmental Protection Agency released in May 1995, lawns and farms are now the main sources of water pollution, replacing sewage and industrial pollution as the prime causes of water contamination. Forty percent of our rivers, streams and lakes are no longer suitable for swimming, fishing or drinking.

WATER DAMAGE

Prediction: *I see unprecedented water damage occurring this year because of erratic and repeating weather patterns. (ECR 1/97)*

January 1997 — California hit with record rain falls and flooding of various areas and rivers;. States of emergency were declared in thirty-seven of California's fifty-eight counties.

February 1997 — Record rains cause floods and evacuations in Illinois and floods cause damage from Dallas/Fort Worth to San Antonio, Texas.

March 1997 — Floods and severe storms kill at least forty people in six states: Arkansas, Mississippi, Kentucky, Tennessee, Ohio and Indiana. Ohio, Kentucky, Illinois and Indiana have the worst floods in thirty years, affecting areas all the way down the Mississippi River, to Louisiana.

April 1997 — North Dakota, South Dakota and parts of Minnesota are declared disaster areas as snow melt-off, rains and severe storms leave unprecedented amounts of water with the worst floods of the century for those areas.

WEATHER

Hurricane Andrew

Prediction: *Florida will have two storms, one coming from the east and one from the west* — *high winds, rain, tornadoes.* (ECR 3/92)

Prediction: *I have mentioned already that I see two hurricanes coming to Florida. I believe one of these will be the largest hurricane that has ever hit Florida. I see one coming in from the east and one coming in through the Gulf Coast. The big one is from the east.* (ECR 6/92)

Prediction: *The first hurricane will cross the Bahamas at approximately twenty-seven degrees latitude, slamming into Florida's east coast. It will be the largest recorded in Florida's history, with winds, at times, exceeding one hundred fifty miles per hour. It is to occur between August 15 and September 27.* (ECR 8/92)

On August 24, 1992, Hurricane Andrew crossed the Bahamas, hitting Florida's east coast with one hundred fifty mile-per-hour winds. According to a CNN broadcast on September 25, 1992, Hurricane Andrew was rated the worst natural disaster in the history of the U.S.

The Great Flood of 1993

Prediction: *The Mississippi is to become a new inland sea. Consider a minimum of fifty miles on either side [of the current riverfront] as unsafe during Tribulation.* (from the *Future Map of the United States, 1998-2001*, published in 1991, and quoted in ECR 4/93)

In July 1993, a *USA Today* headline proclaimed "Rain Will Swell Inland Sea." After weeks and weeks of relentless rain, the Mississippi River flooded throughout the late spring and early summer. Billions of dollars worth of damage was caused up and down the river. Thousands of people were evacuated, and many eventually had to be permanently relocated.

The Blizzard of 1993

Prediction: *Inundations to occur in coastal areas in U.S. from Maine to Florida Keyes, Vancouver to the Baja, Florida's Panhandle to Texas.* (ECR 1/93)

Between January and March of 1993, severe flooding hit Louisiana and California. The "Blizzard of '93" hit the East Coast from the Gulf of Mexico to Maine, billed as the worst storm of the century. Widespread flooding also hit the state of Florida.

GLOBAL WEATHER

Prediction: *Extreme weather pattern changes increase ten-fold in 1994 and 1995. Hardest hit will be the U.S. — the Northwest and West Coast, Texas, and Florida — the United Kingdom, Germany, the former Soviet Union, Africa and Australia.* (ECR 1/94)

Much of California was declared a disaster area because of storms and floods in October 1994.

Florida and Georgia were hit with tornadoes, thunderstorms and Hurricane Alberto in July 1994.

The United Kingdom was hit with flooding in the south and central parts of England in January and February 1994.

Many parts of Germany were hit with flooding from January 1994 through April 1994.

The former Soviet Union reported unusually heavy snow in March 1994, which caused widespread flooding. The same area experienced unusually high temperatures in July — as much as twenty-five degrees above normal.

The entire continent of Africa was hit with severe weather ranging from droughts to massive floods.

In Australia freak storms hit Sydney from January through April 1994, and Perth was hit with the worst storm in twenty years. But as of October 1994, for most of the country, the worst drought in history continues.

In January 1995, unprecedented storms hit California, causing much flooding.

Scotland experienced the worst flooding in recorded history in April 1995, and at the same time England was again hit with flooding.

Prediction: *Earth changes increase globally.* (ECR 1/96)

The world's largest reinsurer, *Munich Re*, released a report in late December 1996, stating that 1996 had seen six hundred major natural disasters which together caused the deaths of some eleven thousand people. The number of disasters in 1996 was thirty more than in 1995. Disasters in 1996 were responsible for approximately $60 billion in property damage. When *Munich Re* compared these numbers with those of the 1960s, they saw an overall increase of four hundred percent, with the increase in cost of property damage estimated at seven hundred percent.

U.S. WEATHER — RAIN

Prediction: *Rain this spring will be record-breaking throughout the U.S.* (ECR 1/95)

By March 1995, San Francisco was already eight inches above its normal yearly rainfall. By April, two-thirds of California's counties had been declared disaster areas because of rains, mud slides, and flooding. Parts of Arizona were inundated with flash floods in March, and in April the Midwest was hit with freezing rain, hail, sleet, snow and thunderstorms. In the same time-period, twenty inches of snow fell in Colorado in April. Louisiana got eighteen inches of rain in just six hours, causing widespread flooding and the evacuation of thousands. Illinois declared twenty-seven counties as disaster areas after severe storms spawned tornadoes and caused massive flooding. Heavy rains also hit Indiana.

U.S. WEATHER — TEMPERATURES

Prediction: *Temperatures nationwide will be unseasonably warm ...* (ECR 1/95)

In June and July 1995, extreme heat was attributed as the main cause of death for at least six hundred seventy people in the nation. During one week in June, more than fifty high temperature records were either tied or broken in the Great Lakes region and New England. From July 25 through August 7, there were several places in Arizona where temperatures reached at least 112 degrees Fahrenheit each day, and on July 28, the temperature reached 124 degrees. Fifty-four people died in Chicago between July 12 and July 15, as temperatures soared, remaining above 90 degrees throughout the nighttime hours. Many parts of California recorded daily average temperatures during this period at over 12 degrees Fahrenheit above the normal range.

EUROPEAN WEATHER

Prediction: *Europe will be very hard hit with severe weather.* (*ECR* 1/95)

In January and February 1995, the Netherlands, Germany, France and Belgium were inundated by the "Floods of the Century." Spain experienced the worst drought of the century, and Great Britain was hit with storms and torrential rains. A heat wave in the Mediterranean in August 1995 was responsible for killing dozens of people.

HURRICANES WORLDWIDE

Prediction: *Fewer named storms than last year, but more violent ones — watch above thirty-five degrees latitude on the East Coast [of the U.S.].*   (*ECR* 7/96)

On July 12, 1996, Hurricane Bertha hit North Carolina just below thirty-five degrees latitude, and left a wide band of devastation northward.

On September 2, 1996, Hurricane Edouard hit New Jersey and southeastern New England with strong winds and heavy rains.

On September 5, 1996, Hurricane Fran hit North Carolina just above thirty-four degrees latitude and then moved north, causing massive damage in North Carolina and Virginia.

On September 13, 1996, Hurricane Hortense threatened the coast of the eastern United States, from Rhode Island to Maine, as it headed northeast with its hundred twenty-five mile per hour winds.

In the 1996 Atlantic Hurricane season, four hurricanes hit at or above thirty-five degrees of latitude: Hurricanes Bertha, Fran, Edouard and Hortense.

Resources

Earth Changes Report

The only source for Gordon-Michael Scallion's predictions and teachings. Published nine times per year, each 8-page newsletter focuses on one of GMS' most recent prophetic visions. Some deal with specific changes that will affect your life today; others bring to light changes affecting life in the near future, as well as the third millennium.

Upcoming reports will feature subjects as diverse as: the effects of Earth's new electromagnetic system on human health; population migrations and relocation; new modalities of healing; self-sufficiency before and after Earth changes; spiritual preparation for the new millennium; intuitive development; Earth's energy grid; previous Earth changes that destroyed Atlantis and Lemuria; communication with extraterrestrials; GMS' Milios Prophecies; annual prophecies for each upcoming year; and GMS' visions of the near-future, in which the communities now forming throughout our world will rebalance and harmonize with the shifted energies of the planet. *ECR* also features the teachings and perspectives of Cynthia Keyes in her column, "Insights."

Earth Changes Report is an interactive publication which offers resources, book reviews, and the "Forum," where readers can write, fax, or E-mail questions and comments to GMS. It is available by single issue or by subscription, exclusively through Matrix Institute.

Future Map of North America

1996 Release — Shows Gordon-Michael Scallion's predicted changes for North America through the year 2012, including:

> Full-size coverage of the continental U.S., Alaska and Hawaii, Canada, Mexico and Central America. Illustrates migration areas, pole-shift information, primary safety lands, and new islands that will rise off the east and west coasts of the U.S.

Map size is 29" x 39" — Available in three formats:
Paper, folded to 8" x 9" — Item No. NMP
Vinyl, folded to 8" x 9" — Item No. NMV
Vinyl, rolled and shipped in a tube — Item No. NMVR

Quantity pricing is available.

Future Map of the World

1996 Release — Shows Gordon-Michael Scallion's predicted global changes from 1998 to 2012, for all continents. Large, wall-size for easy viewing.

Map size is 60" x 46" — Available in two formats:
Paper, folded to 8" x 9" — Item No. WMF
Laminated, rolled and shipped in a tube — Item No. WML
(Due to postal size regulations the laminated, rolled format is not available outside the U.S.)

Quantity pricing is available.

How To Find Us On The Internet

WORLD WIDE WEB ADDRESS

http://www.matrixinstitute.com

E-MAIL ADDRESS

To receive an online catalog:
info@matrixinstitute.com

For Your Personal Journal Notes

For Your Personal Journal Notes

For Your Personal Journal Notes

For Your Personal Journal Notes

For Your Personal Journal Notes

For Your Personal Journal Notes